Walter Benjamin's Archive

"Here we have a man whose job it is to gather the day's refuse in the capital. Everything that the big city has thrown away, everything it has lost, everything it has scorned, everything it has crushed underfoot he catalogues and collects. He collates the annals of intemperance, the capharnaum of waste. He sorts things out and selects judiciously: he collects like a miser guarding a treasure, refuse which will assume the shape of useful or gratifying objects between the jaws of the goddess of Industry." This description is one extended metaphor for the poetic method, as Baudelaire practised it. Ragpicker and poet: both are concerned with refuse.

Walter Benjamin

Walter Benjamin's Archive

IMAGES, TEXTS, SIGNS

Translated by Esther Leslie

Edited by
Ursula Marx
Gudrun Schwarz
Michael Schwarz
Erdmut Wizisla

VERSO
London • New York

The Walter Benjamin Archive
is an Institute of the Hamburg Foundation
for the promotion of knowledge and culture
based in the Academy of Arts Berlin.

This edition published by Verso 2007

1 3 5 7 9 10 8 6 4 2

Verso
UK: 6 Meard Street, London W1F 0EG
USA: 180 Varick Street, New York, NY 10014-4606
www.versobooks.com

Verso is the imprint of New Left Books

ISBN-13: 978-1-84467-196-0

British Library Cataloguing in Publication Data
A catalogue record for this book is available from the British Library

Library of Congress Cataloging-in-Publication Data
A catalog record for this book is available from the Library of Congress

Typeset in Gill Sans Light by Hewer Text UK Ltd, Edinburgh
Printed and bound in Singapore by Tien Wah Press

CONTENTS

Excavation and Memory

Language has unmistakably made plain that memory is not an instrument for exploring the past, but rather a medium. It is the medium of that which is experienced, just as the earth is the medium in which ancient cities lie buried. He who seeks to approach his own buried past must conduct himself like a man digging. Above all, he must not be afraid to return again and again to the same matter; to scatter it as one scatters earth, to turn it over as one turns over soil. For the "matter itself" is no more than the strata which yield their long-sought secrets only to the most meticulous investigation. That is to say, they yield those images that, severed from all earlier associations, reside as treasures in the sober rooms of our later insights—like torsos in a collector's gallery. It is undoubtedly useful to plan excavations methodically. Yet no less indispensable is the cautious probing of the spade in the dark loam. And the man who merely makes an inventory of his findings, while failing to establish the exact location of where in today's ground the ancient treasures have been stored up, cheats himself of his richest prize. In this sense, for authentic memories, it is far less important that the investigator report on them than that he mark, quite precisely, the site where he gained possession of them. Epic and rhapsodic in the strictest sense, genuine memory must therefore yield an image of the person who remembers, in the same way a good archaeological report not only informs us about the strata from which its findings originate, but also gives an account of the strata which first had to be broken through. *SW* 2:2*, p. 576

* Abbreviated sources to be found in bibliography.

Ausgraben und Erinnern

Die Sprache hat es unmißverständlich bedeutet, daß das Gedächtnis nicht ein Instrument für die Erkundung der Vergangenheit ist, vielmehr das Medium. Es ist das Medium des Erlebten wie das Erdreich das Medium ist, in dem die alten Städte verschüttet liegen. Wer sich der eigenen verschütteten Vergangenheit zu nähern trachtet, muß sich verhalten wie ein Mann, der gräbt. Vor allem darf er sich nicht scheuen, immer wieder auf einen und denselben Sachverhalt zurückzukommen – ihn auszustreuen wie man Erde ausstreut, ihn umzuwühlen wie man Erdreich umwühlt. Denn „Sachverhalte" sind nicht mehr als Schichten, die erst der sorgsamsten Durchforschung das ausliefern, um dessentwillen sich die Grabung lohnt. Die Bilder nämlich, welche, losgebrochen aus allen früheren Zusammenhängen, als Kostbarkeiten in den nüchternen Gemächern unserer späten Einsicht – wie Torsi in der Galerie des Sammlers – stehen. Und gewiß ist's nützlich, bei Grabungen nach Plänen vorzugehen. Doch ebenso ist unerläßlich der behutsame, tastende Spatenstich ins dunkle Erdreich. Und der betrügt sich selber um das Beste, der nur das Inventar der Funde macht und nicht im heutigen Boden Ort und Stelle bezeichnen kann, an denen er das Alte aufbewahrt. So müssen wahrhafte Erinnerungen viel weniger

berichtend verfahren als genau den Ort bezeichnen, an dem der Forscher ihrer habhaft wurde. Im strengsten Sinne episch und rhapsodisch muß daher wirkliche Erinnerung ein Bild zugleich von dem, der sich erinnert, geben, wie ein guter archäologischer Bericht nicht nur die Schichten angeben muß, aus denen seine Fundobjekte stammen, und jene andern vor allem, welche vorher zu durchstoßen waren.

Preface

> But when shall we actually write books like catalogues?
>
> *One-Way Street* (SW1, p. 457)

His last archive remains a secret: the briefcase that Walter Benjamin carried over the Pyrenees in September 1940 is lost. Only one document that was transported in it survives—an authenticated letter from May 8, 1940, in which Max Horkheimer confirms Benjamin's membership of the Institute for Social Research in New York and confirms that his researches have proven to be extremely helpful for the Institute. Lisa Fittko, who helped him and other refugees in their escape, attested that Benjamin wanted the briefcase to be saved above everything else; for supposedly his latest manuscript was inside, and it was the most important thing of all, more important even than his own life. It may possibly have contained the theses *On The Concept of History*. Any more detailed information is lacking. What is certain, however, is that the briefcase held some sort of texts by Benjamin. Papers with unknown contents are mentioned in a police report listing the belongings on his person at the time of his death—his last possessions consisted of a watch, a pipe, six photographs, glasses, letters, magazines, and money, which was used to pay off the hotel bill and the costs of the funeral.

If Benjamin had not taken precautions his legacy would have suffered the same fate as the briefcase. It is impossible to imagine the effect that might have had on the reception of his work. The fact that his archive is so bristling with contents today—a fact that is barely comprehensible when viewed against the backdrop of his personal fate—is due to the strategic calculation with which he deposited his manuscripts, notebooks, and printed papers in the custody of friends and acquaintances in various countries. His archives landed in the hands of others, so that their documents might be delivered to posterity. Those who received his work accepted the obligatory nature of their role and faithfully conserved the papers. With the ethos of an archivist Benjamin secured the continued life of his thought, a thought that sought to grasp the present through reading testimonials from the past.

Benjamin's concept of the archive, however, differs from that of the institutionalized archives, whose self-understanding is derived from the origin of the word "archive." "Archive" stems from the Greek and Latin words for "town hall, ruling office," which, in turn, are derived from "beginning, origin, rule." Order, efficiency, completeness, and objectivity are the principles of archival work. In contrast to this, Benjamin's archives reveal the passions of the collector. The remains heaped up in them are reserve funds or something like iron reserves; crucial to life, and which for that reason must be conserved. These are points at which topicality flashes up, places that preserve the idiosyncratic registrations of an author, subjective, full of gaps, unofficial.

Thirteen of Benjamin's archives are presented in what follows. Not all of their contents can be enclosed within briefcases, folders, card indexes or other containers. Something else is transferred alongside their objective significance: Benjamin's archives consist of images, texts, signs, things that one can see and touch, but they are also a reservoir of experiences, ideas, and hopes, all of which have been inventoried and analyzed by their stock taker. His project on the Paris Arcades, a collection of quotations and commentary, was intended to scout the "prehistory of the 19th century" from elements of the everyday world, art, and dreams. It registers types (the flâneur, the dandy, the rag picker, the whore), building forms and places (arcades, boulevards, panoramas, catacombs), materials (iron, glass), the effect of fashion, advertising and the workings of the commodity. For all this Benjamin created "a place in the archives of our memory" (Baudelaire[1]). This entire work of this author can be conceived as an archive of thought, of perceptions, of history and of the arts.

What can be found in these archives? The opening chapter "Tree of Conscientiousness"—a quotation from Benjamin, as are all of the chapter headings in this book—traces Benjamin's activity as an archivist of his own writings. Lists, catalogues, and card indexes, at once meticulous and inventive compilations, have all found their way into the archive. At the chapter's center stands a registry, in which Benjamin rubricated his correspondence and manuscripts according to his own predilections. "Scrappy Paperwork" deals with the word "scrap" (*verzetteln*); and its twofold meaning—as "failure, fragmentary, unachieved," on the one hand, and as a particular method of making information manageable, on the other. Benjamin's legacy consists of hundreds of little scraps; and as such might be associated with *Zettel's Dream* by Arno Schmidt and the little boxes of memoranda in Jean Paul's *Quintus Fixlein*—in a review in 1934 Benjamin claimed that Jean Paul's boxes of memoranda were the archive of art of the Biedermeier period. Small- format manuscripts encouraged Benjamin's inclination to write in a miniscule hand, a trait reminiscent of Robert Walser; the chapter "From Small to Smallest Details" outlines this characteristic aspect of Benjamin's writing. The Russian toys that Benjamin

[1] Charles Baudelaire, "Salon of 1859," in Charles Baudelaire, *The Mirror of Art*, London: Phaidon, 1955.

acquired in Moscow, and described in an illustrated article, are presented under the heading "Physiognomy of the Thing World." These photographs are witnesses to a disappearance, they bring into view remnants of peasant handiwork. "Opinions et Penseés" describes the words and turns of phrase that derive from Stefan Benjamin—an "archive of non-sensuous similarities," constructed and interpreted by the father who tracked the linguistic and intellectual development of his son. Benjamin once described his notebooks as the "daintiest quarters": this line becomes a chapter heading. His notebooks were important tools of his work, for they stored and structured his material and thoughts; every single square centimeter of them seems to have been used. Only a portion of Benjamin's postcard collection has been preserved—this consists of "Travel Scenes" from Tuscany and the Balearics, in relation to which the jottings of an enthusiastic traveler might be read differently. The chapter "A Bow Being Bent" investigates Benjamin's capacity for structuring his research materials and it demonstrates his organization of knowledge in rigorous and eccentric designs—which provide the connecting links between initial ideas and first drafts. Graphic forms are considered here as "Constellations"; spatial, bi-polar, or elliptical orderings, in which concepts or figures of thought exist in charged relationships with each other. Benjamin's sympathy for the figure of the rubbish collector permits a view of the great unfinished *Arcades Project* as "Rag Picking," a practice committed to salvaging everything that is disregarded by history. Taken from Benjamin's bequest, Germaine Krull's photographs of arcades and Sasha Stone's interior studies are presented under the title "Past Turned Space"—public and private bourgeois lives, two sides of the same coin. The chapter "Hard Nuts to Crack" is devoted to Benjamin's delight at word games and brainteasers, which he developed into a small collection of puzzles—he managed to publish some of them, but some were simply exchanged with those of like minds. A puzzle forms the object of the thirteenth chapter: eight reproductions of the Sibyls from the cathedral at Siena. What meaning these held for Benjamin remains obscure; one of the mottos in *The Arcades Project*, taken from the *Aeneid*, gives a pointer—into the underworld.

These would not be Benjamin's archives if the materials did not communicate with one another. Each of these collections is distinctive and yet none of them lies in a closed drawer. Fine threads lead from one to another. The drafts are tangent to the graphic outlines. Puzzles work with the tones of language, with distortions and shifts of meaning—just as do Benjamin's notes on his son Stefan. The toys of the child's world are miniaturized just like his tiny script. The reproductions of the Sibyls are picture postcards as are the views of Italy and Spain. The overarching concept is the archive, to which belong all the scraps, notebooks, the notes for *The Arcades Project*, as well as the photographs and the drafts.

Everything is held together by the genius of the collector, who regarded "being at home in marginal areas" (*GS* III, p. 369) as a characteristic of the modern researcher.

Comprehensiveness was neither possible nor sought after. Certain materials that disappeared between 1933 and 1940 are absent. The most sensitive loss is Benjamin's library, of which only a piteous remainder was delivered to Moscow. The trail of the Heinle brothers' bequest, which Benjamin possessed and which he wished to publish, ends in Berlin. The one essential thing necessary for a reconstruction of Benjamin's radio work is missing: there is no recording of his voice. Equally this presentation of Benjamin's archives dispenses with presenting those items that are already accessible, such as his collection of children's books, or photographs and documents pertaining to his life. A stringent selection had to be made from his research materials. Each of his projects forms an archive in itself, and these are to a large extent preserved: quotations from Baroque literature, poems by Baudelaire, materials for the essay on Goethe's *Elective Affinities*, transcriptions of sonnets by Brecht, radio plays, notes on Eduard Fuchs, the collector and historian, excerpts from the journal *New Age*. Also left out of this book are bibliographies on various fields of research, his photographs of stage sets, drawings by Paul Klee and also—though omitting these was especially hard—his collection of anecdotes pertaining to Kant and the impressions he jotted down during and after consuming drugs.

Collections unlock themselves once a single piece is brought to voice. In the beginning was the exemplary object, which often opens up the way to thought as if by itself. Groups of documents arose. Sibling relationships became visible. The consideration of material and its context in the work delivered insights into an extraordinary bequest and its originator—it generated a portrait of the author from his archive.

Benjamin's mode of working is marked by the techniques of archiving, collecting, and constructing. Excerpts, transpositions, cuttings-out, montaging, sticking, cataloguing and sorting appear to him to be true activities of an author. His inspiration is inflamed by the richness of materials. Images, documents, and perceptions reveal their secrets to the look that is thorough enough. Benjamin was interested in the incidental. He loved to think in marginal areas, in order to push out from there to the center; he liked to use the phrase "most central." His capacity for immersion and his preparedness to make connections allowed him to discover essential things in details. Fragments recombined into new things; this researcher converted them into something distinctive.

Benjamin believed that the basis of collecting does not lie in "exactness," in "silk reeling" or "the complete inventorizing of all data" (*GS* III, p. 216). Peculiar to the collector is "a relationship to objects which does not emphasize their functional, utilitarian value—that is their usefulness—but studies and loves them as the scene, the stage of their fate" (*SW* 2:2, p. 487). Benjamin designates the true passion of the collector as "anarchistic, destructive." He affiliates fidelity to the thing with "the wilfully subversive protest against the typical, classifiable." Possession of a thing generates completely irrational accents. For the collector his item, its origin and past all close ranks as "a magic encyclopedia, a world ordering, whose outline is the fate of the object" (*GS* III, pp. 216f).

The suspicion that what is being dealt with here is historically outbid can be countered by a reference to the note *Excavation and Memory*, a key text on the question of memory. It informs us that to approach a submerged past involves digging. It is advisable to plan one's procedures, but also indispensable to probe cautiously, tentatively, into the dark loam. "And the man who merely makes an inventory of his findings, while failing to establish the exact location of where in today's ground the ancient treasures have been stored up, cheats himself of his richest prize" (*SW* 2:2, p. 576). The concept of "topicality" was no empty phrase for Benjamin.

One of the few who was able to judge that for himself was Jean Selz. Selz got to know Benjamin in 1932 on the Pitiusas, the small sister islands of the Balearics, and he encountered him on Benjamin's home ground: translation, as they rendered parts of *Berlin Childhood* in French. Selz learnt a lot about Benjamin's modes of thinking and working. He experienced how Benjamin traced the graphic form of words. He witnessed how he held his pen. And he discovered the various functions of the notebooks. In retrospect Selz described his extraordinary interlocutor in the following way: "Walter Benjamin was one of the most intelligent men I have ever met in my life. He was perhaps the only one who gave me with so much force the impression that there is a depth of thought where, propelled by rigorous logical reasoning, precise historic and scientific facts inhabit a plane in which they coexist with their poetic counterparts, a plane where poetry is no longer simply a form of literary thought, but reveals itself as an expression of the truth that illuminates the most intimate correspondences between man and the world" (Jean Selz, "Benjamin in Ibiza," p. 366).

"Thirteen—it was a cruel pleasure to stop at this number": Benjamin quotes Marcel Proust, from his cycle *In Search of Lost Time*, two volumes of which he translated together with Franz Hessel. Benjamin had a particular affinity for the number thirteen. He described the thirteen towers of San Gimignano. And he composed five texts that are structured as thirteen theses. Four of these are in *One-Way Street*: *The Writer's Technique in Thirteen Theses*, *Thirteen Theses against Snobs*, *The Technique of the Critic in Thirteen Theses*, *Number 13* and *The Path to Success in Thirteen Theses*.[2] These are poetological reflections, contributions to the self-understanding of writing, judging, and publishing, his main activities. Thirteen features as a magical number, standing for conspiracy and danger, bringing bad luck or good fortune. That last thing was bestowed upon Benjamin's archives. They were saved and it is to be hoped that they will not be forgotten.

Erdmut Wizisla

[2] This final one is in *SW* 2:1, pp. 144-7.

I

Tree of Conscientiousness

Benjamin as Archivist

> Thus the life of a collector manifests a dialectical tension between the poles of disorder and order.
>
> *SW* 2:2, p. 487

> The scruples, sometimes disturbing even to me, with which I view the plan of some sort of "Collected Works" correspond to the archival precision with which I preserve and catalog everything of mine that has appeared in print. Furthermore, disregarding the economic side of being a writer, I can say that for me the few journals and small newspapers in which my work appears represent for me the anarchic structure of a private publishing house. The main objective of my promotional strategy, therefore, is to get everything I write—except for some diary entries—into print at all costs and I can say that I have been successful in this—knock on wood!—for about four or five years.
>
> *Correspondence*, p. 385

> I, however, had something else in mind: not to retain the new but to renew the old. And to renew the old—in such a way that I myself, the newcomer, would make what was old my own—was the task of the collection that filled my drawer.
>
> *SW* 3, p. 403

The "struggle against dispersion," which is the "most deeply hidden motive of the person who collects" (*AP*, p. 211), finds no more pregnant expression than in the archive. Given the insecurities that beleaguered his life, Walter Benjamin led this struggle with particular perseverance and finesse. His own contribution as a collector to the preservation and transmission of his works is not without irony. "I will continue to ensure the completion of your collection of little grasses and stems from my field," Benjamin wrote to his friend Alfred Cohn in 1928, in a statement that predates his departure into exile. "This way, at least, there is the benefit, more for me than you, of there being another complete herbarium somewhere apart from my own" (*GB* III, p. 388). His carefulness stood him in good stead early on, and his friends ensured the conservation of the scripts passed to them as reservoirs of his thought and writing. "But now the moment has come," Benjamin wrote to Gershom Scholem on May 31, 1933, "when you must allow me to shake a few meager fruits from the tree of conscientiousness which has its roots in my heart and its leaves in your archive" (*Benjamin/Scholem Correspondence*, p. 53).

Benjamin was extremely conscientious not only in distributing and conserving his works. The archival logging of his manuscripts and collections was an equally important task. He compiled a catalog (which is no longer in existence) of the contents of his library (*Correspondence*, p. 306) and he kept a notebook with meticulous details of his reading since graduation from high school (*Correspondence*, p. 268). This catalog, preserved in a small black leather lined notebook, begins with entry number 462 (the previous list of items is missing) and registers Benjamin's reading from the age of twenty-two, in 1917, until 1939: it ends with Robert Hichens' *Le Toque noire* (1939), which bears the number 1712. Another notebook preserves bibliographical lists on various themes such as "Romantic Journals," "Gnomic Science," "Mythological Research," and "Greek and Roman Literature." Numerous card indexes and scraps of paper with addresses, excerpts, and literature lists are likewise preserved. Benjamin ordered some of these odds and ends thematically, separated into envelopes marked with lists of their contents (fig. 1.1). A note on a slip of paper in the bequest mentions a "friendship book with quotation entries" (WBA 210/12), which Benjamin must have once possessed. And lastly there are also catalogs detailing the contents of his archive. An early inventory, left behind in his apartment when he fled Berlin, is presented here (figs 1.2 and 1.3). It is written in black ink on a chamois-colored piece of paper, which is folded in the middle to make a double sheet. Additional corrections, addenda, crossings out, and colored marks indicate that Benjamin contributed to it over a long period of time and reworked it on several occasions. The itemization it provides is a research tool, a floor plan of Benjamin's archive. On the basis of this inventory, the life and writing of Benjamin can be traced in model form.

The inventory comprises thirty groups. Predominant amongst them is correspondence but there are also headings for manuscripts by others, personal and business documents, and his own writings. His writings are classified according to thematic aspects relating to content, as well as partly in relation to their written format ("printed," "only in handwriting," "typewritten"). The arrangement is systematic, "but according to a surprising coherence that is incomprehensible to the profane" (*GS* III, pp. 216f). Measured against any conventional system, Benjamin's ordering appears distorted, affected by subjective memories and meanings. His classifications—including "Letters from deceased people except for Fritz Heinle and Rika Seligson" and "Letters from all living male correspondents except for relatives and Gerhardi, Blumenthal, Sachs, Wolf Heinle / In addition letters from Jula

[Cohn]"—evidence a personal relationship to the material, in which the writers continue to live. It is as if only certain people might be brought together, while others must be kept apart from each other or be given their own separate place. These living connections break through the "mild boredom of order" (*SW* 2:2, p. 486), recognizing in things less their "functional, utilitarian value" than the "scene, the stage, of their fate" (*SW* 2:2, p. 487).

Each of the archival containers—folders, files, envelopes, cases, and boxes—is precisely described by an indication of the brand (Sönneken), color, size, provenance ("cardboard envelope from *The Demons*"), as well as any material peculiarities ("with crest," "extendable") or breakages ("torn in half"). These containers are aids in systematizing the material. At the same time, they offer protection against damage: they stow away and preserve the papers stored in them, holding them together in one place. For Benjamin, the securing of his archive was an important task in several regards. Mechanical damage to papers was mended with thin strips of vellum or the edges of sheets of stamps or, as in one case, sewn with needle and thread (figs 1.4 and 1.5). In the mid-1930s he arranged for *The Arcades Project* to be photographically reproduced and he sent the images to the Institute for Social Research in New York for safekeeping. He made transcriptions of his writings (or had them made) and sent them to friends and colleagues with the request, "please store the manuscript carefully" (*GB* I, p. 452). When it came to requests for their return or for them to be sent on to someone else, he asked, on various occasions, that they be insured, and indicated the estimated value. His "Memorandum on the Mexican Seminar," for example, which he requested Scholem return, was assessed by him immodestly "at a value of 400M" (*GB* I, p. 453). According to an early note written in Berlin, he stored photographs "in the large bureau—middle compartment, small drawer at the bottom on the right" (fig. 1.6). He also owned a "magazine chest" (WBA 210/12). In the last apartment he inhabited in Berlin there was a locked manuscript cupboard (see *GB* IV, p. 90), in which Benjamin kept the residues of his life and writing, the "masked" things of his existence, ordered "in drawers, chests, and boxes" (*SW* 3, p. 403).

While the inventory evidences the significance that Benjamin attributed to his own writings, it provides just as precisely confirmation of the loss of documents from the years prior to exile. Some things listed were destroyed or are assumed missing—such as a large part of the correspondence, including letters from Grete Radt, his parents, Franz Sachs, Wolf Heinle, and other friends from the milieu of the youth movement. Whether and which of the "Philosophical works, Fragments" are lost is very difficult to ascertain. Proofs of published writings, which Benjamin most probably kept in the brown cardboard box with a crest on it, have survived. In a letter to Scholem on October 28, 1931 Benjamin indicates the "archival precision with which I preserve and catalog everything of mine that has appeared in print" (*Correspondence*, p. 385). Presumably this is a reference to the *Catalogue of My Published Works*, which is amongst the papers of the bequest (fig. 1.7). This consists of ten written sheets, some of which have writing on the reverse side and it collates—if not quite exhaustively—436 entries from the years 1911 to 1939. It is to be assumed that he arranged for a secretary to type up the copy that is in the archive (Ts. 2379–2393). Up until 1928 every entry was also individually transferred to an index card (WBA 218). Benjamin collected sheets of his published work, snipped them out (or received them as offprints) and then stuck them to large sheets with gummed strips. These were then furnished with details of sources and corrections, additions, and observations (fig. 1.8).

Through all of this careful ordering and classification of his papers, the compilation of bibliographic catalogs, the lists of themes and books, the collections of excerpts and notes, a mode of work is documented, which aims at something far more than the mere securing and stock-taking of knowledge. Benjamin's archive represents a reserve of drafts, thoughts, and quotations. And yet what is collected is not only supposed to be held in safekeeping: it is also to be used productively and grounded in the present. For, as Benjamin notes in *Excavation and Memory*, "he who merely makes an inventory of his findings, while failing to establish the exact location of where in today's ground the ancient treasures have been stored up, cheats himself of his richest prize" (*SW* 2:2, p. 576)

Figures

1.1 Envelope for literature lists and notes on various themes.

1.2 and 1.3 Early inventory of Walter Benjamin's archive—Manuscript on a double sheet, two sides.

1.4 and 1.5 Book list on the reverse side of a form from the Bibliothèque Nationale. The parts of the sheet of paper that have come away along the perforation have been sewn together again, presumably by Walter Benjamin.—Manuscript, one page, with materials on reverse.

It is presumed that this list of books belongs to the work for *The Arcades Project*. It lists titles on history, technology, architecture, photography, fine arts, and literature. These include: the several volumes of *History of Iron in its Technological and Cultural-Historical Context* by Ludwig Beck (1897ff), *The Tragedy of the Technological Epoch* by Otto Veit (1935), *Karl Marx* by Auguste Cornu (1934), the Goncourt Brothers' *Journal*, Houben's *Conversations with Heine*, books by Fourier, Balzac, Alexandre Dumas (*père*), and others.

1.6 Archival notes—Manuscript, two sides; shown here, page 1.

1.7 *Catalogue of My Published Works* (1911–1939)—Manuscript, thirteen sides; shown here, page 1. Compare *GS* VII.1, pp. 477–9.

1.8. Discussion of Gabriele Eckehard, *The German Book in the Epoch of the Baroque*. On the top right-hand corner Benjamin has noted: "The Lit[erary] World VI, 23/6 June 1930"—printed, one side. Compare *GS* III, pp. 236f.

1.9 Walter Benjamin's Paris address book (1930s)—shown here, pp. 33 verso and 34 recto.

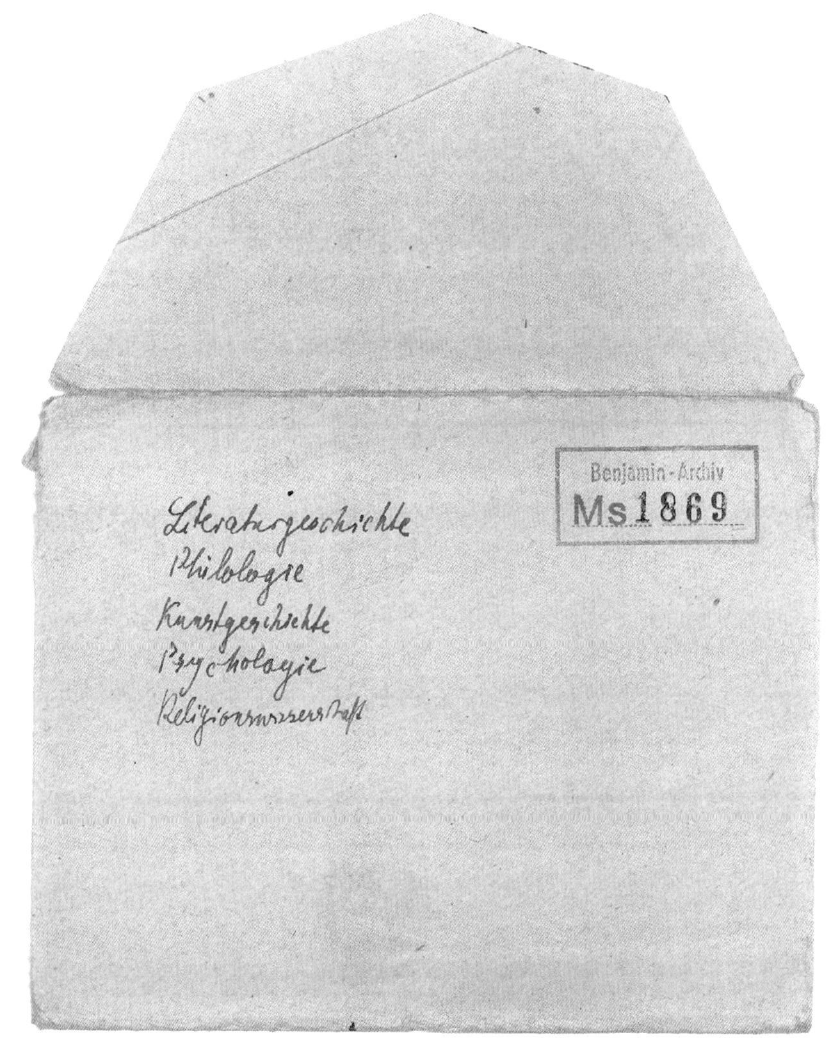
Benjamin-Archiv
Ms 1869
Literaturgeschichte
Philologie
Kunstgeschichte
Psychologie
Religionswissenschaft

Fig. 1.1

Fig. 1.1

Literary history
Philology
Art history
Psychology
Religious science

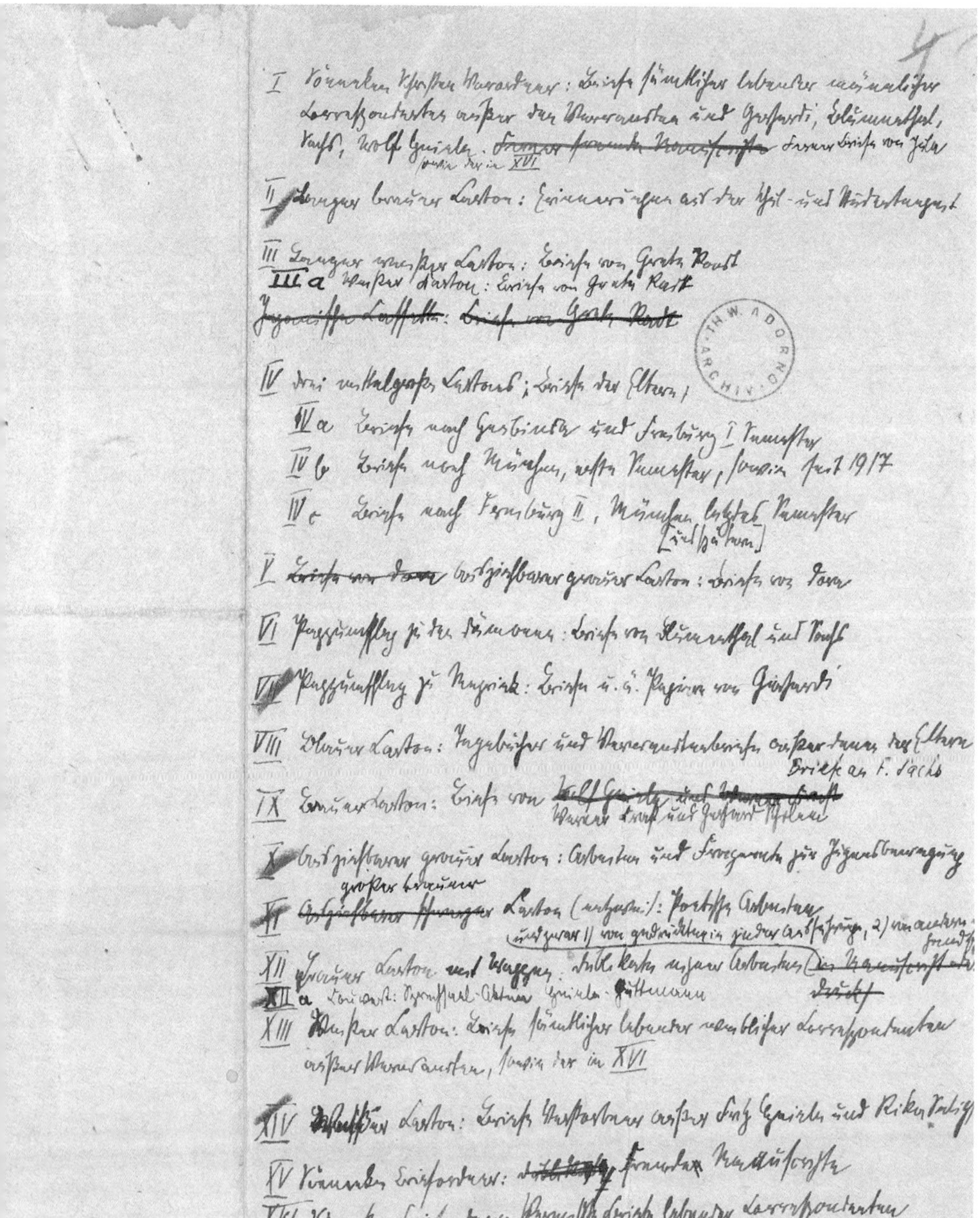

Fig. 1.2

Fig. 1.2

I Sönneken writings expanding file: Letters from all living male correspondents except for relatives and Gerhardi, Blumenthal, Sachs, Wolf Heinle. ~~In addition manuscripts by others' hands~~ In addition letters from Jula plus those in XVI

II Long brown cardboard box: Memories from school and university days

III Long white cardboard box: Letters from Grete Radt

IIIa White cardboard box: Letters from Grete Radt

~~Japanese casket: Letters from Grete Radt~~

IV Three medium-sized cardboard boxes; letters from parents,
IVa Letters to Haubinda and Freiburg, I Semester
IVb Letters to Munich, first semester, as well as 1917 and after
IVc Letters to Freiburg II, Munich final semester [and later]

V ~~Letters from Dora~~ Extendable grey cardboard box: Letters from Dora

VI Cardboard envelope from *The Demons*: Letters from Blumenthal and Sachs

VII Cardboard envelope from Meyrink: Letters and other papers from Gerhardi

VIII Blue cardboard box: Diaries and letters from relatives except for those from parents

Letters to F. Sachs

IX Brown cardboard box: Letters from ~~Wolf Heinle and Werner Kraft~~ Werner Kraft and Gerhard Scholem

X Extendable grey cardboard box: Writings and fragments on the youth movement

Large brown

XI ~~Extendable black~~ cardboard box (torn in half): Poetic works
Namely 1) published in any version, 2) others that are only handwritten

XII Brown cardboard box with crest: Duplicates of own works (~~in manuscript or print~~)

XIIa Envelope: Lecture-hall files Heinle—Guttmann

XIII White cardboard box: Letters from all living female correspondents except for relatives, plus those in XVI

XIV White cardboard box: Letters from deceased people except for Fritz Heinle and Rika Seligson

XV Sönneken letter file: ~~Duplicates~~, Manuscripts by other people

XVI Sönneken letter file: Miscellaneous letters from living correspondents

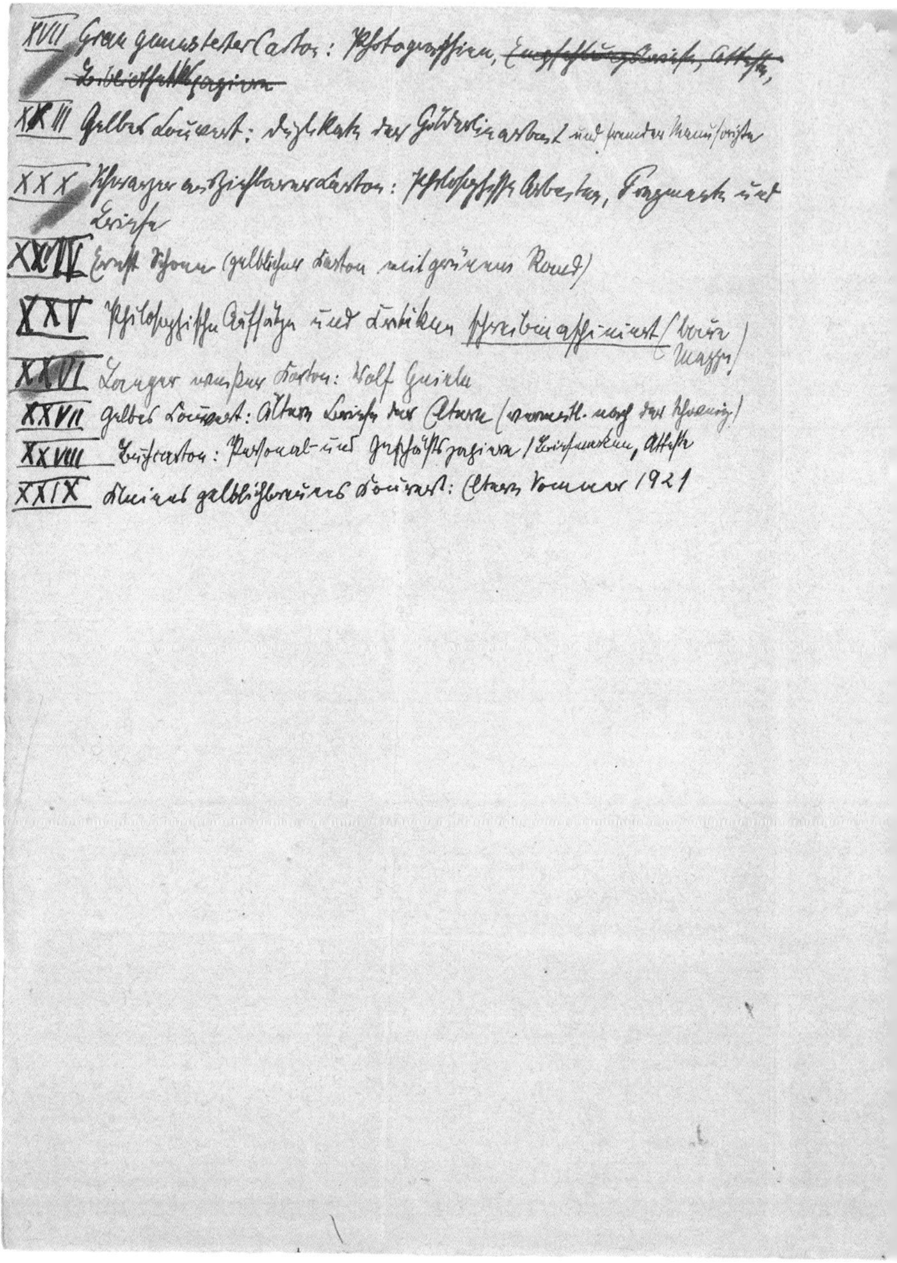

XVIII Grau gemusterter Carton: Photographien, ~~[illegible]~~

XXIII Gelbes Couvert: Duplikate der Hölderlinarbeit und fremder Manuskripte

XXX Schwarzer [illegible] Carton: Philosophische Arbeiten, Fragmente und Briefe

XXIV Ernst Schoen (gelblicher Carton mit grünem Rand)

XXV Philosophische Aufsätze und Kritiken schreibmaschiniert (braune Mappe)

XXVI Langer [illegible] Carton: Wolf Heinle

XXVII gelbes Couvert: Alte Briefe der Eltern (namentl. nach der Schweiz)

XXVIII [illegible]carton: Personal- und Geschäftspapiere / [illegible], Atteste

XXIX Kleines gelblichbraunes Couvert: Eltern Sommer 1921

Fig. 1.3

Fig 1.3

XVII Grey patterned cardboard box: Photographs, ~~letters of recommendation, certificates;, library papers~~

XXIII Yellow envelope: Duplicates of the Hölderlin work and manuscripts by others

XXX Black extendable cardboard box: Philosophical works, fragments and letters

XXIV Ernst Schoen (yellowy cardboard box with green edging)

XXV Philosophical essays and critiques typewritten (blue folder)

XXVI Long white cardboard box: Wolf Heinle

XXVII Yellow envelope: Older letters from parents (probably after Switzerland)

XXVIII Book box: Personal and business papers/stamps, certificates

XXIX Small, yellow-brown envelope: Parents Summer 1921

Toussenel: Mammifères de France (3e éd) illustré par Emile Bayard 1868

Hackländer: Die Damenwahl

Revue internationale ed Carlos de Roode [illegible] Mario Proth

Journalists: Journal [über Photographie] über Meryon]

Cleuziou: L'oeuvre de Delacroix

L Beck: Geschichte des Eisens 3 B de Braunschweig 1898

Escholier: Daumier

Courbet: L'apôtre Jean Journet

Franz Schnabel: Deutsche Geschichte im 19ten Jahrhundert III (Erfahrungswissenschaften und Technik) Freiburg 1935 (Herder)

Panofsky [Schrift über die Perspektive]

Amelia [Victor Hugo et Advokat]

B[r]isson et Ribeyre: Les journaux de France

Paris 1936

Otto Veit: Die Tragik des technischen Zeitalters Berlin 1935

R Ruyer: L'humanité de l'avenir d'après Cournot Paris 1930

[Bemerkungen über la réserve et les rythmes des métiers]

Gautier: Vorrede zu Mademoiselle de Maupin [gegen den Journalismus]

Fourier: Les Tartufes du progrès [gegen Saint-Simon]

N Grosl: Théorie du mouvement perpétuel Paris 1825

Alexandre Dumas (père): Mémoires VIII p 242 (gegen Eisenbahnen)

A Cornu: Karl Marx Paris 1934

E Ténot: Les provinces en décembre 1851
Paris en décembre 1851

H Castille: Les massacres de juin

Vermorel: Les hommes de 1848
: L'opposition

A Kirrmann: La Chimie d'hier et d'aujourd'hui Paris [über J-B Dumas]

Rassenfosse et Guében: Des alchimistes aux briseurs d'atomes Liège

Fig. 1.4

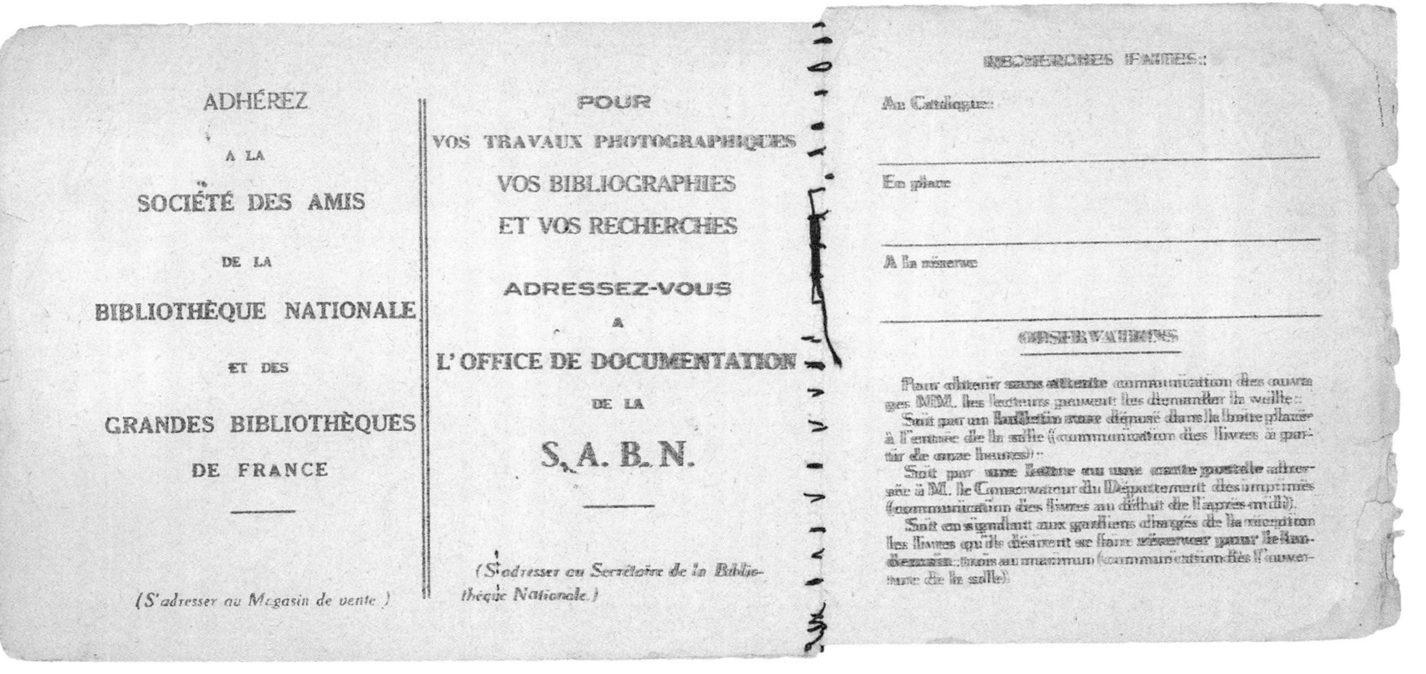

ADHÉREZ

A LA

SOCIÉTÉ DES AMIS

DE LA

BIBLIOTHÈQUE NATIONALE

ET DES

GRANDES BIBLIOTHÈQUES

DE FRANCE

(S'adresser au Magasin de vente.)

POUR

VOS TRAVAUX PHOTOGRAPHIQUES

VOS BIBLIOGRAPHIES

ET VOS RECHERCHES

ADRESSEZ-VOUS

A

L'OFFICE DE DOCUMENTATION

DE LA

S. A. B. N.

(S'adresser au Secrétaire de la Bibliothèque Nationale.)

RECHERCHES FAITES :

Au Catalogue :

En place

A la réserve

OBSERVATIONS

Pour obtenir sans attente communication des ouvrages MM. les lecteurs peuvent les demander la veille :

Soit par un bulletin rose déposé dans la boîte placée à l'entrée de la salle (communication des livres à partir de onze heures) ;

Soit par une lettre ou une carte postale adressée à M. le Conservateur du Département des imprimés (communication des livres au début de l'après-midi).

Soit en signalant aux gardiens chargés de la réception les livres qu'ils désirent se faire réserver pour le lendemain : trois au maximum (communication dès l'ouverture de la salle).

Fig. 1.5

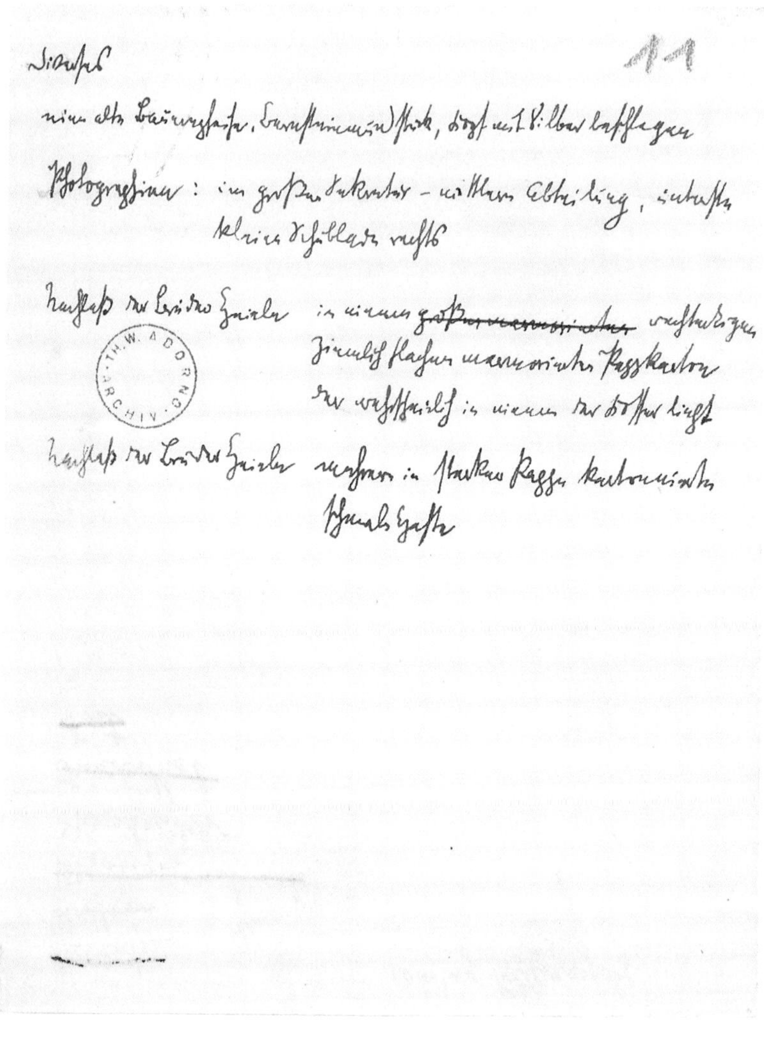

Diverses 11

eine alte Bauernjacke, [illegible], [illegible] mit Silber beschlagen

Photographien: im großen Sekretär – mittlere Abteilung, unterste kleine Schublade rechts

Nachlaß der Brüder Heinle in einem ~~großen marmorierten~~ rechteckigen ziemlich flachen marmorierten Pappkarton der wahrscheinlich in einem der Koffer liegt

Nachlaß der Brüder Heinle mehrere in starker Pappe kartonierte Schnellhefter

Fig. 1.6

Fig. 1.6

Miscellany
An old farmer's pipe, amber mouthpiece, bowl studded with silver

Photographs: in the large bureau—middle compartment,
small drawer at the bottom on the right

Heinle brothers' bequest in a ~~large marbled~~ rectangular
quite flat marbled cardboard box
which probably is in one of the cases

Heinle brothers' bequest several slim notebooks covered in stiff cardboard

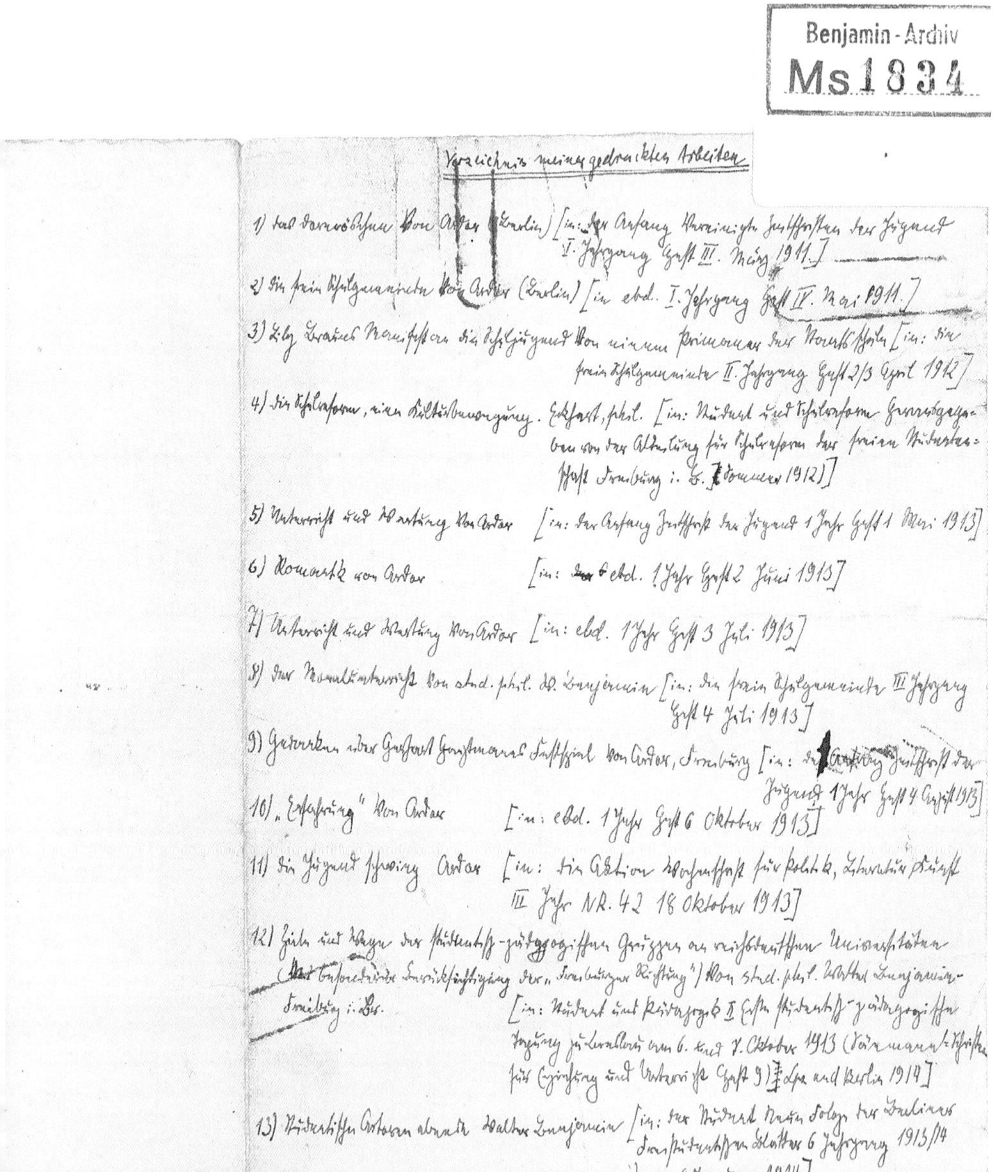

Verzeichnis meiner gedruckten Arbeiten

1) Das Dornröschen von Ardor (Berlin) [in: Der Anfang Vereinigte Zeitschriften der Jugend I. Jahrgang Heft III. März 1911.]

2) Die freie Schulgemeinde von Ardor (Berlin) [in ebd. I. Jahrgang Heft IV. Mai 1911.]

3) [illegible] [illegible] Manifest an die Schuljugend von einem Primaner der [illegible] Schule [in: Die freie Schulgemeinde II. Jahrgang Heft 2/3 April 1912]

4) Die Schulreform, eine Kulturbewegung. Eckhart, phil. [in: Student und Schulreform Herausgegeben von der Abteilung für Schulreform der freien Studentenschaft Freiburg i. B. Sommer 1912]

5) Unterricht und Wertung von Ardor [in: Der Anfang Zeitschrift der Jugend 1 Jahr Heft 1 Mai 1913]

6) Romantik von Ardor [in: ebd. 1 Jahr Heft 2 Juni 1913]

7) Unterricht und Wertung von Ardor [in: ebd. 1 Jahr Heft 3 Juli 1913]

8) Der Moralunterricht von stud. phil. W. Benjamin [in: Die freie Schulgemeinde III Jahrgang Heft 4 Juli 1913]

9) Gedanken über Gerhart Hauptmanns Festspiel von Ardor, Freiburg [in: Der Anfang Zeitschrift der Jugend 1 Jahr Heft 4 August 1913]

10) „Erfahrung" von Ardor [in: ebd. 1 Jahr Heft 6 Oktober 1913]

11) Die Jugend schwieg Ardor [in: Die Aktion Wochenschrift für Politik, Literatur, Kunst III Jahr NR. 42 18 Oktober 1913]

12) Ziele und Wege der studentisch-pädagogischen Gruppen an reichsdeutschen Universitäten (mit besonderer Berücksichtigung der „Freiburger Richtung") von stud. phil. Walter Benjamin–Freiburg i. Br. [in: Student und Pädagogik II Heft studentisch-pädagogische Tagung zu Breslau am 6. und 7. Oktober 1913 (Teubners Schriften für Erziehung und Unterricht Heft 9) Lpz und Berlin 1914]

13) Studentische Autorenabende Walter Benjamin [in: Der Student [illegible] der Berliner Freistudentischen Blätter 6 Jahrgang 1913/14 Nr. 9 9 Januar 1914]

14) Erotische Erziehung (Anlässlich des letzten studentischen Autorenabends in Berlin) Ardor [in: Die Aktion Wochenschrift für Politik, Literatur, Kunst IV Jahr NR 3 17 Januar 1914]

Fig. 1.7

Fig. 1.7
Catalogue of My Published Works

The publications listed here are as follows: his pseudonymous publications for the youth movement magazine *Der Anfang* [The Beginning]: *Sleeping Beauty* published in March 1911; *The Free School Community* from May 1911; the two-part *Teaching and Evaluation* from May–July 1913; *Romanticism* from June 1913; *Thoughts on Gerhart Hauptmann's Festival* from August 1913; and *Experience* from October 1913.

Listed also: *School Reform, A Cultural Movement*, published in a Free Students' publication on students and school reform in 1912; *Moral Education* in *The Free School Community* journal; *Youth Was Silent*, published in the journal *Action* in 1913; *Aims and Methods of the Student-Pedagogic Groups at the Universities of the German Reich*, published in a collection of papers from a student conference in 1914; *Students' Author Evenings* published in *The Student* in 1914; and *Erotic Education (On the Occasion of the Latest Students' Author Evening in Berlin)*, which appeared in *Action* in 1914.

GABRIELE ECKEHARD: DAS DEUTSCHE BUCH IM ZEITALTER DES BAROCK

Ullstein, Berlin

Es ist selten, daß Sammler als solche sich der Oeffentlichkeit vorstellen. Sie wünschen als Wissenschaftler, als Kenner, zur Not auch als Besitzer zu passieren, aber sehr selten als das, was sie vor allem doch sind: als Liebhaber. Diskretion pflegt ihre stärkste, Freimut ihre schwächste Seite zu sein. Wenn ein großer Sammler den Prachtkatalog seiner Schätze veröffentlicht, repräsentiert er zwar seine Sammlung, in den seltensten Fällen aber sein Sammlergenie. Von diesen Regeln bildet das vorliegende Buch eine ~~begrüßenswerte~~ Ausnahme. Ohne gerade Katalog zu sein, repräsentiert es eine der stattlichsten Privatsammlungen deutscher Barockliteratur; ohne gerade Entstehungsgeschichte der Sammlung zu sein, enthält es die Impulse, aus denen sie sich gebildet hat. Man redet so gerne von dem „persönlichen Verhältnis", das ein Sammler zu seinen Sachen habe. Im Grunde scheint diese Wendung eher geschaffen, die Haltung, die sie anerkennen will, zu bagatellisieren, sie als unverbindliche, als liebenswürdig-launische hinzustellen. Sie führt irre. Am ehesten aber wird man die Gemeinde der wahren Sammler als die der Zufallsgläubigen, der Zufallsanbeter zu bezeichnen haben. Nicht nur darum, weil sie alle wissen, daß ihr Besitz sein bestes dem Zufall dankt, sondern weil sie in ihren Besitztümern selber den Spuren des Zufalls nachjagen, weil sie Physiognomiker sind, die da glauben, daß nichts so Ungereimtes, Unberechenbares, Unvermerktes den Dingen zustoßen könne, daß es in ihnen seine Spuren nicht hinterließe. Diese Spuren sind es, denen sie nachgehen: der Ausdruck des Geschehenen entschädigt sie tausendfach für die Unvernunft des Geschehens. — Soviel um anzudeuten, warum es die Sammlerin und nicht nur die Verfasserin dieser Schrift rühmt, wenn wir sie eine Ader an der Physiognomik nennen. Was sie vom Einband, von der Druckweise, der Erhaltung, dem Preis, der Verbreitung der Werke, mit denen sie es zu tun hat, aufzeichnet, sind ebenso viele Verwandlungen zufälligen Geschickes in mimischem Ausdruck. So von Büchern zu reden, wie sie es tut, ist das Vorrecht des Sammlers. Hoffen wir, daß dem Beispiel, das hier — bis in Ausstattung und Illustration hinein — gegeben wird, so viele folgen, als wenige ihm vorangingen.

W. B.

Fig. 1.8

Fig. 1.8

Gabriele Eckehard: *The German Book in the Baroque Epoch*
Ullstein, Berlin

Handwritten marginalia:
Top right:
The Lit World
VI, 23
6 June 1930

It is rare for collectors to present themselves to the public. They hope to be regarded as scholars, connoisseurs, if needs be as owners too, but very rarely as that what they above all are: lovers. Discretion appears to be their strongest side, frankness their weakest. When a great collector publishes the glorious catalogue of his treasures he may be displaying his collection, but only in the rarest cases does he display his genius for collecting. The present book provides a welcome exception from these rules. Without exactly being a catalogue, it showcases one of the most impressive private collections of German Baroque literature. Without exactly being a history of the mode of acquisition of the collection, it contains the impulses out of which it was built. Many love to speak of the "personal relationship" that a collector has to his things. Fundamentally this phrase appears rather designed to trivialize the attitude that it wants to recognize, placing it as tentative, as agreeably moody. It is misleading. + It would be better to characterize the community of genuine collectors as those who believe in chance, are worshippers of chance. Not only because they each know that they owe the best of their possessions to chance, but also because they themselves pursue the traces of chance in their riches, for they are physiognomists, who believe that everything that befalls their items, no matter how illogical, wayward or unnoticed, leaves its traces. These are the traces that they pursue: the expression of past events compensates them a thousandfold for the irrationality of events.—All this is said in order to indicate why it is not just the author of this work but also the collector who is honored, when we designate her a connoisseur of physiognomy. What she records about the binding, the printing mode, the conservation, the price and the distribution of the works with which she deals, are likewise many such transformations of coincidental fate into mimetic expression. To speak of books as she does is the prerogative of the collector. We hope that the example that is given here—right down to the layout and illustrations—is followed by many, unlike the few who preceded.++

Handwritten amendments: "laudable" substituted for "welcome"

+ Collectors may be loony—though this in the sense of the French *lunatique*–according to the moods of the moon. They are playthings too, perhaps—but of a goddess—namely τυχη.

++ That amongst these few, though, the best—Karl Wohfskehl—is a lover of the Baroque shows that, for the true book collector, few similarly adequate objects of his love exist apart from precisely these books stemming from the German Baroque epoch.

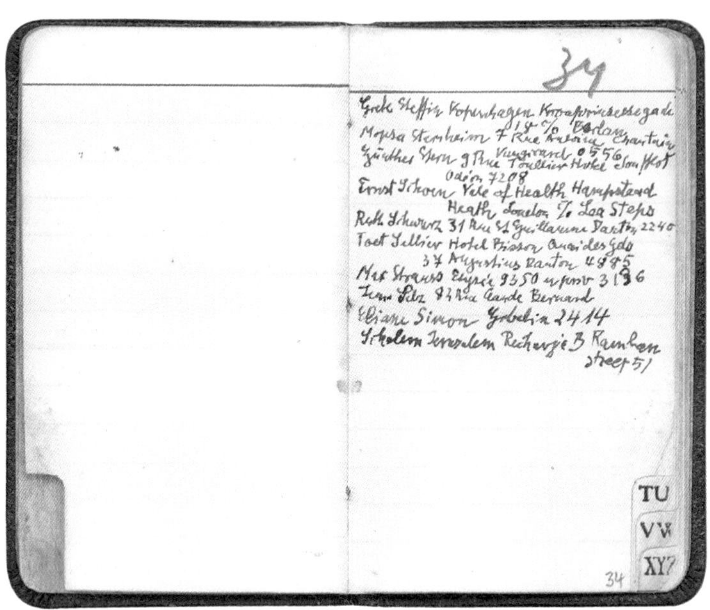

Fig. 1.9

Fig. 1.9

A page from Benjamin's Paris address book of the 1930s.
The names listed here: Margarete Steffin, Mopsa Sternheim, Günther Stern, Ernst Schoen, Ruth Schwarz, Toet Sellier, Max Strauss, Jean Selz, Eliane Simon and Gershom Scholem.

2

Scrappy Paperwork

Collecting and Dispersal

> For someone whose writings are as dispersed as mine, and for whom present conditions no longer allow the illusion that they will be gathered together again one day, it is a genuine endorsement to hear of a reader here and there, who has been able to make himself at home in my scraps of writings, in some way or another.
>
> *GB* IV, p. 394

> The card index marks the conquest of three-dimensional writing, and so presents an astonishing counterpoint to the three-dimensionality of script in its original form as rune or knot notation. (And today the book is already, as the present mode of scholarly production demonstrates, an outdated mediation between two different filing systems. For everything that matters is to be found in the card box of the researcher who wrote it, and the scholar studying it assimilates it into his own card index.)
>
> *SW* I, p. 456

Even though Benjamin's audience was not exactly small in the second half of the 1920s, the difficulties of existence as a freelance author were familiar to him: the necessity to secure money to live on; arising from this the imperative of lobbying editors and publishers; the merciless circuits of acquiring, executing, and delivering commissions; the impossibility of pursuing larger projects, because writing for subsistence money gobbled up all of his time. "Shameful hack paperwork" was the name he gave his commissions in a letter in September 1928, and he let it be known that even this was to be kept at a certain level in order that it not "revolt him." He did not lack in opportunities to publish bad stuff, but he did lack the courage needed to write it, he claimed (*GB* III, p. 414). His reviewing and his work for radio are, therefore, not to be seen purely as chores. A tolerably stable system of public activity collapsed, prior indeed to February 1933, once the press and radio were brought under a new political line. In exile in France, the opportunities for earning an income reduced dramatically, even though Benjamin was capable of writing in the tongue of his host land. Indeed Paris of all places was the one place where he could barely procure the cost of living: "There are places where I could earn a minimal income, and places where I could live on a minimal income, but not a single place where these two conditions coincide" (*Correspondence*, p. 402). How could he ever finance the primary researches for the books on Baudelaire and the arcades, which, after all, could only be undertaken in the Bibliothèque Nationale? In a letter dated July 20, 1938, Benjamin told his acquaintance Kitty Marx-Steinschneider, a resident of Jerusalem, of the difficulties of engaging with a larger project after months of unstable existence and countless obstacles. "I got behind with my ongoing projects and this always led to more or less disjointed scribbling, which then kept me on the go again for quite some time" (*Correspondence*, p. 568).[1]

The word "paperwork" indicates—as the formulation "income paperwork" (*GB* III, p. 414) makes clear—a certain disdain for the results of the work. "I had to make a start on something new, something quite different and was handicapped by journalistic-diplomatic scribbles" (*GB* III, p. 321), as he put it as early as January 1928, prior to the appearance of *One-Way Street*. Benjamin liked to describe those works that kept him from other work as "allotria." In similar fashion, he used the term "scrap" (*verzetteln*): as "disperse," "hack up," "lose," "waste"—regarding the scrap as a handicap or hindrance preventing him from making something new, working on something else, doing something "essential." He used his last bit of money to amalgamate his books, which were split between Berlin and Paris, at Brecht's house in Svendborg, "so as not to lose hold of my library by virtue of its being spread [*Verzettelung*] throughout Europe" (*Correspondence*, p. 450), as he told Gershom Scholem in July 1934. In January 1934, when he sent the manuscript of *Berlin Childhood around 1900* to Hermann Hesse (who had praised *One-Way Street* highly), he bemoaned that fact that, owing to his distance from Germany and the powerlessness that it implied, he was abandoned to an editorial that "did not accommodate" the manuscript "under its title or author, but rather printed it in scraps as individual contributions to the newspaper supplements" (*GB* IV, p. 334). The counter-image to this, which was never actually achieved, would be something completed, concentrated, collected, and undivided. *Berlin Childhood* counted for Benjamin as scrapped. It was one of his "shattered books" (*Correspondence*, p. 512).[2]

Benjamin acknowledged with gratitude every effort to safeguard his manuscripts. He appreciated a bibliographic mention of his works, published by the historian and theologian Karl Thieme in a journal titled *Religious Reflection*:

---

1 "Disjointed scribbling" is the Jacobsons' translation of *verzettelter Schreiberei*, heading of this chapter. I have chosen "scrappy paperwork" instead.

2 Translation amended (from "frustrated book projects") to convey sense in this context.

it was "a genuine endorsement to hear of a reader here and there, who has been able to make himself at home in my scraps of writings, in some way or another" (*GB* IV, p. 394). He saw himself "in a span of history and life," as he explained to Scholem in February 1935, "in which the final collecting together of the infinite scraps of my production seems less conceivable, indeed more improbable than ever" (*GB* V, p. 47). It was impossible for him to gather the scraps together, but it is owing to his calculations and the conscientiousness of his friends, that the improbable was still possible after his death. His bequest bears witness to the dogged attempt to write under adverse conditions.

And it tells the story of an extraordinary writing project in which aestheticism and pragmatism are held in balance. Benjamin used the choicest materials. But to an increasing degree, his life situation made any luxury in his working conditions impossible. In exile, it would seem, economic need dictated that everything he got his hands on be used (or re-used): the reverse sides of letters sent to him, postcards or an invitation to review, library forms, travel tickets, proofs, an advertisement for "S. Pellegrino," prescription pads discarded by his friend Fritz Fränkel, doctor and drug connoisseur (figs 2.3–2.9). The formats are fascinating: some scraps are no bigger than 4.5cm × 9cm. But Benjamin was able to utilize every last square millimeter. And he left behind a wealth of compressed sheets, notes, scraps, on which his great work unfolds richly detailed.

The structure of Benjamin's bequest is not only indebted to necessity. It exhibits idiosyncrasies in its modes of production, peculiar methods of thought and writing. "An economy of scraps just like in my family," a distant relation exclaimed recently on seeing Benjamin's condensed notes. Benjamin wrote constantly. When an idea occurred to him he did not delay its writing down by seeking out the right piece of paper, but rather used the nearest suitable thing at hand. In this way key thoughts are fixed in passing, "scrawled down," often on the margins of other works or directly interleaved in them (figs 2.10 and 2.11). And of course he knew the meaning of the concept "*verzetteln*" prevalent in library science or lexicography: "to excerpt," "to disperse things that belong together into individual slips or into the form of a card index."

The court library at Vienna introduced a card index catalog around 1780, because the bound catalog could not accommodate the flood of entries. Parish registers are entered on slips or even card, in order to be able to deploy the individual entries independently of the place of their transmission, and to be able to order them according to different criteria. Transfer to individual scraps or cards makes possible lexical projects such as the Goethe-Dictionary, which began to index the Weimar edition on slips of paper in 1946. Slips or their stronger sisters, index cards—of which the *Journal for Organisation* declared in 1929, "cards can do everything"—stand out because of their flexibility, and thus they represent modernity.

Benjamin recognized the artistic potential of this method of sorting: Mallarmé named as his own "a working instrument for poetry in the form of a card file" (*SW* 4, p. 117). In the section "Attested Auditor of Books", in *One-Way Street*, Benjamin points out a revolution in the administration of knowledge. The present mode of scholarly production demonstrates that the book is already "an outdated mediation between two different filing systems": "For everything that matters is to be found in the card box of the researcher who wrote it, and the scholar studying it assimilates it into his own card index" (*SW* 1, p. 456). Benjamin repeatedly treated the elements of his text according to the principle of building blocks: he copied them out, cut them out, stuck them on new sheets of paper and arranged them anew, long before such procedures became established in electronic word-processing under the name "copy and paste"—and before the appearance of the German computer program *Zettelwirtschaft [Paper Jumble]*, which was developed to order and re-order notes. Benjamin's idea of composing a work entirely of quotations ensures that the material within the collection can remain mobile, elements can be shifted at will. At the outset all material is of equal value: knowledge that is organized in slips and scraps knows no hierarchy.

Figures

2.1 *Types of Knowledge* (1921)—Manuscript, one side. Compare *GS* VI, p. 48.

2.2 *Language and Logic I* (1921)—Manuscript, one side. Compare SW I, p. 272.

2.3 and 2.4 Notes for *Franz Kafka* (1934)—Manuscript, one side, with reverse side (extract). Compare *GS* II.3, p. 1207.

2.5 and 2.6 *Proust and Kafka*. Notes for *Franz Kafka* (1934)—Manuscript, one side, with reverse side. Compare *GS* II.3, p. 1221.

2.7 *What is Aura?*—Manuscript, one side.

2.8 and 2.9 Bibliographic notes—Manuscript, one side, with reverse side. These bibliographical notes on a purchase voucher are probably connected to Benjamin's montage of letters for the 150th anniversary of the French Revolution, which appeared in the journal *Europe* on July 15, 1939 under the title "Allemands de quatre-vingt-neuf."

Itemized here are, amongst other things, the biography of Seume by Oskar Planer and Camillo Reißmann (1898), the books *Biedermeier in Chains* (1924) and *Prohibited Literature from Classical Times to the Present* (1925) by Heinrich Hubert Houben, Gustav Landauer's *Letters from the French Revolution*, Herder's *Letters for the Advancement of Humanity*, Benjamin's "Introduction to Jochmann," *Correspondence* by Georg Forster and a letter from Jochmann to Kant.

2.10 and 2.11 Note for *On the Concept of History*:
"Marx says that revolutions are the locomotives of world history. But perhaps it is quite different. Perhaps revolutions are what happens when the humanity travelling in this train snatches at the emergency brake." (c. 1940)—Manuscript, one side, with reverse side. The reverse side appears to show calculations relating to the cost of a lunch. Compare *GS* I.3, p. 1232.

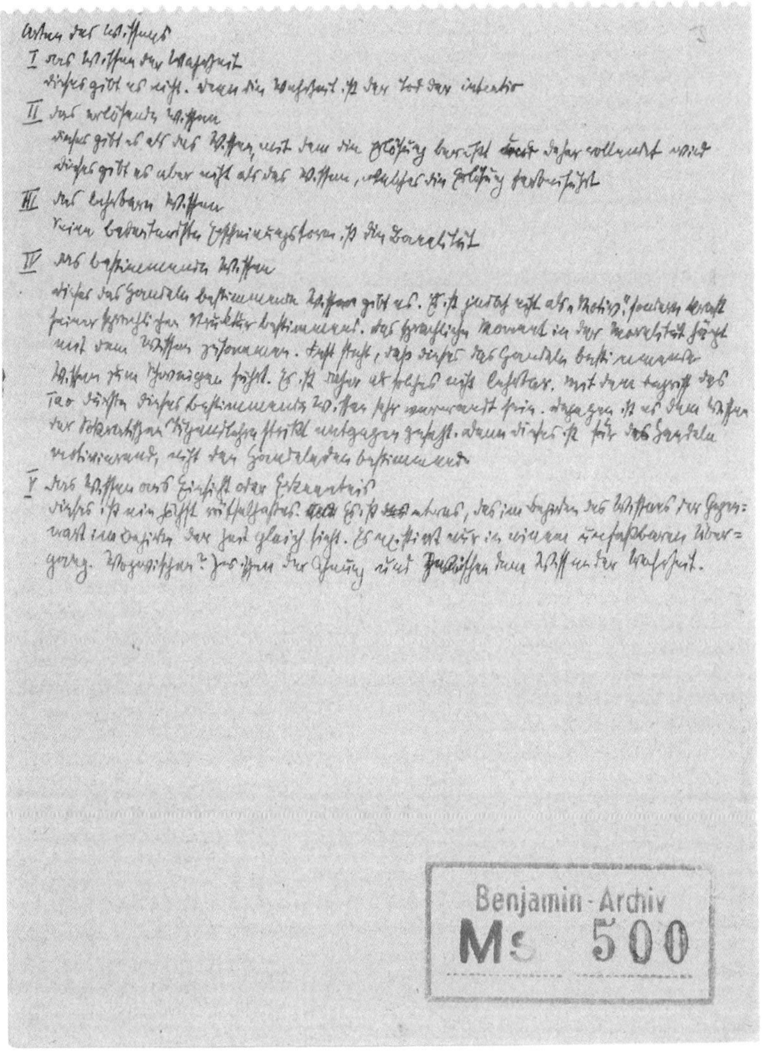

Arten des Wissens

I Das Wissen der Wahrheit

Dieses gibt es nicht. Denn die Wahrheit ist der Tod der intentio

II Das erlösende Wissen

Dieses gibt es als das Wissen, mit dem die Erlösung beruht ~~durch~~ daher vollendet wird
Dieses gibt es aber nicht als das Wissen, welches die Erlösung herbeiführt

III Das lehrbare Wissen

Seinen charakteristischen Erscheinungsformen ist die Totalität

IV Das bestimmende Wissen

Dieses das Handeln bestimmende Wissen gibt es. Es ist jedoch nicht als „Motiv", sondern kraft seiner sprachlichen Struktur bestimmend. Das sprachliche Moment in der Moralität hängt mit dem Wissen zusammen. Fest steht, daß dieses das Handeln bestimmende Wissen zum Schweigen führt. Es ist daher als solches nicht lehrbar. Mit dem Begriff des Tao dürfte dieses bestimmende Wissen sehr verwandt sein. Dagegen ist es dem Wissen der sokratischen Tugendlehre strikt entgegengesetzt. Denn dieses ist für das Handeln motivierend, nicht das Handeln bestimmend

V Das Wissen durch Einsicht oder Erkenntnis

Dieses ist ein höchst rätselhaftes. ~~Es~~ Es ist etwas, das im Begriffe des Wissens der Gegenwart im Begriffe der Zeit gleich liegt. Es existiert nur in einem unfaßbaren Übergang. Mysterien? Zwischen der Schauung und Zwischen dem Wissen der Wahrheit.

Fig. 2.1

Fig. 2.1

Types of Knowledge

I The knowledge of truth
This does not exist. For truth is the death of intention

II Redemptive knowledge
This is the knowledge that dawns with redemption, which is thereby completed
But it is not the knowledge that precipitates redemption

III Teachable knowledge
Its most significant form of appearance is banality

IV Determining knowledge
There is knowledge that determines action. It is, however, not determining as a "motive," but rather due to the force of its linguistic structure. The linguistic moment in morality is connected to knowledge. It is absolutely certain that this knowledge that determines action leads to silence. Therefore, as such, it is not teachable. This determining knowledge is closely related to the concept of Tao. This is in direct contradiction to knowledge in Socrates' Doctrine of Virtue. While this is motivating for action, it does not determine those who act.

V Knowledge from insight or perception
This type is highly enigmatic. In the region of knowledge, it is something that resembles the present in the region of time. It exists only as an ungraspable transition. From what to what? Between foreboding and the knowledge of truth.

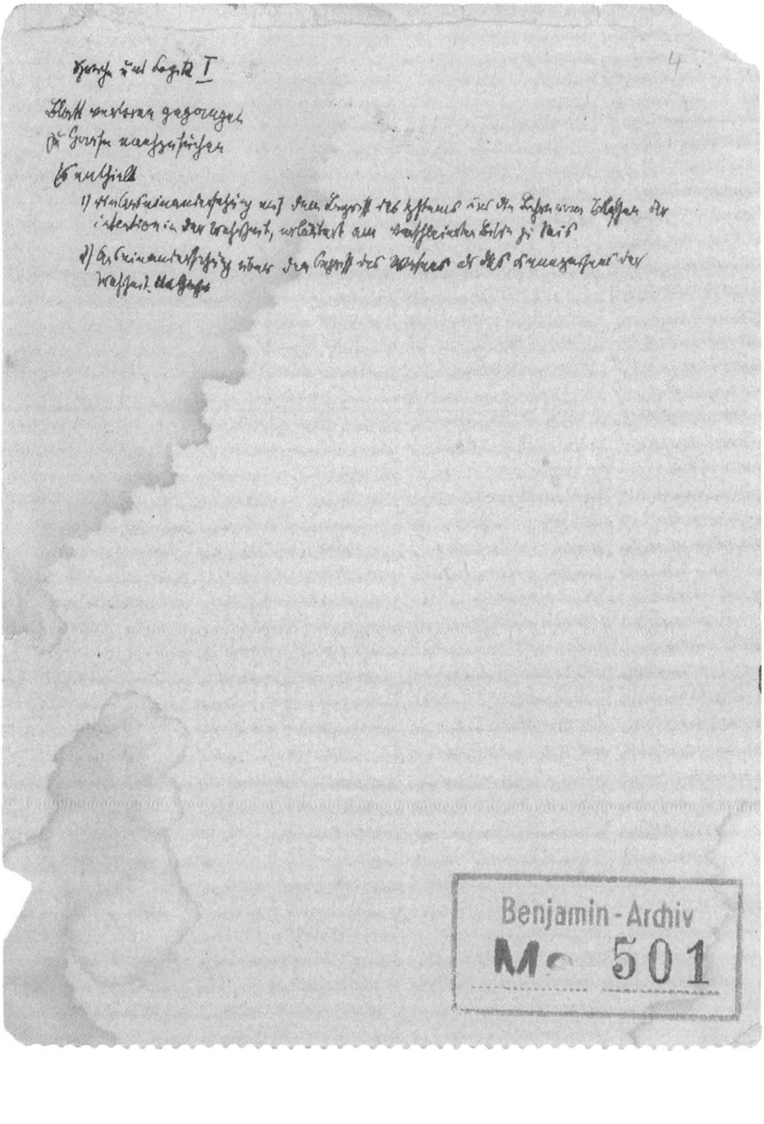

Fig. 2.2

Fig. 2.2

I

Sheet of paper has gone missing; must look for it at home. It contained:

1. The discussion of the concept of "system" and the doctrine of the extinguishing of intention in the truth, explained in terms of the veiled image of Sais.
2. Discussion of the concept of "essence" as the mark of truth.

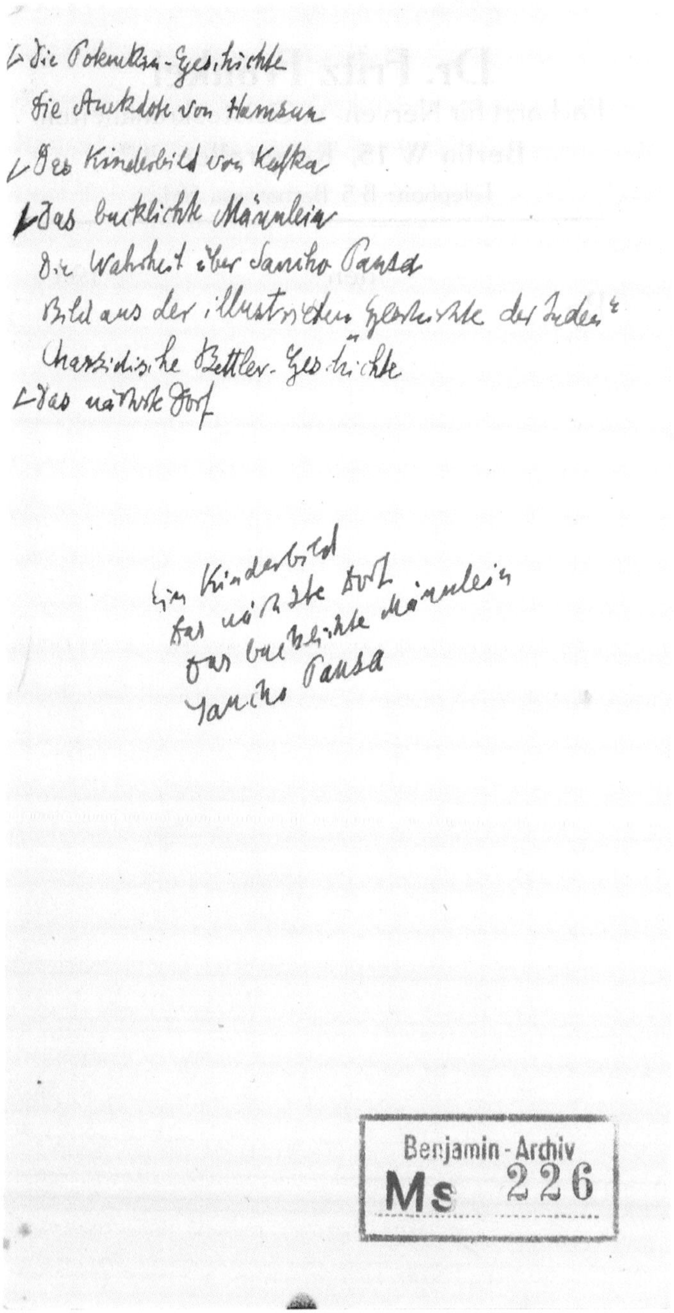

Die Potemkin-Geschichte
Die Anekdote von Hamsun
Das Kinderbild von Kafka
Das bucklichte Männlein
Die Wahrheit über Sancho Pansa
Bild aus der illustrierten Geschichte der Juden
Chassidische Bettler-Geschichte
Das nächste Dorf

Ein Kinderbild
Das nächste Dorf
Das bucklichte Männlein
Sancho Pansa

Fig. 2.3

Dr. Fritz Fränkel
Facharzt für Nerven- u. Geisteskrankheiten
Berlin W 15, Kaiserallee 207
Telephon: B 5 Barbarossa 5312

den 193

Rp.

Fig. 2.4

Fig. 2.3

The Potemkin Story
The anecdote from Hamsun
The childhood photograph of Kafka
The little hunchback
The truth about Sancho Panza
Picture from the illustrated *History of the Jews*
Hasidic beggar story
The Next Village

A childhood photograph
The Next Village
The little hunchback
Sancho Panza

Fig. 2.4

Dr Fritz Fränkel
Medical Specialist for
Nervous and Mental
Illnesses
207 Kaiserallee,
West Berlin 15
Telephone: B5
Barbarossa 5312

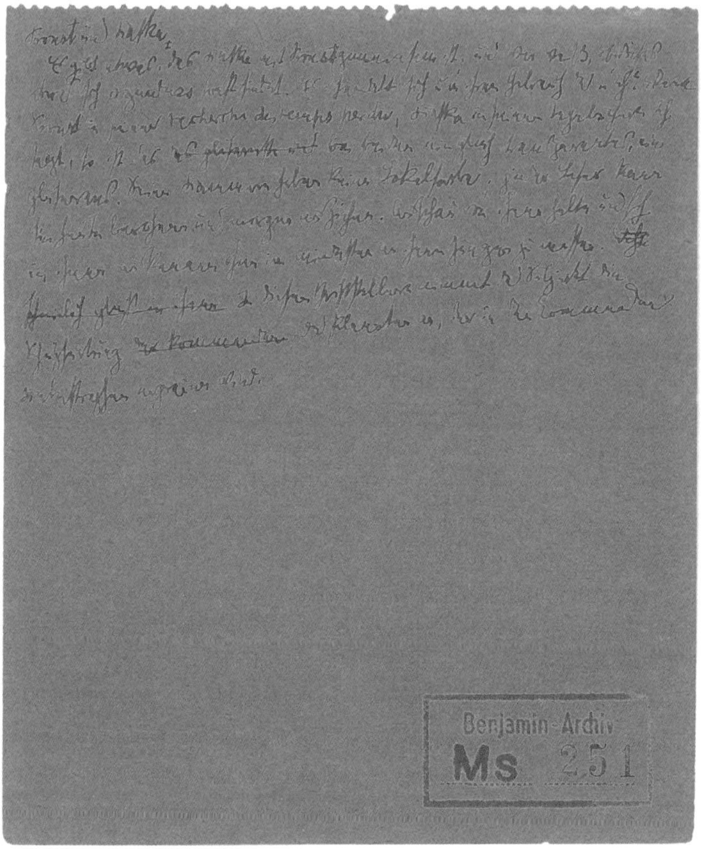

Fig. 2.5

Fig. 2.5

Proust and Kafka
There is something that Proust has in common with Kafka and who knows whether this can be found anywhere else. It is a matter of how they use "I." When Proust, in his *Recherche du temps perdu*, and Kafka, in his diaries, use I, for both of them it is equally transparent, glassy. Its chambers have no local coloring; every reader can occupy it today and move out tomorrow. You can survey them and get to know them without having to be in the least attached to them. In these authors the subject adopts the protective coloring of the planet, which will turn grey in the coming catastrophes.

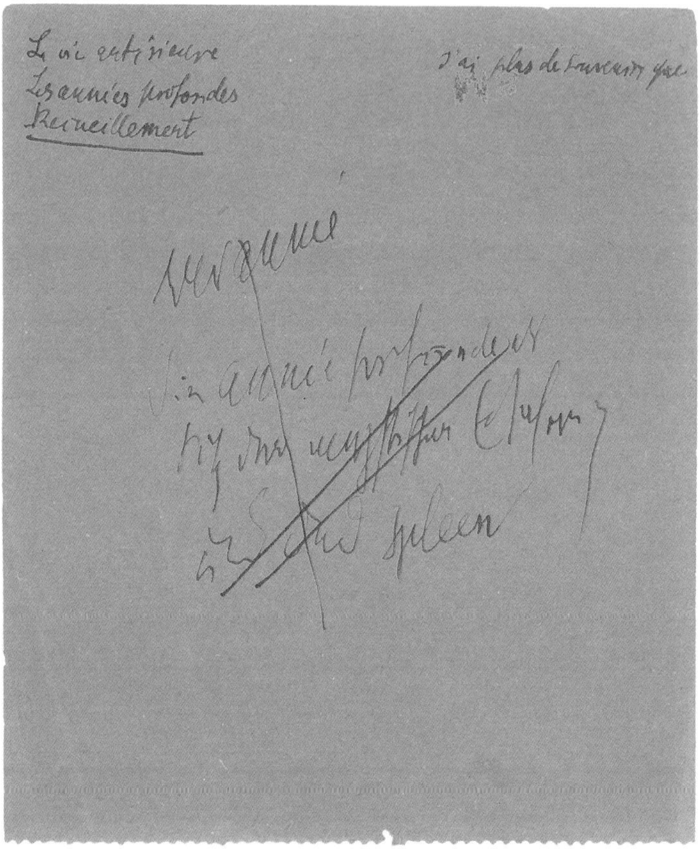

La vie extérieure
Les années profondes
Recueillement

J'ai plus de souvenirs que

Fig. 2.6

Fig. 2.6

La vie antérieure
Les années profondes
Recueillement

J'ai plus de souvenirs que

Redonnée [?]
The année profonde as
seat of mystical experience
and of spleen

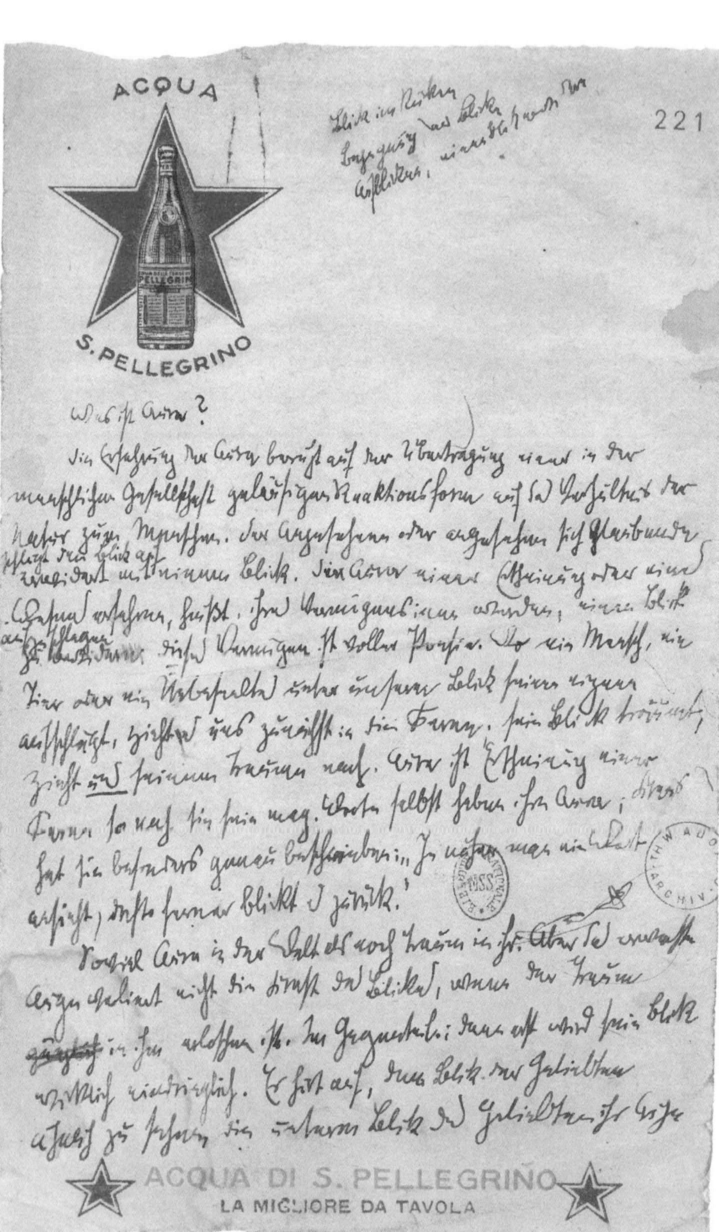
ACQUA

S. PELLEGRINO

221

Was ist Aura?

ACQUA DI S. PELLEGRINO

LA MIGLIORE DA TAVOLA

Fig. 2.7

Fig. 2.7

Eyes staring at one's back
Meeting of glances
Glance up, answering a glance

What is Aura?

The experience of aura rests on the transposition of a form of reaction normal in human society to the relationship of nature to people. The one who is seen or believes himself to be seen [glances up] answers with a glance. To experience the aura of an appearance or a being means becoming aware of its ability [to pitch] to respond to a glance. This ability is full of poetry. When a person, an animal, or something inanimate returns our glance with its own, we are drawn initially into the distance; its glance is dreaming, draws us after its dream. Aura is the appearance of a distance however close it might be. Words themselves have an aura; Kraus described this in particularly exact terms: "The closer one looks at a word, the greater the distance from which it returns the gaze."

As much aura in the world as there is still dream in it. But the awakened eye does not lose the power of the glance, once the dream is ~~totally~~ extinguished in it. On the contrary: it is only then that the glance really penetrates. It ceases to resemble the glance of the loved one, whose eye, under the glance of the lover

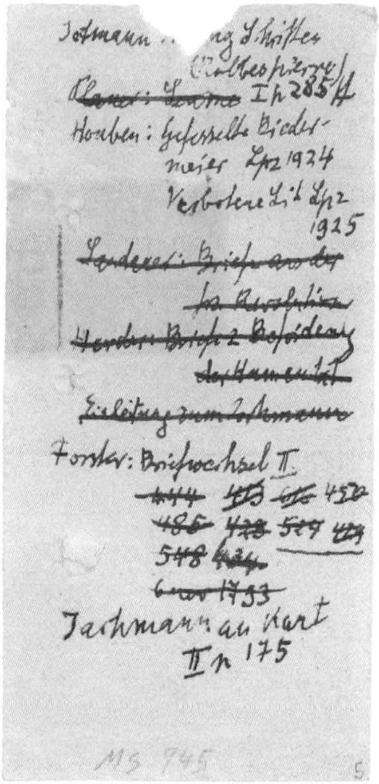

Jochmann: [illegible] Schriften
(Robespierre)
[illegible] I p 285 ff
Houben: Gefesselte Bieder-
meier Lpz 1924
Verbotene Lit Lpz
1925
Forster: Briefwechsel II
452
Jachmann an Kant
II p 175

MS 945

5

Fig. 2.8

Fig. 2.9

Marx sagt, die Revolutionen sind die
Lokomotive der Weltgeschichte. Aber
vielleicht ist dem gänzlich anders. Vielleicht
sind die Revolutionen der Griff
des in diesem Zuge reisenden
Menschengeschlechts nach der
Notbremse.

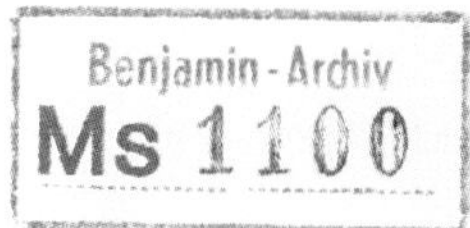

Fig. 2.10

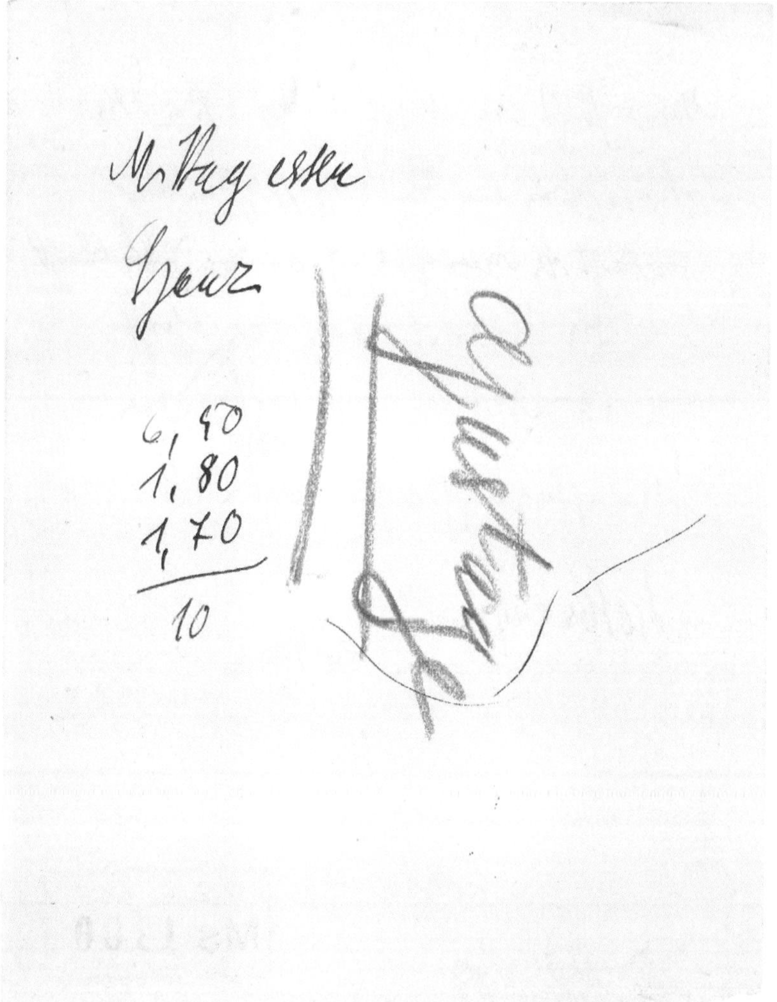

Fig. 2.11

3

From Small to Smallest Details

Micrographies

> Walter's teeninesses do not allow my ambition to rest. I can do it too [...]. As you see my writing is getting bigger again, a sign, I suppose, that I should stop writing such nonsense.
>
> Dora Sophie Benjamin to Gershom Scholem, *GB* II, p. 198

> I'll bring with me a new manuscript—one, tiny, book—that will surprise you.
>
> *GB* IV, p. 144

> He who has once begun to open the fan of memory never comes to the end of its segments. No image satisfies him, for he has seen that it can be unfolded, and only in its folds does the truth reside—that image, that taste, that touch for whose sake all this has been unfurled and dissected; and now remembrance progresses from small to smallest details, from the smallest to the infinitesimal, while that which it encounters in these microcosms grows ever mightier.
>
> *SW* 2:2, p. 597

> Memory does this: lets the things appear small, compresses them. Land of the sailor.
>
> Ms. 863v

For Benjamin, writing was not only a means of securing his thoughts, but also an object and theme of theoretical reflection. Perfect writing should flow as if from itself: "If the smoke from the tip of my cigarette and the ink from the nib of my pen flowed with equal ease, I would be in the Arcadia of my writing" (*SW* I, p. 463). High-quality paper, particular pens, ink, and nibs, and, furthermore, specific spatial preconditions were important prerequisites for a non-resistant and smoothly running flow of writing. In a letter to Siegfried Kracauer, for example, Benjamin reports on the acquisition of a new fountain pen, an "enchanting creation, with which I can fulfill all my dreams and develop a productivity which was impossible in the days of the now desiccated—nib" (*GB* III, p. 262).

But in order to aid the cogitations in finding their way to an appropriate realization on paper, some resistance is necessary. The route from inspiration to thought to phrasing to writing is to be hindered. The writer, according to Benjamin, should keep the "pen aloof from inspiration," and "it will then attract with magnetic power. The more circumspectly you delay writing down an idea, the more maturely developed it will be on surrendering itself" (*SW* I, p. 458). Flow and delay must coincide, in order both to satisfy dreams and propose ideas.

Benjamin's characteristically small handwriting, his graphic minimalism, which compelled him to concentration, deliberateness, and exactness, can be located within this context. His miniaturized script is reminiscent of Robert Walser's "pencil system," which he used to help him write again, once his abilities had dwindled. From 1924 Walser began "to jot in pencil, to sketch, to dilly-dally" (Walser, cited from Morlang, p. 58) his first intuitions, prior to writing his texts cleanly in pen. He tried to solve his "writer's block" by a resistance-less pencil gliding on paper, forming quite blurred, almost illegible characters. Benjamin's manuscripts, despite similarities in appearance, are the expression of a diametrically opposed method. While Walser learnt "to play, poeticize" once more (Walser, cited from Morlang, p. 58) in the small and the smallest details, attempting to unlock the open space of childish light-heartedness, so as to allow script and language to flow, for Benjamin it is a matter of the "placing" of script, the composition of thoughts. The small here is not childhood re-attained and imitated, but, rather, a product of adult reflection and concentration. Even in the choice of writing implement—Benjamin wrote mostly with a fountain pen—this other face of writing is expressed. Jean Selz recalls "such a small handwriting that he never found a pen that was fine enough, which forced him to write with the nib upside down" (Selz, p. 355)—such a posture in writing is directed against the stroke and flow of script.

The manuscripts in Benjamin's bequest document how up until around 1917–1918 his writing was somewhat larger and using wider swings than in later periods. But it is not really possible to date his manuscripts from the size and style of the script. Benjamin's handwriting does not develop in a uniform way. It varies. It is almost always precise and fine; even in notes that were intended only for his own eyes he rarely renounced "definition or accuracy" (Scholem, *Benjamin*, p. 177). In spite of the density of script, the compressing together of signs in the smallest space, he hardly ever wrote carelessly. The letters measure between one and around 7mm. Benjamin's penchant for small script developed in particular in the 1920s. One example is a sharp polemic against Fritz von Unruh's *Wings of Nike* (1925) titled "Peace Commodity," which appeared on May 21, 1926 in the *Literary World*. With each letter measuring from one to 1.5mm, the fair copy is difficult to decipher with the naked eye (fig. 3.1). The same is true of an early draft of

The Arcades of Paris (1928/1929), which Benjamin jotted on a sheet of fine handmade paper of an exceptionally lengthy format and folded in the middle (fig. 3.2). The 22cm of sheet allowed him to write eighty-one lines. Scholem has already noted Benjamin's "never-realized ambition to get a hundred lines onto an ordinary sheet of notepaper" (Scholem, "Benjamin," p. 177) and reports on how his fascination was aroused by two grains of wheat in the Museum Cluny in Paris, "on which a kindred soul had inscribed the complete 'Shema Israel'" (Scholem, "Benjamin," p. 177). In many cases it looks as if he intended to completely cover the page with writing (fig. 3.3). On the other hand, "giant letters" can be found in Benjamin's hand too (*GB* II, p. 446). Some letters and work manuscripts are even composed within "normal" dimensions. But these are exceptions.

Like Walser, Benjamin is an aesthetician of the written sheet; the manuscript should appeal to the eye as a textual image. The manuscript of the gloss *Dream Kitsch*, a "short consideration of the Surrealists" (*GB* III, p. 116), from 1925, which Benjamin thought was too difficult to be published in the *Literary World*, is remarkable both for the small size of the writing and for the format of the sheet: the text, which is separated into narrow columns, is strikingly reminiscent of a newspaper layout (fig. 3.4). The visual aspects of a manuscript of an early sonnet on the death of Christoph Friedrich Heinle (1894–1914) convey an expression of the contents. In the contrast between the small script and the size of the sheet, Benjamin's grief at the loss of his friend, and the loneliness and abandonment of those left behind, is graspable in the form of an image (fig. 3.5).

The spatial density of what is written corresponds to the economy of expression, a precise, laconic style. In this is expressed an ethic of "creative modesty typical of the person who lives wholly inside his subject and who is utterly incapable of viewing it complacently from the outside" (*SW* 1:1, p. 131).

Benjamin's small handwriting acts as a restriction, but with positive intent—for the writer as much as for the reader. Just as the writer is forced to attend to each letter, so too for those who are addressed "this objectionable writing style is like nothing else an expression of my most friendly disposition" (*GB* II, p. 399). But it is not simply an expression of this ethos, but also a claim to it and on it. Benjamin expects of readers such a great deal of concentration and effort that they might well object. He places objects in the way of a too rapid reading. But finally (also) in return he promises objects that impel readers to new thought. Benjamin's micrographies do not open up to casual readings—and he self-consciously inscribed in them recognition of their magnitude and significance.

Benjamin had a predilection for "the unassuming, the tiny, and the playful" (*SW* 2:1, p. 114). The world of experiences and things familiar to childhood, including his own memory of these, apparently trivial and marginal themes, the small format of the gloss, thesis, miniatures, puzzles, reports, and aphorisms—all these are manifestations of the small thematized over and over again in Benjamin's work. In these Benjamin achieves his ambition "to present in the briefest literary utterance something complete in itself" (Scholem, "Benjamin," p. 177). His aesthetic of the small is aimed at the particular, which "carries the whole in miniature form" (*GS* III, p. 51). Only "in the analysis of the small individual moment" might the "crystal of the total event" be discovered (*AP*, p. 461).

On June 9, 1926 Benjamin wrote to Jula Radt-Cohn: "You will see that—starting about a week ago, I have once more entered a period of small writing, in which, even after long intervals, I always find some kind of home again, and into which I should like to entice you. If you perceive this little box as homely, then nothing should prevent you from becoming its Princess. (You do know the 'New Melusine', don't you?)" (*GB* III, p. 171). In Goethe's fairytale *The New Melusine*, an allegorical tale in *William Meister's Journeyman Years*, the magic box harbors a wonderful realm that has shrunk to a miniature, and is constantly exposed to the dangers of ruin and disappearance. Just as an air of secrecy and fragility surrounds the casket in Goethe, so too Benjamin's tiny handwriting appears enigmatic and fragile. It bars the reader from direct access to what is written, and initially it can only be experienced sensuously, through the expressive power of the writing's image; only once it has been deciphered can its contents unfurl. Like the casket it preserves something precious, which disguises itself in the form of a miniature. It parades "the pantomime of the entire nature and existence of mankind, in microcosmic form" (*SW* 2:1, p. 134).

Figures

3.1 *Peace Commodity* (1926). Critique of Fritz von Unruh's *Wings of Nike* (1925)—Manuscript, three sides; shown here, page 1. Compare *GS* III, pp. 23–5.

3.2 Draft of *The Arcades of Paris* (c. 1928/1929)—Manuscript on one double page; shown here, page 1. Compare AP, pp. 873–6.

3.3 Draft of "Moscow" (c. spring 1927)—Manuscript, one side.
The manuscript contains drafts for the article "Moscow," published in the journal *Die Kreatur* in 1927. Benjamin was in Moscow from December 1926 until February 1927, having traveled there in order to visit the Latvian director Asja Lacis, who had fled to the Soviet capital for political reasons and was recuperating in a sanatorium following an illness. Benjamin recorded striking experiences and impressions of his visit in his *Moscow Diary*, which he also used as the basis of his article. The notes depicted here relay observations on Moscow city life—lively descriptions of traffic, the Kremlin, street traders, and the proletarian quarter with its youth groups.

3.4 *Dream Kitsch: Gloss on Surrealism* (c. 1925)—Manuscript, two sides; shown here, page 1. Compare *SW* 2:1, pp. 3–5.

3.5 Sonnet, untitled. From the cycle of 73 sonnets on the death of Christoph Friedrich Heinle—Manuscript, one side. Compare *GS* VII.1, p. 56.

3.6 Letter to Florens Christian Rang from 27 January 1923—Manuscript, two sides; shown here, page 1. Compare *GB* II, pp. 309f.

3.7 *Language and Logic II* (1921)—Manuscript, two sides; shown here, page 1. Compare *SW* 1, pp. 272–3.

Fig. 3.1

Fig. 3.1

Peace Commodity

"Leafing through your volumes!"

From 1920 to 1923, in Rome, in Zurich, in Paris—in short, whatever place outside of German soil one might have happened to land upon—German products could be found for half the price that one would usually have paid for the same goods abroad, or indeed in Germany itself. Poorly assembled goods for an impoverished population who were no longer capable of normal consumption were thrown into the dumping ground of the inflation era, placed on the European market as "peace commodities" at bargain prices. Around that time the barriers began to lift again and the traveling salesman set off on tour. One had to live on clearance sales and the higher the dollar rose, the greater was the circulation of export goods. At the height of the catastrophe it included intellectual and cultural goods too. For, even if the financial benefit was smaller, turnover raised the prestige of the entrepreneur. The Kantian idea of eternal peace—long undeliverable in a spiritually bankrupt Germany—was right in the first ranks of those spiritual export articles. Uncheckable in its manufacture, a slow seller for the previous ten years, it was available at unbeatable prices. It was a heaven-sent opportunity to smooth the way for more serious export. No thought was given to the genuine quality of its peace. Immanuel Kant's raw, homemade weave of thought had indeed proven itself to be highly durable, but it did not appeal to a broader public. It was necessary to take account of the modern taste of bourgeois democracy. The cloth of the peace flag was tie-dyed, its white, threadbare weave brightly patterned and, given all the signs and symbols, it was difficult—this will be found to be corroborated—for the green of hope to stand out from the bellicose red of the lobster, the blue of faithfulness from the drab brown of the roast turkey. In such a form this renovated weave of a pacifism in all the colors of the world's ways—which was sated in other ways too—was to be unveiled before the international public. And just as one expects that the simplest apprentice can throw out, fold, and prepare the bales of cloth according to the rules, so too the gentleman who markets this gaily colored pile, for good or for evil, has to drape himself in the colors of the universe and hold in front of the customer's nose the world of God which he sells in pieces. All that was necessary was to find the traveling salesman who also had at his immediate disposal the required vim of gesticulation, such as has the journalist with his triply loosened wrist and pen. That the reserve lieutenant was formerly popularly perceived as a traveling salesman is well known. He was easily imported into "better circles." This is also thoroughly true of Mr von Unruh, who, in 1922, as a traveling salesman going from city to city for eternal peace, processed the Paris position. Of course—and this was accordingly so apt that Mr von Unruh himself bridled at moments—his import into French circles some years ago at Verdun did not occur without furore, not without commotion, not without the spilling of blood. Be that as it may, the report that he presents—*Wings of Nike: The Book of a Journey*—implies that his contact with his customer base has persisted, even when he presented for inspection peace commodities rather than heavy munitions. It is not equally as certain whether it can be assured that the publication of this travel journal—a list of his customers and done deals—is of use to the broader course of business. For barely had it occurred before the commodity began to be returned from Paris.

In any case it is extremely instructive to examine Mr von Unruh's pacifism more closely. Since the supposed convergence of the moral idea and that of right, on whose presupposition the European proof of the Kantian gospel of peace rested, began to disconnect in the mind of the nineteenth century, German "peace" has pointed more and more to metaphysics as the place of its foundation. The German image of peace emanates from metaphysics. In contrast to this it has long been observed that the idea of peace in West European democracies is a thoroughly worldly, political, and, in the final instance, juristically justifiable one. Pax is for them the ideal of international law. To this corresponds, in practical terms, the instrument of the arbitration court and its treaties. The great moral conflict of an unlimited and reinforced right to peace with an equitable peace, the diverse ways in which this theme has been instrumentalized in the course of history, are not up for discussion in Mr von Unruh's pacifism, just as indeed the world-historical events of this hour remain unaddressed. And "in terms of the philosophical politics of France"—Florens Christian Rang analyzed them for the Germans (in his final work *German Shelters*, the most truthful critique of war and post-war literature and one of the greatest political works ever, and of which out of the entire German daily press only the *Frankfurter Zeitung* took note in any sort of adequate fashion): its rigor matched by its humanity, its precision detracting not in the least from its depth—here, though, "philosophical politics" fuses in Unruh's pathos with idealistic waffle. "Tout action de l'esprit est aisée si elle n'est plus soumise au réel"—that is how Proust phrases the old truth. Mr von Unruh has heroically wrestled himself free from reality. In any case, the great formal dinners are the only international facts that his new pacifism takes into account. His new international is hatched in the peace of the communal digestion and the gala menu is the magna carta of the future peace of nations. And just as a cocky sidekick might smash a valuable vessel at a love feast, so the thin terminology of the Königsberg philosopher dispatches to the devil with the kick of a jackboot, and what remains is the innerness of the heavenly eye in its attractive alcoholic glassiness. The image of the gifted blabbermouth with a teary look, as Shakespeare alone could capture!—The great prose of all evangelists of peace spoke of war. To stress one's own love of peace is always the close concern of those who have instigated war. But he who wants peace should speak of war. He should speak of the past one (is he not called Fritz von Unruh,[1] the one thing about which he would remain silent), and, above all, he should speak of the coming one. He should speak of its threatening plotters, its powerful causes, its terrifying means. And yet this would be perhaps the only discourse against which the salons, which allowed Mr von Unruh entry, remain completely hermetically sealed? The much pleaded peace, which is already in existence, proves, when seen by daylight, to be the one—the only "eternal," known to us—which those enjoy who have commanded in war and who wish to set the tone at the peace party. For this is what Mr von Unruh has become too. "Woe" his Cassandra-like gobbledegook clamors over all who have realized at the correct moment—that is roughly between the fish and the roast—that "inner conversion" is the only acceptable revolt and that the

[1] *Unruh* means "unrest" in German.

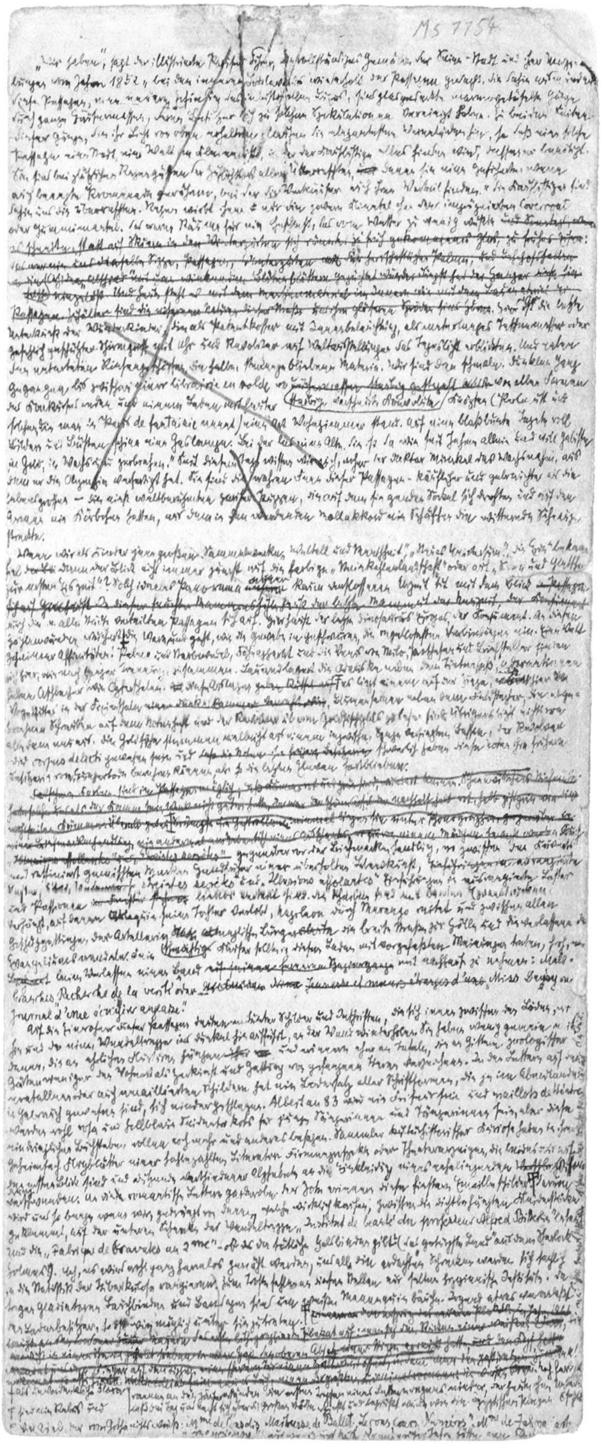

Fig. 3.2

Fig. 3.2

"In speaking of the inner boulevards," says the *Illustrated Guide to Paris*, a complete picture of the city on the Seine and its environs from the year 1852, "we have made mention again and again of the arcades which open onto them. These arcades, a recent invention of industrial luxury, are glass-roofed, marble-paneled corridors extending through whole blocks of buildings, whose owners have joined together for such enterprises. Lining both sides of these corridors, which get their light from above, are the most elegant shops, so that the arcade is a city, a world in miniature, in which customers will find everything they need. During sudden rainshowers, the arcades are a place of refuge for the unprepared, to whom they offer a secure, if restricted, promenade—one from which the merchants also benefit." The customers are gone, along with those taken by surprise. Rain brings in only the poorer clientele without waterproof or mackintosh. These were spaces for a generation of people who knew little of the weather and who, on Sundays, when it snowed, would rather warm themselves in the winter gardens than go out skiing. Glass before its time, premature iron: it was one single line of descent—arcades, winter gardens with their lordly palms, and railroad stations, which cultivated the false orchid "adieu" with its fluttering petals. They have long since given way to the hangar. And today, it is the same with the human material on the inside of the arcades as with the materials of their construction. Pimps are the iron bearings of this street, and its glass breakables are the whores. Here was the last refuge of those infant prodigies that saw the light of day at the time of the world exhibitions: the briefcase with interior lighting, the meter-long pocket knife, or the patented umbrella handle with built-in watch and revolver. And near the degenerate giant creatures, aborted and broken-down matter. We followed the narrow dark corridor to where—between a discount bookstore, in which colorful tied-up bundles tell of all sorts of failure, and a shop selling only buttons (mother-of-pearl and the kind that in Paris are called *de fantaisie*)—there stood a sort of salon. On a pale-colored wallpaper full of figures and busts shone a gas lamp. By its light, an old woman sat reading. They say she has been there alone for years, and collects sets of teeth "in gold, in wax, and broken." Since that day, moreover, we know where Doctor Miracle got the wax out of which he fashioned Olympia. They are the true fairies of these arcades (more salable and more worn than the life-sized ones): the formerly world-famous Parisian dolls, which revolved on their musical socle and bore in their arms a doll-sized basket out of which, at the salutation of the minor chord, a lambkin poked its curious muzzle.

All this is the arcade in our eyes. And it was nothing of all this. They <the arcades> radiated through the Paris of the Empire like grottoes. For someone entering the Passage des Panoramas in 1817, the sirens of gaslight would be singing to him on one side, while oil-lamp odalisques offered enticements from the other. With the kindling of electric lights, the irreproachable glow was extinguished in these galleries, which suddenly became more difficult to find—which wrought a black magic at entranceways, and peered from blind windows into their own interior. It was not decline but transformation. All at once, they were the hollow mold from which the image of "modernity" was cast. Here, the century mirrored with satisfaction its most recent past. Here was the retirement home for infant prodigies …

When, as children, we were given those great encyclopedic works *World and Mankind, New Universe, The Earth*, wouldn't our gaze always fall, first of all, on the color illustration of a "Carboniferous Landscape" or on "Lakes and Glaciers of the First Ice Age"? Such an ideal panorama of a barely elapsed primeval age opens up when we look through the arcades that are found in all cities. Here resides the last dinosaur of Europe, the consumer. On the walls of these caverns, their immemorial flora, the commodity, luxuriates and enters, like cancerous tissue, into the most irregular combinations. A world of secret affinities: palm tree and feather duster, hair dryer and Venus de Milo, prosthesis and letter-writing manual come together here as after a long separation. The odalisque lies in wait next to the inkwell, priestesses raise aloft ashtrays like patens. These items on display are a rebus; and <how> one ought to read here the birdseed kept in the fixative-pan from a darkroom, the flower seeds beside the binoculars, the broken screws atop the musical score, and the revolver above the goldfish bowl—is right on the tip of one's tongue. After all, nothing of the lot appears to be new. The goldfish come perhaps from a pond that dried up long ago, the revolver will have been a corpus delicti, and these scores could hardly have preserved their previous owner from starvation when her last pupils stayed away.

Never trust what writers say about their own writings. When Zola undertook to defend his *Thérèse Raquin* against hostile critics, he explained that his book was a scientific study of the temperaments. His task had been to show, in an example, exactly how the sanguine and the nervous temperaments act on one another—to the detriment of each. But this explanation could satisfy no one. Nor does it explain the unprecedented admixture of colportage, the bloodthirstiness, the cinematic goriness of the action. Which—by no accident—takes place in an arcade. If this book really expounds something scientifically, then it's the death of the Paris arcades, the decay of a type of architecture. The book's atmosphere is saturated with the poisons of this process, and its people are destroyed by them.

One knew of places in ancient Greece where the way led down into the underworld. Our waking existence likewise is a land which, at certain hidden points, leads down into the underworld—a land full of inconspicuous places from which dreams arise. All day long, suspecting nothing, we pass them by, but no sooner has sleep come than we are eagerly groping our way back to lose ourselves in the dark corridors. By day, the labyrinth of urban dwellings resembles consciousness; the arcades (which are galleries leading into the city's past) issue unremarked onto the streets. At night, however, under the tenebrous mass of the houses, their denser darkness bursts forth like a threat, and the nocturnal pedestrian hurries past—unless, that is, we have emboldened him to turn into the narrow lane.

Falser colors are possible in the arcades; that combs are red and green surprises no one. Snow White's stepmother had such things, and when the comb did not do its work, the beautiful apple was there to help out—half red, half poison-green, like cheap combs. Everywhere stockings play a starring role. Now they are lying under phonographs, across the way in a stamp shop; another time on the side table of a tavern, where they are watched over by a girl. And again in front of the stamp shop opposite, where, between the envelopes with various stamps in refined assortments, manuals of an antiquated art of life are lovelessly dispensed—*Secret Embraces* and *Maddening Illusions*, introductions to outmoded vices and discarded passions. The shop windows are covered with vividly colored Epinal-style posters, on which Harlequin betroths his daughter, Napoleon rides through Marengo, and, amid all types of standard artillery pieces, delicate English burghers travel the high road to hell and the forsaken path of the Gospel. No customer ought to enter this shop with preconceived ideas; on leaving, he will be the more content to take home a volume: Malebranche's *Recherche de la vérité*, or *Miss Daisy: The Journal of an English Equestrienne.*

To the inhabitants of these arcades we are pointed now and then by the signs and inscriptions which multiply along the walls within, where here and there, between the shops, a spiral staircase rises into darkness. The signs have little in common with the nameplates that hang beside respectable entryways but are reminiscent of plaques on the cages at zoos, put there to indicate not so much the dwelling place as the origin and species of the captive animals. Deposited in the letters of the metal or enameled signboards is a precipitate of all the forms of writing that have ever been in use in the West. "Albert at No. 83" will be a hairdresser, and "Theatrical Tights" will probably be silk tights, pink and light blue, for young chanteuses and ballerinas; but these insistent letterings want to say something more, something different. Collectors of curiosities in the field of cultural history have in their secret drawer broadsheets of a highly paid literature which seem, at first sight, to be commercial prospectuses or theatrical bills, and which squander dozens of different alphabets in disguising an open invitation. These dark enameled signs bring to mind the baroque lettering on the cover of obscene books.—Recall the origin of the modern poster. In 1861, the first lithographic poster suddenly appeared on walls here and there around London. It showed the back of a woman in white who was thickly wrapped in a shawl and who, in all haste, had just reached the top of a flight of stairs, where, her head half turned and a finger upon her lips, she is ever so slightly opening a heavy door to reveal the starry sky. In this way Wilkie Collins advertised his latest book, one of the greatest detective novels ever written, *The Woman in White.* Still color<less>, the first drops of a shower of letters ran down the walls of houses (today it pours unremittingly, day and night, on the big cities) and was greeted like the plagues of Egypt.—Hence the anxiety we feel when, crowded out by those who actually make purchases, wedged between overloaded coatstands, we read at the bottom of the spiral staircase: "Institut de Beauté du Professeur Alfred Bitterlin." And the "Fabrique de Cravates au Deuxième"—Are there really neckties there or not? ("The Speckled Band" from Sherlock Holmes?) Of course, the needlework will have been quite inoffensive, and all the imagined horrors will be classified objectively in the statistics on tuberculosis. As a consolation, these places are seldom lacking institutes of hygiene. There gladiators wear orthopedic belts, and bandages are wrapped round the white bellies of mannequins. Something induces the owner of the shop to circulate among them on a frequent basis.—Many are the aristocrats who know nothing of the Almanach de Gotha: "Mme. de Consolis, Ballet Mistress—Lessons, Classes, Numbers." "Mme. de Zahna, Fortuneteller." And if, sometime in the mid-Nineties, "we had" asked for a prediction, surely it would have been: the decline of a culture.

Fig. 3.3

Fig. 3.4

Fig. 3.4

Dream Kitsch
Gloss on Surrealism

No one really dreams any longer of the Blue Flower. Whoever awakes as Heinrich von Ofterdingen today must have overslept. The history of the dream remains to be written, and opening up a perspective on this subject would mean decisively overcoming the superstitious belief in natural necessity by means of historical illumination. Dreaming has a share in history. The statistics on dreaming would stretch beyond the pleasures of the anecdotal landscape into the barrenness of a battlefield. Dreams have started wars, and wars, from the very earliest times, have determined the propriety and impropriety—indeed, the range—of dreams.

No longer does the dream reveal a blue horizon. The dream has grown gray. The gray coating of dust on things is its best part. Dreams are now a shortcut to banality. Technology consigns the outer image of things to a long farewell, like banknotes that are bound to lose their value. It is then that the hand retrieves this outer cast in dreams and, even as they are slipping away, makes contact with familiar contours. It catches hold of objects at their most threadbare and timeworn point. This is not always the most delicate point: children do not so much clasp a glass as snatch it up. And which side does an object turn toward dreams? What point is its most decrepit? It is the side worn through by habit and patched with cheap maxims. The side which things turn toward the dream is kitsch.

Chattering, the fantasy images of things fall to the ground like leaves from a Leporello picture book, *The Dream*. Maxims shelter under every leaf: "Ma plus belle maîtresse c'est la paresse," and "Une médaille vernie pour le plus grand ennui," and "Dans le corridor il y a quelqu'un qui me veut à la mort." The Surrealists have composed such lines, and their allies among the artists have copied the picture book. *Répétitions* is the name that Paul Eluard gives to one of his collections of poetry, for whose frontispiece Max Ernst has drawn four small boys. They turn their backs to the reader, to their teacher and his desk as well, and look out over a balustrade where a balloon hangs in the air. A giant pencil rests on its point in the windowsill. The repetition of childhood experience gives us pause: when we were little, there was as yet no agonized protest against the world of our parents. As children in the midst of that world, we showed ourselves superior. When we reach for the banal, we take hold of the good along with it—the good that is there (open your eyes) right before you.

For the sentimentality of our parents, so often distilled, is good for providing the most objective image of our feelings. The long-windedness of their speeches, bitter as gall, has the effect of reducing us to a crimped picture puzzle; the ornament of conversation was full of the most abysmal entanglements. Within is heartfelt sympathy, is love, is kitsch. "Surrealism is called upon to reestablish dialogue in its essential truth. The interlocutors are freed from the obligation to be polite. He who speaks will develop no theses. But in principle, the reply cannot be concerned for the self-respect of the person speaking. For in the mind of the listener, words and images are only a springboard." Beautiful sentiments from Breton's *Surrealist Manifesto*. They articulate the formula of the dialogic misunderstanding—which is to say, of what is truly alive in the dialogue. "Misunderstanding" is here another word for the rhythm with which the only true reality forces its way into the conversation. The more effectively a man is able to speak, the more successfully he is misunderstood.

In his *Vague de rêves* [Wave of Dreams], Louis Aragon describes how the mania for dreaming spread over Paris. Young people believed they had come upon one of the secrets of poetry, whereas in fact they did away with poetic composition, as with all the most intensive forces of that period. Saint-Pol-Roux, before going to bed in the early morning, puts up a notice on his door: "Poet at work."—This all in order to blaze a way into the heart of things abolished or superseded, to decipher the contours of the banal as rebus, to start a concealed William Tell from out of wooded entrails, or to be able to answer the question, "Where is the bride?" Picture puzzles, as schemata of the dreamwork, were long ago discovered by psychoanalysis. The Surrealists, with a similar conviction, are less on

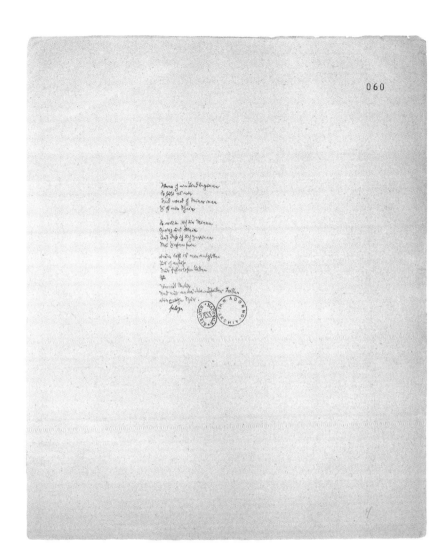

Fig. 3.5

Fig. 3.5

When I begin a song
It sticks
And if I become aware of you
It is an illusion

And thus love wanted you
Humble and small
So that I win you
With being alone

Therefore you slipped from me
Until I learnt
Only flawless petitions

Betray nature
And only enraptured steps
The ~~eternal~~ trace.
blessed

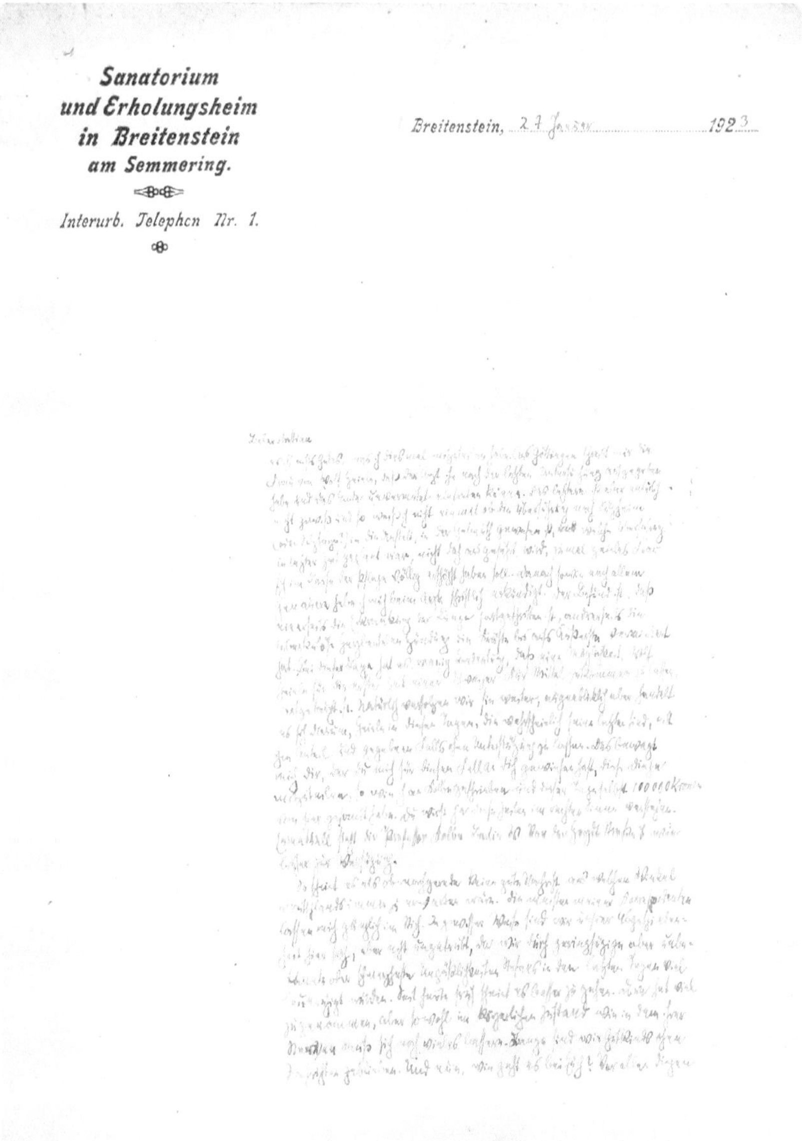

Sanatorium
und Erholungsheim
in Breitenstein
am Semmering.

Interurb. Telephon Nr. 1.

Breitenstein, 27 Jänner 1923

[illegible]

Fig. 3.6

Fig. 3.6

Sanatorium
and Convalescence Home
in Breitenstein at Semmering

Interurb. Telephone no.1
Breitenstein January 27, 1923

Dear Christian

I have nothing good to report this time. Wolf Heinle's wife has written to me from Göttingen to inform me that the doctor gave up on him after the last examination and the end may burst in at any time. The latter is, of course, uncertain and so I do not know whether transportation to Sülzheim to the hospital, where Helmuth was, a transportation that was indeed planned recently, has been carried out after all, the more so as Heinle's wife must have completely exhausted herself through caring for him. I have written a letter asking the doctor about this and all further particulars. The diagnosis states that the lung disease is advanced, on the one hand, and, on the other, the tuberculous inflammation of the heart sac has fully sapped his energy. In this situation it is fairly irrelevant that now there is a chance of means for Wolf Heinle to undergo his first Swiss cure. Of course we will pursue this further, but at the moment it is a matter of not leaving Heinle without his due and, if necessary, support, in these days, which are probably his last. This moves me, as you requested I do in such a case, to relate these details to you, just as I have written to Kolbe and in the last few days I myself have sent 100,000 krone from here. I am sure you will understand these lines correctly. Should you need him, Professor Kolbe, 7 Von der Heydt Street, West Berlin, is, as before, at your disposal.

And so it seems as if there is well-nigh no good news at all to be expected from whatever corner of Germany. Most of my correspondents have left me completely in the lurch. In a certain respect we are quite glad of our isolation here, however not untroubled, as we have been greatly disturbed in the last few days by Stefan's minor but unfamiliar and painful ailments. Since this morning things seem to be somewhat better. Dora has put on a lot of weight, but there still needs to be much more improvement in her bodily state, as well as that of her nerves. We have not heard [from] the Gutkinds in a long time. Well now, how are you and yours? Above all

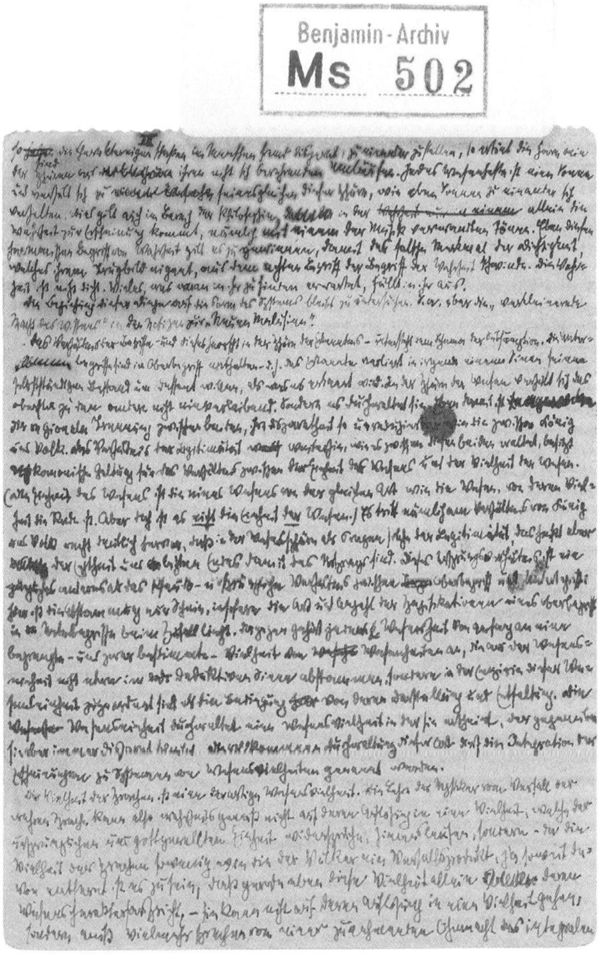

Fig. 3.7

Fig. 3.7

II

... and so the characteristics of human beings are to be counterpoised as alien to one another, and so the harmony of the spheres resounds from their orbits, which do not come into contact with one another. Every essential being is a sun and relates to beings like itself, as suns in fact relate to one another. This also applies in the realm of philosophy, which is the only realm in which the truth becomes manifest, namely with a sound like music. And this is the harmonic concept of truth, which we must acquire so that the false quality of watertightness that characterizes its delusion vanishes from the authentic concept, the concept of truth. The truth is not watertight. Much that we expect to find in it slips through the net.

The relation of these things to the forms of a system remains to be investigated. See, too, the "veiling power of knowledge" in the notes to "The New Melusine."

The relation between concepts—and this relation governs the sphere of knowledge—is one of subsumption. The lower concepts are contained in the higher ones—that is to say, in one sense or another what is known loses its autonomy for the sake of what it is known as. In the sphere of essences, the higher does not devour the lower. Instead, it rules over it. This explains why the regional separation between them, their disparateness, remains as irreducible as the gulf between monarch and people. The legitimacy that characterizes their relations possesses canonical validity for the relation between the unity of essence and the multiplicity of essences. (The unity of essence is of the same kind as the essence of whose multiplicity we are speaking. But it is *not* the unity *of* the essences.) The relation between monarch and people makes very clear that in the sphere of essence questions of legitimacy are questions of authenticity and ultimately of origins. In this context, the question of origins is quite different from the pseudo-question of origins in the relations between concept and subconcept. For here the derivation is an illusion, since the mode and number of specifics of the concept that occur in the subconcept are a matter of chance. In contrast, every essence possesses from the outset a limited—and moreover determinate—multiplicity of essences, which do not derive from the unity in a deductive sense but are empirically assigned to it as the condition of its representation and articulation. The essential unity reigns over a multiplicity of essences in which it manifests itself, but from which it always remains distinct. A thoroughgoing system of control of this sort can be called the integration of manifestations into systems of multiple essences.

The multiplicity of languages is such a plurality of essences. The doctrine of the mystics concerning the degeneration of the true language stands on false ground if it bases its argument on the dissolution into many languages. That multiplicity would simply amount to the contradiction of a primordial and God-willed unity, but the multiplicity of languages is not the product of decadence any more than is the multiplicity of peoples, and indeed is so far removed from any such decay that we might be justified in asserting that this multiplicity expresses their essential character. Therefore, this doctrine should not focus on the dissolution into many languages as the primary issue, but, rather, must speak of the fact that the integral power to rule becomes increasingly impotent.

4

Physiognomy of the Thingworld

Russian Toys

Benjamin's deep, inner relationship to things he owned—books, works of art, or handcrafted items, often of rustic construction—was evident. For as long as I knew him, even during my last visit with him in Paris, he loved to display such objects, to put them into his visitors' hands, as he mused over them aloud like a pianist improvising at the keyboard. [...] In the twenties he was apt to offer philosophical reflections as he brought forth a toy for his son.

Scholem, *Walter Benjamin: The Story of a Friendship*, p. 47

Toy is handtool—not artwork.

Ms. 604

On February 23, 1927 Benjamin wrote to Siegfried Kracauer: "A lovely collection of photos (toys of Russian origin) should now have reached you in Frankfurt. I am offering them to the *Illustriertes Blatt*" (*Moscow Diary*, p. 129). Almost three years later the essay on "Russian Toys" was published, not there, but in the *South West German Radio Gazette*—in a "cut version" as Benjamin noted on his proof copy (fig. 4.17). Included with it were six photographs referred to in the text and taken from the "lovely collection" that has been preserved amongst Benjamin's papers. The essay and the images in this little collection transported the toys across "Russian borders" (*GS* IV.2, p. 624) to bring them closer to a German readership. They offered samples from a material culture, a thingworld, which Benjamin had got to known during his stay in Moscow in December 1926 and January 1927.

The inclusion of images changes the status of the text, prompting a reciprocal effect. The interplay of text, documentary images, and image captions was an important element of the publication for Benjamin. This is demonstrated by notes on the Russian toys and the photo captions, found in the bequest (Mss 602–607). More explicitly than in the shortened essay (whose manuscript has not survived), they deal with the physiognomic aspects of the toy world.

Four of the six photographs reproduced in the *South West German Radio Gazette* were retouched before they appeared in print, as a glance at the originals makes clear. By airbrushing and the imposition of a stencil, the background is neutralized, in order to excerpt the objects from the surroundings, allowing them to emerge more clearly.

During his stay in Moscow—Benjamin traveled to the Soviet Union in order to visit his girlfriend Asja Lacis (1891–1979)—he visited the Kustarny Museum (for regional art), which held in its larger room a collection of Russian toys, predominantly from the nineteenth century. Benjamin organized for the photographing of objects that especially interested him. A shop where children's toys could be purchased was attached to the museum. *Moscow Diary* also relates an excursion to Sergiev, a center for toy manufacture about 70km from the capital, where Benjamin bought toys. He was a connoisseur and passionate collector. The small decorated sewing machine (fig. 4.2) and the spherical samovar colored like an apple (fig. 4.3) were acquired in Moscow, as he noted in his diary (compare *Moscow Diary*, p. 83 and p. 68). None of his colorful toy collection is extant in the archive. The photos—the reduced stock remaining in the bequest—represent a residue. They are traces of disappearance.

Traditional Russian toys themselves—according to Benjamin's observation at the end of his essay—also adopt the form of a residue. They are witnesses to a disappearing folk culture, manufactured in a peasant cottage industry, which is under threat. Benjamin says it explicitly of the clay dolls from the north of Russia: their "highly fragile condition" (*Moscow Diary*, p. 124) in material terms corresponds to the fragility of their whole existence. This brightly colored clay toy has been rescued by collections, has "found a safe asylum" in the museum (*Moscow Diary*, p. 124). Technological-industrial development renders uncertain how long it can survive outside the museum's cabinets.

Three sheets are found in Benjamin's bequest with information in Russian on eleven toys, signed by N[ikolaj Dmitrievič] Bartram (1873–1931 [1934?]), the director of the Moscow Toy Museum (fig 4.13). These notes were in front of Benjamin when he wrote the captions on the reverse of the photos (unusually for him in Latin script). But only part of his captions stem from "a German translation of Bartram's notes" (*GS* IV.2, p. 1051). The more expansive Russian notes refer to a large degree to toys that are not amongst those photographed in Benjamin's bequest. These could be toys belonging to the museum, of which Benjamin might have ordered photos but which he did not receive (compare *Moscow Diary*, p. 120).

The captions for the images name the objects; they locate them regionally, socially, and temporally; provide data on their provenance (e.g. "Governorate of Vladimir" or "Viatka Doll"), on their political and social origin ("Peasant work," "Work of Siberian prisoners") and the age of the toy. The names of artists or makers are not given. There are details of the material composition and the technique of manufacture, also the size, the noise or sound it makes, and, on one occasion, the color (which the photo sadly cannot convey). The straw doll (fig. 4.8) reminds Benjamin of a cultic-fetishistic context, the magical or religious function, which similar objects once possessed. The reference to the simplification of the Viatka doll (fig. 4.4), which allows the horse and the rider to merge into one another—"with the horse's head and neck already gone" (*SW* 2:2, p. 814)—reveals Benjamin's physiognomically attuned look.

Two photos in the bequest do not have captions. These show a festive pyramidal arrangement of toys, books, and candles (figs. 4.14 and 4.15). The construction, or the whole table, was turned 180 degrees for the second image, in order to record the reverse side. We see Russian toys depicted and are able to recognize the drummers and the Viatka dolls once more. It is to be assumed that Benjamin owned these toys—the sewing machine and the samovar. Under what conditions these photos were made is less clear. Christmas in Moscow? Is it a table of gifts for Daga, the daughter of Asja Lacis, who was born in 1919? We do not know. It is also not known what Stefan Benjamin received from his father, when he returned with toys from Moscow. We do know of other presents, given two years earlier: "Yesterday, on the first night of Hanukkah, Stefan received a train set, as well as a splendid Indian costume, one of the most beautiful toys to have come on the market in a long time: colorful feather headdresses, axes, chains. Since someone else happened to give him an African mask for the same occasion, this morning I saw him dancing toward me in a grandiose getup" (*Correspondence*, p. 258).

Figures

4.1 *Moscow Diary* (December 9, 1926–February 1, 1927). Benjamin has obliterated the title *Moscow Diary* and replaced it with *Spanish Journey*.—Manuscript, eleven double and six single sheets; shown here, page 1. Compare *Moscow Diary*, p. 9.

4.2 to 4.12 Photographs of Russian toys with Benjamin's captions.

4.13 Nikolai Dmitrievic Bartram, "Notes on Russian Toys" (January 30, 1927)—Manuscript, three sides; shown here, page 1.
The first page of the Russian notes by Nikolaj Dmitrievič Bartram contains information about the playthings in figs 4.5, 4.6, and 4.10 of this book: N1 provides information on the "furniture set for a doll's house" that was made out of tiny pieces of wood between 1860–1880 by Siberian prisoners. "Bacchus on a billy-goat" (N2) is made of papier mâché. According to Bartram it was manufactured in Moscow around 1907 and is situated in the Moscow Toy Museum. The "horsey" described in N3 measured 12 zoll, and was big enough for a child to sit on.

4.14 and 4.15 Table with Russian toys (presumably 1926/1927)—photographs

4.16 Notes for *Russian Toys*—Manuscript, one side.

4.17 *Russian Toys*. On the left-hand corner Benjamin has noted: "*South West German Radio Gazette* VI, 2/10 January 1930, cut version, see manuscript"—one side. Compare *Moscow Diary*, pp. 123–4.

[1]

Fig. 4.1

Fig. 4.1

Spanish Journey

December 9. I arrived December 6th. In the train I had made a mental note of the name and address of a hotel in case there should be nobody waiting for me at the station. (At the border they had made me pay extra to travel first class, claiming there were no more seats in second.) I was relieved that there was no one there to see me emerge from the sleeping car. But there was no one at the platform gate either. I was not overly upset. Then, as I was making my way out of the Belorussian-Baltic railway station, Reich appeared. The train had arrived on time, not a second late. We loaded ourselves and the two suitcases into a sleigh. A thaw had set in that day, it was warm. We had only been underway a few minutes, driving down the broad Tverskaia with its gleam of snow and mud, when Asja waved to us from the side of the street. Reich got out and walked the short remaining distance to the hotel, we took the sleigh. Asja did not look beautiful, wild beneath her Russian fur hat, her face somewhat puffy from all the time she had spent bedridden. We stopped off briefly at the hotel and then had tea in a so-called pastry shop near the sanatorium. I filled her in about Brecht. Then Asja, who had slipped away during a rest period, took a side entrance back into the sanatorium in order to escape notice while Reich and I went in by the main stairs. Here, for the second time, encountered the custom of removing one's galoshes. The first time had been at the hotel, even though it involved no more than checking in the luggage; they had promised us a room that night. Asja's roommate, a hefty textile worker, was absent, I would see her for the first time the following day. Here we were, alone together for the first time under the same roof for a few minutes. Asja was looking at me very affectionately. An allusion to the decisive conversation in Riga. Then Reich accompanied me back to the hotel, we had a bite in my room, and went to the Meyerhold Theater. It was the first dress rehearsal for *The Inspector General.* I was unable to get a ticket despite Asja's efforts on my behalf. So I strolled up Tverskaia in the direction of the Kremlin for half an hour and came back, carefully spelling out the shop signs, carefully proceeding over the ice. Then, very tired (and, very likely, sad), I returned to my room.

On the morning of the 7th, Reich came to fetch me. Itinerary: Petrovka (to register with the police), the Kameneva Institute (for a 1.50 ruble seat at the Institute of Culture; talked, moreover, with their local German representative, an utter ass), then via Herzen Street to the Kremlin, passing in front of the totally botched Lenin mausoleum and then on to the scenic view of the St. Isaac Cathedral. Return via Tverskaia, following Tverskoi Boulevard to Dom Herzena, the headquarters of the Organization of Proletarian Writers, VAPP. A good meal, which I barely appreciated, given the exertion which the walk in the cold had involved. Kogan was introduced to me and expounded on his Rumanian grammar and his Russian–Rumanian dictionary. The tales Reich tells, which in the course of our long walks I am often too tired to listen to with both ears, are endlessly vivacious, filled with anecdotes and specifics, sharp and amusing. Stories about a bureaucrat who works for the Treasury Department, and goes on vacation at Easter and celebrates mass as a pope. And then: the one about the conviction of a seamstress who struck her alcoholic husband dead, and the hooligan who attacked a male and female student on the street.

Hölzernes Modell einer Nähmaschine. Dreht man die Kurbel, so geht der Nagel auf und nieder und erzeugt im Auffallen ein klapperndes Geräusch, das dem Kinde den Rhythmus der Nähmaschine vorstellt. Bauernarbeit.

Fig. 4.2

Fig. 4.2

Wooden model of a scwing machine. If one turns the wheel the needle goes up and down and as it strikes it makes a clattering sound that suggests to the child the rhythm of a sewing machine. Peasant handicraft.

a) Samowar (gelb, rot und grün) als Behang für den Weihnachtsbaum

b) Trommler – gibt ein knatterndes Geräusch von sich und bewegt die Arme, wenn man die Kurbel rechts unten dreht

Fig. 4.3

Fig. 4.3

a) Left, samovar (yellow, red, and green) as Christmas-tree decoration.
b) Drummer—makes a rattling sound and moves its arms when one turns the crank on the bottom right-hand corner.

Interessant ist der Vergleich dieser beiden Wjatka-Puppen.
Das Pferd, das auf dem einen Modell noch sichtbar ist,
ist auf dem nebenstehenden schon mit dem Manne verschmol-
zen. Volkstümliches Spielzeug strebt nach vereinfachten Formen.

Fig. 4.4

Fig. 4.4

It is interesting to compare the two Viatka dolls. The horse, which is still visible on one model, has merged with the man on the one next to it. Demotic toys strive for simplified forms.

Möbelgarnitur für die Puppenstube. Arbeit sibirischer Sträflinge aus dem 19ten Jahrhundert. Das Zusammenfügen der winzigen Holzstückchen erfordert unsägliche Geduld

Fig. 4.5

Fig. 4.5

Furniture set for a doll's house. Work of Siberian prisoners from the nineteenth century. Assembly of the tiny pieces of wood demands untold patience.

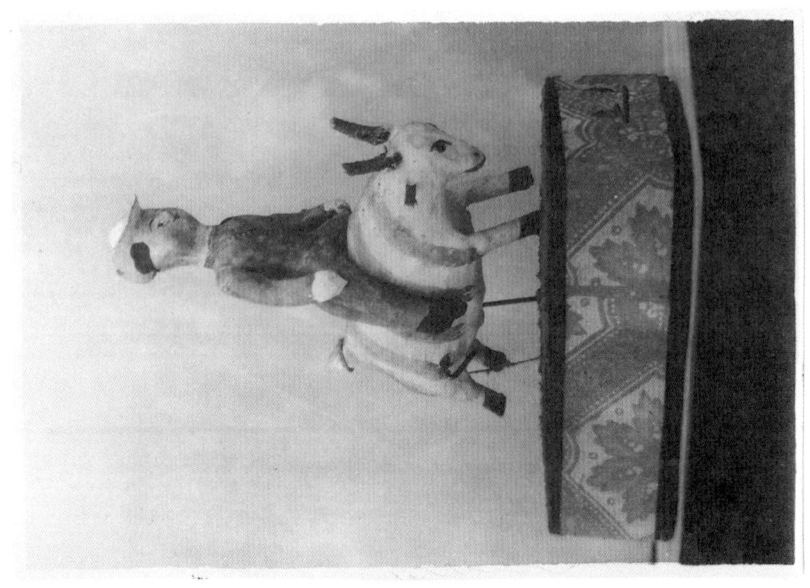

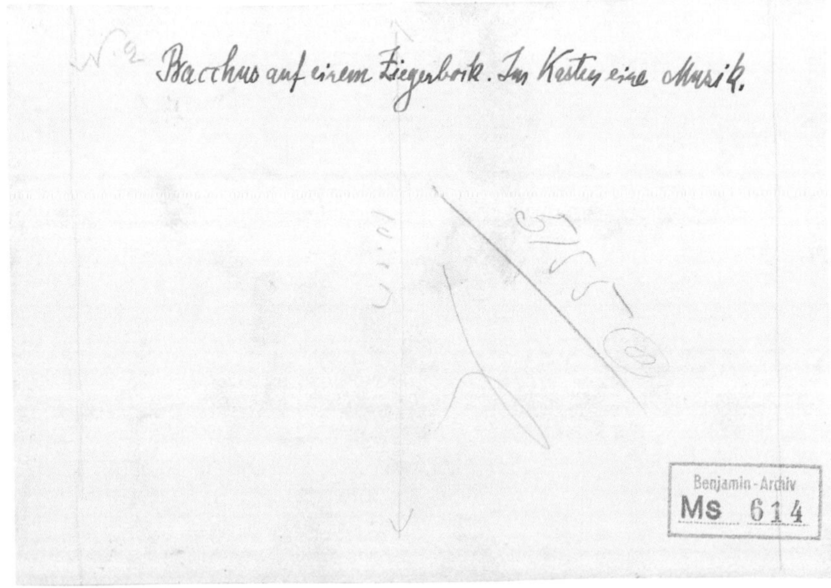

N. 2 Bacchus auf einem Ziegenbock. Im Kasten eine Musik.

Fig. 4.6

Fig. 4.6

Bacchus on a billy goat. Music in the casket.

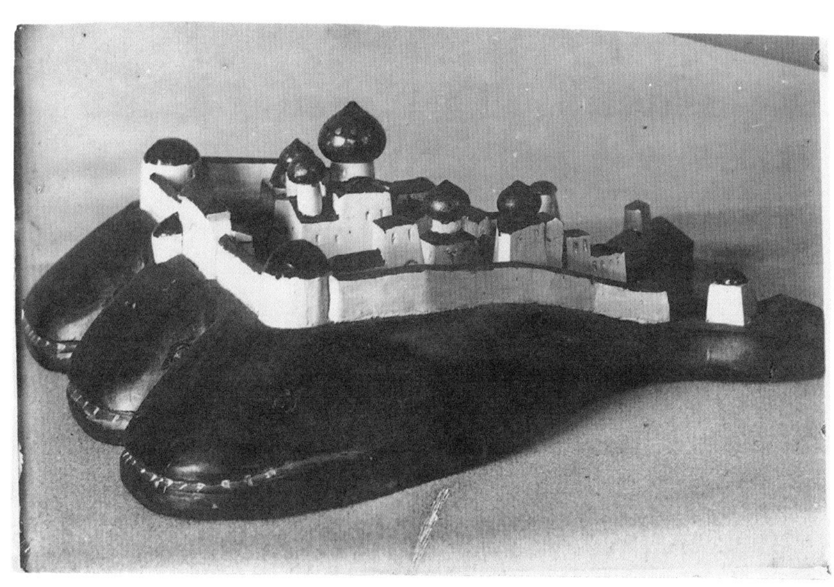

Die Erde auf drei Walfischen. Von einem neueren Künstler aus Holz verfertigt. Das Motiv entstammt
einer russischen Sage
N. 9
Benjamin-Archiv
Ms 616

Fig. 4.7

Fig. 4.7

The earth on three whales. Made out of wood by an artist. The motif stems from a Russian tale.

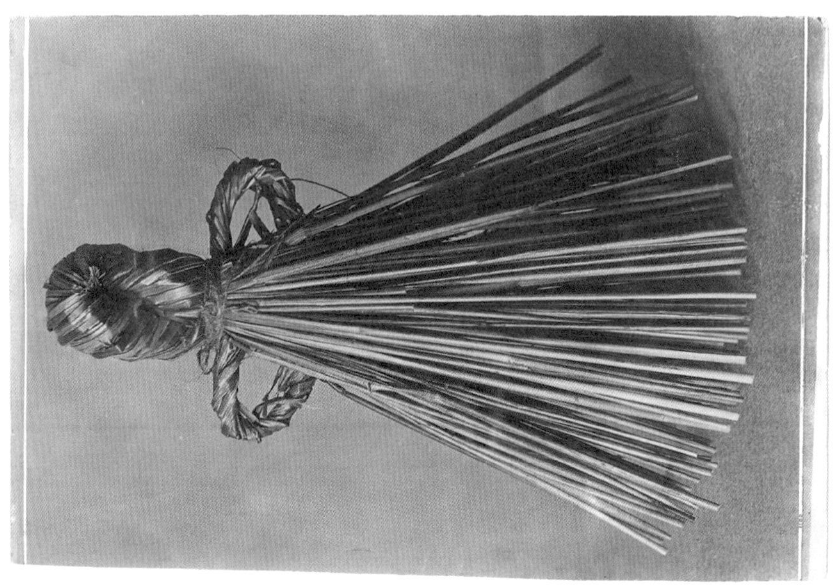

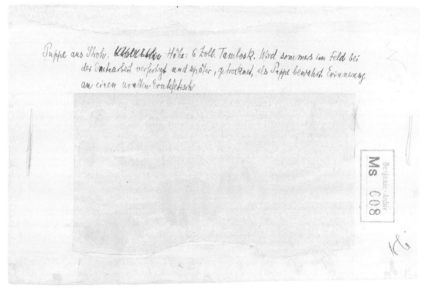

Puppe aus Stroh. [illegible] Höhe: 6 Zoll. Tambosk. Wird sommers im Feld bei der Erntearbeit verfertigt und später, getrocknet, als Puppe bewahrt. Erinnerung an einen uralten Erntefetisch

Fig. 4.8

Fig. 4.8

Straw doll. Height: 6 zoll. Tambosk. Made in the summer in the field during harvcsting and, later, once dried out, kept as a doll. Reminder of an ancient fetish of the harvest.

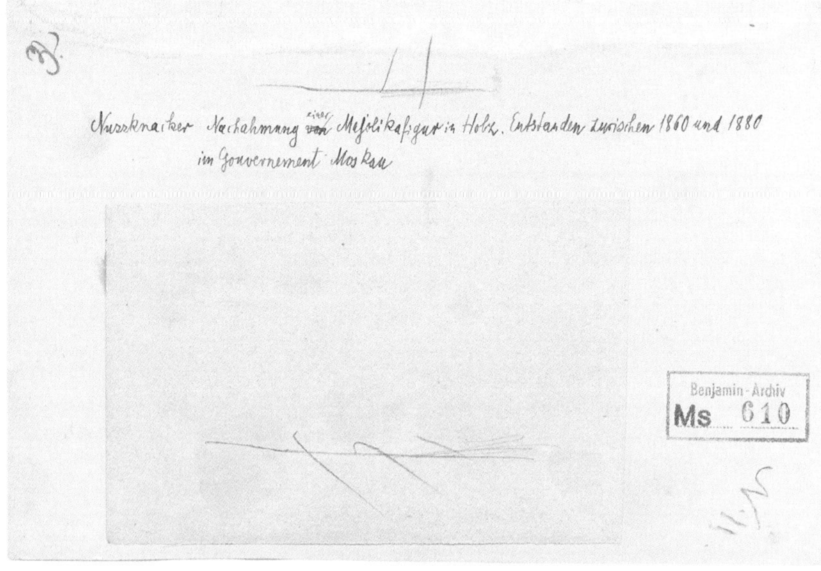
3.
Nussknacker Nachahmung einer Majolikafigur in Holz. Entstanden zwischen 1860 und 1880
im Gouvernement Moskau
Benjamin-Archiv
Ms 610

Fig. 4.9

Fig. 4.9

Nutcracker. Imitation of a majolica figure in wood. Made between 1860 and 1880 in the governorate of Moscow.

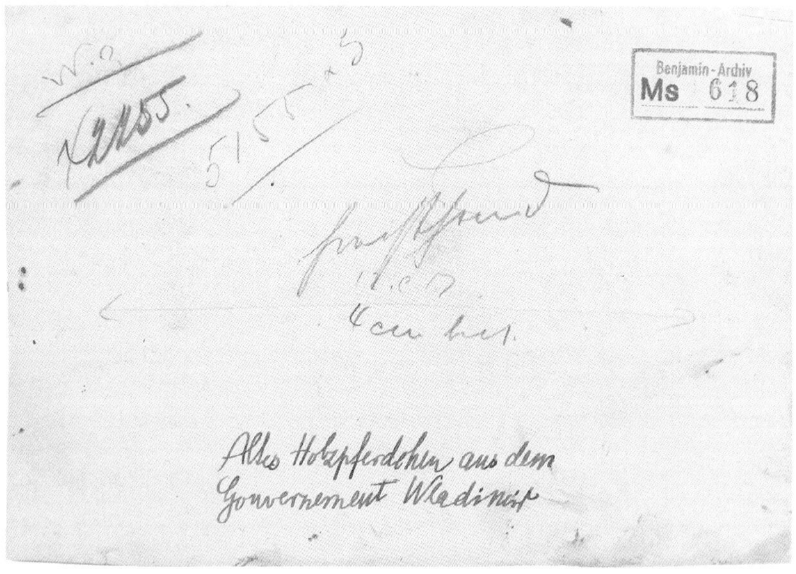
Benjamin-Archiv
Ms 618
Altes Holzpferdchen aus dem
Gouvernement Wladimir

Fig. 4.10

Fig. 4.10

Old wooden horsey from the governorate of Vladimir.

X2255

Benjamin-Archiv
Ms 609

Droschke mit zwei Pferden bespannt. Holzschnitzerei aus dem Gouvernement Wladimir ca. 1860/1870

Fig. 4.11

Fig. 4.11

Carriage stringed with two horses. Wood carving from the governorate of Vladimir, c. 1860/1870.

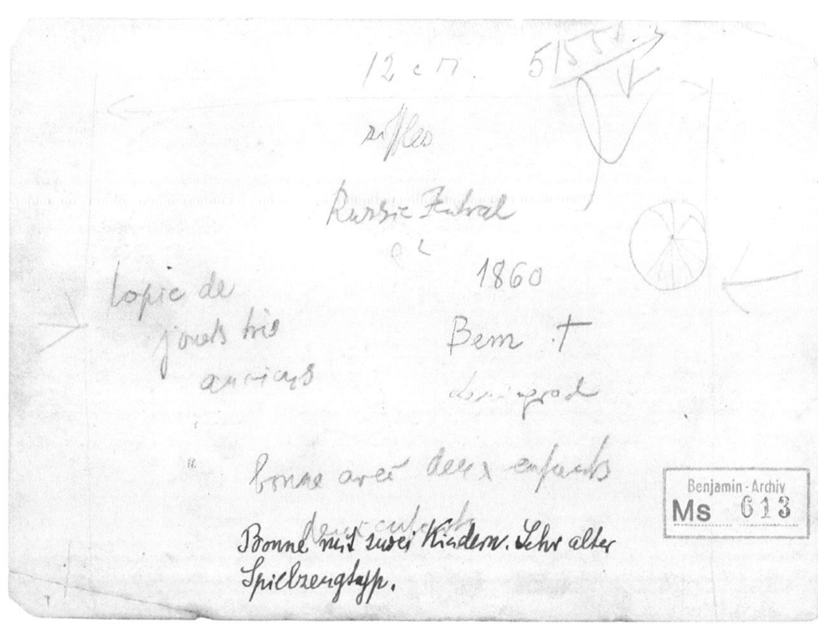
12 cm.
1860
bonne avec deux enfants
Bonne mit zwei Kindern. Sehr alter Spielzeugtyp.
Benjamin-Archiv
Ms 613

Fig. 4.12

Fig. 4.12

Nanny with two children. Very old type of toy.

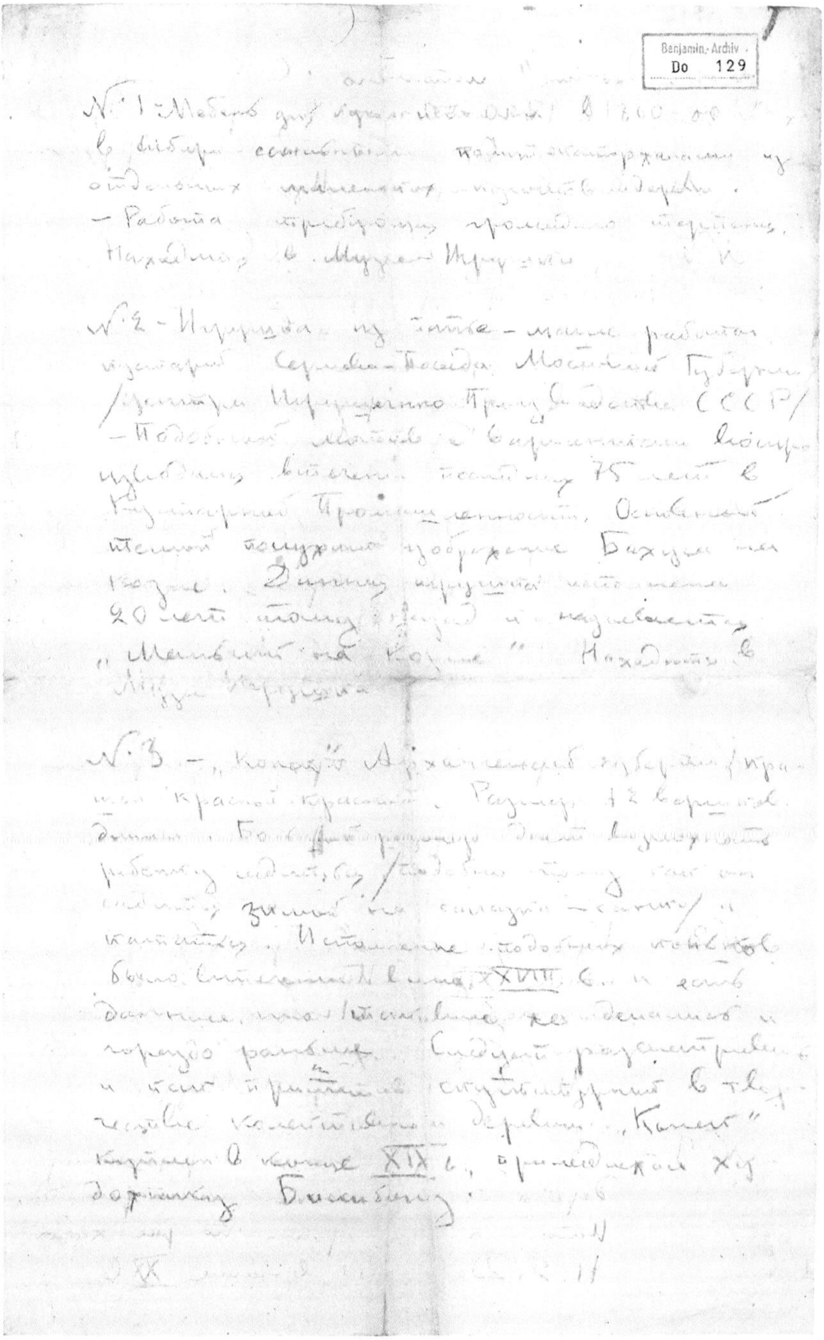

№ 1 – Набор для [illegible] в 1800-ых г., в выборе сочетаний [illegible] из отдельных [illegible] в [illegible]. – Работа [illegible]. Находится в Музее Игрушки.

№ 2 – Игрушка из папье-маше работы игрушечника Сергиева-Посада Московской Губернии /центра Игрушечного Производства СССР/ – Подобные мотивы с вариациями воспроизводились впервые лет 75 тому назад в кустарной промышленности. Основной темой послужило изображение Бахуса на бочке. Данная игрушка изготовлена 20 лет тому назад и называется „Мальчик на бочке". Находится в Музее Игрушки.

№ 3 – „Конёк" Архангельской губернии /крашеный красной краской. Размер 12 вершков. [illegible] ребенку [illegible] /подобно тому как он [illegible] зимой на салазки – санки/ и катается. Изготовление подобных коньков было отмечено в нач. XVIII в. и есть данные, [illegible] и гораздо раньше. Следует рассматривать и этот пример [illegible] в творчестве [illegible] деревни. „Конек" [illegible] в конце XIX в., принадлежащий художнику Билибину.

Fig. 4.13

Figs 4.14 and 4.15

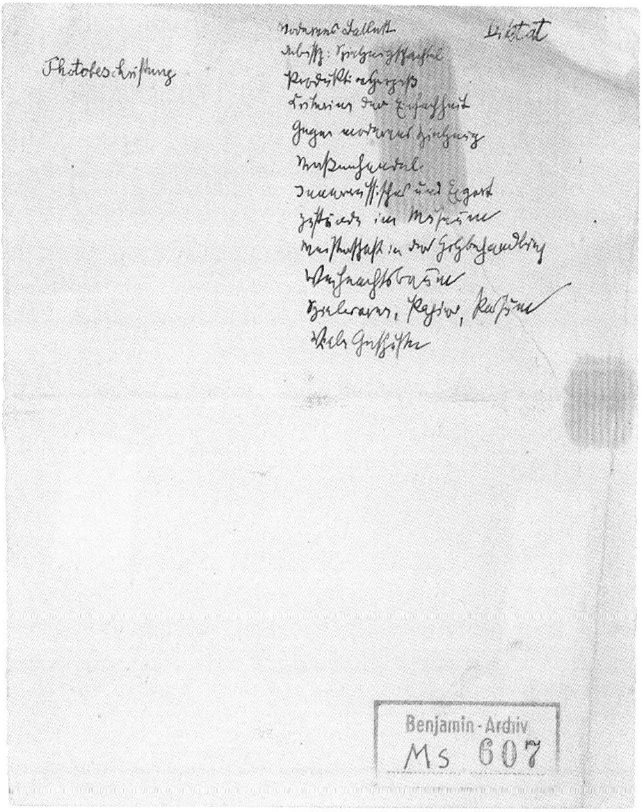

Photobeschriftung

Diktat

Fig. 4.16

Fig. 4.16

	Modern ballet	dictation
	Debussy: Toy box	
Photo caption	Production process	
	Criterion of simplicity	
	Against modern toys	
	Street trading	
	Internal Russian and export	
	Conditions in the museum	
	Mastery in fashioning wood	
	Christmas tree	
	Toys, paper, perfume	
	Lots of shops	

Russische Spielsachen

Holzpferdchen. Bauernschnitzerei aus dem Gouvernement Wladimir.

Ursprünglich geht das Spielzeug aller Völker aus der Heimindustrie hervor. Der primitive Formenschatz des niederen Volkes, der Bauern und Handwerker bildet gerade für die Entwicklung des Kinderspielzeugs bis in die Gegenwart hinein die gesicherte Grundlage. Daran ist auch nichts Wunderbares. Der Geist, aus welchem die Erzeugnisse hervorgehen, der ganze Herstellungsprozeß und nicht nur sein Ergebnis ist ja dem Kind im Spielzeug gegenwärtig, und es versteht natürlich einen primitiv erzeugten Gegenstand viel besser als einen, der aus einem komplizierten Industrieverfahren herstammt. Hierin liegt nebenbei gesagt denn auch der berechtigte Kern in dem modernen Streben, „primitives" Kinderspielzeug herzustellen. Wenn dabei nur nicht unsere Kunstgewerbler gar zu oft vergäßen, daß primitiv auf Kinder nicht die konstruktiven, schematischen Formen wirken, sondern vielmehr der ganze Aufbau seiner Puppe oder seines Hündchens, soweit es nämlich sich vorstellen kann, wie sie gemacht sind. Das will es gerade wissen, das stellt ihm erst zu seinen Sachen die lebendige Beziehung her. Weil es beim Spielzeug nun einmal darauf ankommt, so darf man sagen, daß von allen Europäern vielleicht allein die Deutschen und die Russen das eigentliche Genie des Spielzeugs haben.

Allbekannt, nicht nur in Deutschland, sondern in der ganzen Welt — die deutsche Spielzeugindustrie ist die internationalste — sind die winzigen Puppen- und Tierreiche, die Bauernstübchen in einer Streichholzschachtel, die Archen Noahs und die Schäfereien, wie sie in thüringischen, erzgebirgischen Dörfern, auch in der Gegend von Nürnberg gemacht werden. Russisches Spielzeug aber ist im allgemeinen unbekannt. Seine Erzeugung ist nur wenig industrialisiert, und außerhalb der russischen Grenzen ist wenig mehr von ihr verbreitet als die stereotype Figur der „Baba", des kegelförmigen Stückchen Holz, das, über und über bemalt, eine Bauersfrau darstellt.

In Wahrheit ist russisches Spielzeug das reichste, mannigfaltigste von allen. Die 150 Millionen Menschen, die das Land bewohnen, verteilen sich auf Hunderte von Völkerschaften, und alle diese Völker haben wiederum eine mehr oder minder primitive, mehr oder minder entwickelte Kunstübung. So gibt es Spielzeug in Hunderten verschiedener Formensprachen, in den allerverschiedensten Materialien. Holz, Ton, Knochen, Stoff, Papier, Papiermaché treten allein oder in Kombinationen auf. Holz ist das wichtigste unter diesen Materialien. Fast überall in diesem Lande der großen Wälder hat man in seiner Behandlung — im Schnitzen, Färben und Lackieren — eine unvergleichliche Meisterschaft. Von den einfachen Hampelmännern aus weißem und weichem Weidenholz, von den naturwahr geschnitzelten Kühen, Schweinen, Schafen bis zu den kunstvoll mit leuchtenden Farben bemalten, lackierten Schatullen, auf denen der Bauer in seiner Troika, Landleute, die um einen Samowar versammelt sind, Schnitterinnen oder Holzfäller bei der Arbeit dargestellt sind und weiter bis zu großen Monstregruppen, plastischen Wiedergaben alter Sagen und Legenden, füllen hölzernes Spielzeug, hölzerne Spielereien in den vornehmsten Straßen von Moskau, Leningrad, Kiew, Charkow, Odessa Laden an Laden. Die größte Sammlung davon besitzt das Moskauer Spielzeugmuseum. Drei Schränke des Museums stehen voll mit tönernem Spielzeug aus dem nördlichen Rußland. Der bäuerliche, robuste Ausdruck dieser Puppen aus dem Gouvernement Wjatka steht einigermaßen im Kontrast zu ihrer höchst gebrechlichen Beschaffenheit. Aber sie haben die weite Reise heil überstanden. Und es ist gut, daß sie im Moskauer Museum ein sicheres Asyl bezogen haben. Denn wer weiß, wie bald auch dieses Stück Volkskunst dem Siegeszug der Technik, welcher Rußland heute durchquert, noch standhalten kann. Schon soll die Nachfrage nach diesen Dingen zumindest in den Städten verstummen. Aber dort oben in ihrer Heimat leben sie sicher noch, werden im Bauernhause selber nach wie vor am Feierabend geknetet, mit leuchtenden Farben gestreift und gebrannt.

Dr. Walter Benjamin.

Links: Samowar (gelb, rot und grün) als Baumschmuck. Rechts: Trommler knattert und beugt den Arm, wenn man an der Kurbel unten dreht.

Puppe aus Stroh, Höhe 6 Zoll (Tobolsk). Wird Sommers im Feld bei Erntearbeiten gefertigt und getrocknet aufbewahrt. Erinnerung an uralten Erntefetisch.

Nußknacker. Nachahmung einer Majolika-Figur in Holz. Gouvernement Moskau ca. 1860.

Hölzernes Modell einer Nähmaschine (Bauernarbeit). Dreht man die Kurbel, so geht der Nagel auf und nieder und erzeugt im Auffallen das rhythmische Geräusch der Nähmaschine.

Droschke mit zwei Pferden bespannt. Holzschnitzerei aus dem Gouvernement Wladimir um 1860.

Fig. 4.17

Fig. 4.17

Russian Toys
The toys of all cultures were products, initially, of a cottage industry. The stock of primitive forms in use by the lower groups in society, the peasants and the artisans, provided the sure foundation for the development of children's toys up to the present. There is nothing remarkable about this. The spirit from which these products emanate—the entire process of their production and not merely its result—is alive for the child in the toy, and he naturally understands a primitively produced object much better than one deriving from a complicated industrial process. Herein, incidentally, lies the legitimate basis of the modern trend to produce "primitive" children's toys. If only our artisans would not so often forget when doing this that it is not the constructive, schematic forms that appear primitive to the child, but rather the total construction of his doll or his toy dog, insofar as he can imagine how it is made. This is just what he wants to know; this first establishes his vibrant relationship with toys. Precisely because of this, one could say, perhaps, that only the Germans and the Russians, of all Europeans, possess the real genius for making toys.

The German toy industry is the most international. The tiny doll and animal kingdoms, the matchbox farmhouse rooms, the Noah's arks, and the sheep pens as they are made in the villages of Thuringia and the Erzgebirge, as well as in the Nuremberg region, are universally known, not only in Germany, but throughout the entire world. On the other hand, Russian toys are generally unknown. Their production is barely industrialized and they are hardly disseminated beyond the Russian borders, except for the stereotyped figure of the "Baba," the cone-shaped piece of wood, that, painted over and over again, represents a peasant woman.

In fact Russian toys are the finest, most diversified of all. The 150 million people who inhabit the country are composed of hundreds of nationalities, and all of these in turn have a more or less primitive, more or less accomplished artistic skill. Thus toys are produced in hundreds of different stylistic idioms, of the most diverse materials. Wood, clay, bone, textiles, paper, papier-mâché appear alone or in combinations. Wood is the most important among these materials. There is an incomparable mastery of its handling—of carving, coloring, and lacquering—almost everywhere in this land of great forests. From the simple jumping-jacks of soft, white willowwood; from the lifelike carved cows, pigs, and sheep to the lacquered jewelry caskets on which the peasant in his *troika*, countryfolk gathered around a samovar, women harvesters, or woodcutters at work are artfully painted with glowing colors; to huge groups of monsters, sculptured renderings of old sagas and legends—wooden toys, wooden gadgets fill shop after shop in the most elegant streets of Moscow, Leningrad, Kiev, Kharkov, and Odessa. The Moscow Toy Museum owns the largest collection. Three cabinets of the museum are filled with clay toys from northern Russia. The robust rural expression of these dolls from the Viatka district stands in contrast to their highly fragile condition. They have, nevertheless, survived the long journey. And it is good that they have found a safe asylum in the Moscow museum. For who knows how long even this kind of folk art can withstand the triumphant progress of technology which today sweeps across Russia. Already the demand for these things has supposedly died, at least in the cities. But in the farmhouse the clay is still kneaded at day's end, painted with glowing colors, and fired; in their homeland, surely, these toys still live on.

5

Opinions et Pensées

His Son's Words and Turns of Phrase

> There is an old nursery rhyme that tells of Muhme Rehlen. Because the word *Muhme* meant nothing to me, this creature became for me a spirit: the mummerehlen. The misunderstanding disarranged the world for me. But in a good way: it lit up paths to the world's interior. The cue could come from anywhere.
>
> Thus, on one occasion, chance willed that *Kupferstichen* [copperplate engravings] were discussed in my presence. The next day, I stuck my head out from under a chair; that was a *Kopf-verstich* [a head stick-out]. If, in this way, I distorted both myself and the word, I did only what I had to do to gain a foothold in life. Early on, I learned to disguise myself in words, which were really clouds. The gift of perceiving similarities is, in fact, nothing but a weak remnant of the old compulsion to become similar and to behave mimetically. In me, however, this compulsion acted through words. Not those that made me similar to models of good breeding, but those that made me similar to dwelling places, furniture, clothes.
>
> *SW* 3, pp. 390–1

Over many years Benjamin logged the language and games of his son Stefan (November 4, 1918–February 6, 1972). Stefan's expressions were collated in a notebook that conserves a small archive of a child's linguistic world. The entries, which in many cases are dated, reach right up until March 1932. It would seem that most are written down in retrospect, recalled in memory at various times. This is indicated, for example, by the heading "Words ~~and Sentences~~ prior to 27 November, 1921," underneath which appears a list of original infantile word forms (fig. 5.2). The sonnet "On 6 January 1922" prefaces the notes that have survived in Benjamin's bequest (compare *GS* VII.1, p. 64). This is followed by "Early Names and Verses for Stefan," affectionate appellations, terms of endearment, and infantile pseudonyms. The notes comprise a wealth of distorted word forms and witty unexpected formulations, which result in an amusing vocabulary book, fragments of a childish lexicon; children's rhymes and songs, belonging to the rhythm of the young family's life; infantile *bon mots*, questions and expressions; a hoard of his son's formulations, turns of phrase, and rituals of play, gestures; dialogues, tales, and stories by Stefan; brief communications by letter to his father as well as a short essay. The notes comprise a cheerful inventory, a collection of quotations and scenes from life with a growing child. They are documents of childish linguistic fantasy, early experiments in language, which found in the father an enthusiastic observer.

On January 14, 1926 Benjamin wrote to Gershom Scholem: "I have written down my son's 'opinions and thoughts' in a notebook since the day he was born. Needless to say, because of my many absences it is not terribly long, but nonetheless lists a few dozen unusual words and expressions. I am thinking of having it typed and one of the few copies would be intended for you" (*Correspondence*, p. 288). Benjamin's reference to his son's "opinions et pensées," as if he were a famous and celebrated person, is not without irony—it appears to be a parodic quotation of book titles such as, for example, *Lessing's Thought and Opinions, Michel de Montaigne's Thought and Opinions on All Manner of Things, Vie, opinions et pensées de Lazare Carnot, l'organisateur de la victoire* or *Opinions, pensées, maxims extraites des ouvrages de Louis-Napoléon Bonaparte*. But Benjamin does not use "opinions et pensées" simply ironically. The notes on Stefan do not merely detail light-hearted nonsense, linguistic curiosities, and playful oddities. Irrespective of all the amusement that his words must have provided for the father, Benjamin was serious. He wanted to present the small collection to Scholem's archive; he thought it worthwhile transposing them into typewritten form. Stefan's expressions were for him the speaking proof of the child's world picture, thought, and knowledge.—Neither in Benjamin's bequest nor in Scholem's collection are there typewritten versions of the notes. In addition the cover of the "little book" in which Benjamin placed his notes is missing. The literary remains hold only sixteen single sheets torn out of the notebook. For the large part these chequered sheets have writing on both sides.

In the nineteenth century intellectuals such as Hippolyte Tain or Charles Darwin recorded in their studies their own observations of infantile use of language. In the twentieth century Jean Piaget did this systematically, and he developed a wide-ranging theory of infantile development from observing, for the most part, his own three children. Of course, Benjamin's fragmentary postscripts have another meaning. They are not directed toward a documentation of the acquisition of language, but rather toward specific aspects of infantile thinking and speaking—the detours in which it goes astray. Losing oneself in language. Benjamin latches onto the distorting effects of children's language. For him, linguistic blunders and misunderstandings do not find their meaning in being corrected.

The distortions of language effected by the child are manifold. Words are disguised—torn, twisted, substituted, confused. "Africa" becomes "Affica," "photograph" turns into "gratophoph," "university" becomes "fursity." Words shrink. Stefan transformed "university library" into "unilibry." Imaginative word inventions, mixed forms and analogies appear. If the word "*Grausamkeiten*," gruesomeness, exists, whose first syllable is the word for gray, then "Grünsamkeiten," a green version, must also be possible. And the parents—Dora Sophie and Walter—engage themselves in the masquerade of words; they too are embroiled in its game. Benjamin, who had a love of word games and anagrams, clearly participated with an attentive, co-inventive joy. He maintains the sonically derived misunderstandings of the child in his ear, notes the surprising metaphorical turns of phrase that Stefan uses. For him language presents itself as shot through with similarities and correspondences. An unlimited play of relationships comes to the fore in infantile speaking.

It was not only the memories of his own childhood, but also the example of his own child that was in Benjamin's mind when he described the misunderstandings and distortions of the child's linguistic world in *The Mummerehlen*. Benjamin composed this vignette from *Berlin Childhood around 1900* in 1932, the same date as the final entry on Stefan. *The Mummerehlen* is contiguous with *Doctrine of the Similar*, which was written at the beginning of 1933. Here Benjamin connects his linguistic-theoretical considerations to the theory of the mimetic faculty. This theoretical sketch (and its later version, *On the Mimetic Capability*) is not unrelated to the notes on his son. Benjamin pinpoints children's play as the schooling of the mimetic faculty—and he develops a view of language that does not reduce it to instrumental usage. It is not consumed in its semiotic function of meaning and communication. Rather language (and writing) is to be seen as a deployment of the mimetic faculty, as "an archive of nonsensuous similarities, of nonsensuous correspondences" (*SW* 2:2, p. 697).

The speech and activity of the child, which Benjamin logged observantly in his little notebook, may be everyday in nature, and yet often enough he spots something at work in the background of this play. To cite just one example, here is a little scene, which was presumably related to the parents by Grete Rehbein, the family's housemaid.

"We were away from the house—this was after several days in which I had pressed very strongly for peace in the apartment because of some work I was doing—he is alone in the kitchen with Grete. He says: 'Grete be very quiet. He must do his work now. Very quiet.' With that he ascends the dark staircase, opens both doors and goes into his dark room. When Grete comes after him some time later, she sees him standing quite still in the darkness. He says: 'Grete do not disturb him. He really has to work.'"

Benjamin described this scene in his notebook. It illustrates for him essential aspects of infantile activity. Stefan presents a performance that follows the example of his absent father. He identifies with him, acts in front of Grete as an adult who has to do something. He becomes the absent father, who must work and may not be disturbed. Standing still in the darkness Stefan plays at intellectual work. And in fact the game represents this work, follows a dark necessity. For Stefan has indeed to work something through. He was compelled by his father to renounce, and that is what the work that he now does affords. Passive concernment is reversed in an assertion of independence. Climbing the staircase Stefan ascends to adulthood, figures himself now as the father. And, conversely, Grete, who follows him, appears in the position of the child.—Benjamin wrote about infantile play (and its relationship to work) in various texts. These contain considerations that demonstrate, in particular, how the everyday life of the family, their interactions in the domestic setting, the play of the son, all played a role in his thought.

Figures

5.1 Stefan and Dora Sophie Benjamin (February 1921)—Photograph.

5.2 Notes on Stefan Benjamin (c. 1919 until 1932)—Manuscript, sixteen pages (thirty-one sides); shown here, page 5: "Words prior to 27 November, 1921."[1]

5.3 Notes on Stefan Benjamin (1928/1929). Above the strips of paper that have been glued in Benjamin noted: "Stefan cuts out money. To do this he clips out the figures and mint-marks from little strips of paper."

5.4 Notes on Stefan Benjamin (1929 and 1932).
His son's "homemade stamps" are glued onto the sheet.
[Ms. 1284]

[1] Throughout this manuscript a variety of solutions have been employed to convey the puns and distortions of language. Puns have been reproduced as accurately as possible. Shifts of consonants have tried to imitate something of the sonic effect, even when different letters are involved. Where it has been impossible to render the punning effect into English, an interpolation is made in the text, in italics. Otherwise, efforts have been made to transfer at least something of Stefan's linguistic inventiveness into English.

Fig. 5.1

On 6 January, 1922

What is the name of the guest who even if he also hurts
Bestows the mistress with house and tribulations
And yet so speedily those gates
Open up for him as a flimsy door does for the wind?

His name is discord which returns
Whether it has long emptied table and chambers
A threefold household deity cleaves to the soul
Uniquely true now: Sleep tears and the child

Yet each day a swordless sheaf
Cuts the old scar of the waking one
And before it cradles consolation in new slumbers

The source of the tears is long run dry
Only the smile of the child its customs
Are able to invite hope into the house.

[Ms. 1270 recto]

Early names and verses for Stefan

Stefanze Stefanserich Houselion (when he was laying on his stomach after bathing in Bern) Mr Silly Mr Treasure (after a wooden doll that I had named in the same way)

Woofy woofy
Snouty snouty

One foot is called Felefoot (Philip Foot), the other is Franz Foot.
When he was brought in the room in swaddling clothes he was called Babysausage Snought, Snoughting, Zeppel [?],[2] Soul, Gob, Sweetielamb. In very early days, in Switzerland also: Bushi, Bushonnili

[2] Where the manuscript is unclear the editors have added [?] after the word or words in question. Some other editorial interpolations are also between square brackets in sans serif.

Bessalien[?] good dolly / dance with mama now
Dance now you good Sweetielamb / for mama is still there
He child (from the Swiss days)

The most charming game that we observed him at in the earliest days, I suppose at around one year old—we only saw this once—was when sitting at his play table he grabbed a little dachshund by the tail and—leaning out of his little chair—first leftwards, then rightwards swung it in the air three times, such that the dog's head was close to the floor. It was very nice to see how he tried to transfer the dog's tail, which was in his left hand, into his right one.

The first word that he uttered meaningfully was: "qui-a." He raised his finger, just as Dora did, when she said "quiet" to him.

For a period, when we were lifting him at night during his sleep, and he did not fully[?] wake up, telepathic phenomena came quite clearly to the fore in the daytime; he spoke of things that Dora or Grete [Rehbein] were thinking of at that moment, every now and then expanded on ~~features in a~~ unknown features in a fairytale (In the *Wolf and the Seven Kids*~~)~~ the youngest one hidden in the clock case).This phenomenon stopped once we did not pick him up anymore at night.

There was a time when he wanted to be known only by a particular name and was something in particular: a boy or a mimi, or a Steffie (or an Ingrid?)—a Rafaela, mummy, etc.

[Ms. 1270 verso]

For a very short period he imitated lifeless objects, e.g. a pear, by coiling himself up on the ground.

5

Worte und Sätze vor dem 27 November 1921

Fig. 5.2

[Ms. 1271 recto]

Words ~~and sentences~~ prior to 27 November 1921

Schring (spring)
Tetecin (medicine)
a lesh (flesh)
Sipper-supper[?] (alphabetic character)
Tysix (seventy-six)
a railway line
a writey (pencil)
a mimi (little girl)
Uncle Dusky (after Walter:)
Balli Podott (blackcurrants)
a tone (from; tower (?) chimney on a locomotive)
image boar [*Bildschwein*] (wild boar [*Wildschwein*], that he saw in an image and that I named for him)
a little step
Children's school (Kindergarten)
Belbrückstraße (Delbrückstraße)
Oulish (ugly, evil; from ghoulish, but co-determined by owl)
Fursity (university)
Tu[?] (meat, derived from noodles. Very early)
Ell (instead of "tell a story," at first without about[?])
Fish-baba (banana, from the Swiss days)
Bai (very early; ball)
Dancetupper ("a dance tupper" railway sleeper[?] ?? Sometimes one was made from little men. [round dance??])
Little Red Riding Head
Dandals (sandals)
Bitterfly (butterfly)
Papsize (capsize; a game, in which Dora continually knocks him down each time he gets up, while standing in the bed or on the floor.)
Pamsret (trumpet)
Coclate (chocolate)
Zolad[?] (salad)
Bowwowsiko (dog)
Creation by Dora
a letter (piece of paper)
Günther (any ill-mannered boy)
Auntie Glow (single-handedly)
Podot (compote)
Fromesser (professor)
Doctorman (a male doll)
Miggay (midday (meal))
Bowwow-lion (instead of lion)
Vird Keets (parakeet, once it was explained to him that it was a bird)
Len[?] (horse) (very early)
Ista (sister [Toni])
Mommy (my mother)
Papa (my father)
Catatoes, Tatatoes (potatoes)
Cap (male member)
Thatte (thanks, early)
the warm and the cold outbacker (meaning is unclear; possibly he means the drainpipes, which he thought were the staircase to the kitchen)
Beta (Bertha, very early)
Affika (Africa, place where the apes [*Affen*] are)
Glasstern (lantern)
Fi (for~~)~~, stuck for a very long time)
Motitive (locomotive)
Once again (this doesn't mean "the same one" after a story or song but "more")
Applemarine (later "margarine") means mandarin
Bagschool (satchel)
Ragerman (gas balloon for playing with)
Bug (picture book)
Conek(ek)er (conker)
Little birds (pieces that fall to the ground when cutting nails. Coined by ~~Dora~~ who?)
Kaper (paper)
Ingrid (well-behaved child, name of children from the children's home where he went at the age of two and a half.)
Small bell (moon)
Building bick (building brick) also: buildingbock
Round (fairground with music; probably from "turning round")
Lala (called "Empress" by me, because it was bought at the Emperor department store. His earliest doll in Bern)
Wolf Bow Wow
Mama keet (parakeet)
Ga(r)ki (garden)
Ballin[?] (Berlin)
Momma (Dora's mother)
Kiss (his name not only for the actual kiss but also anything damp, fruit juice[?] etc. on his face)
Abdolutely (absolutely)
Ung-Ung-train (electric tram)
Puff-Puff train (railway train)
Kabai[?] (make) (tickle)
Shoos (shoes)
Corn (cord)
a lake Halen (made in the garden in sandcastles. In general "a" also served in the early days, for the first three and a half years or so, as the definite article)
a baked opple (baked apple)
The hornses (instead of: the horns)
a heru (hare name for the rabbit, that he was given by Ernst Schoen.[3] In response to the question what is its name, he said: a heru or a rabb. (It was lively)

[3] Ernst Schoen was a long-standing friend of Benjamin. Dora had an affair with him for a while in 1921 and thus he is one of the reference points in Benjamin's essay on Goethe's *Elective Affinities*.

[Ms. 1271 verso]

Words since December 1921

Souldoll
Dickybardy (when he heard that was wrong: Dickyburd)
Outnumbering } situated in a "joke" as edible.
Undernumbering }
Breadmeat (Butter with sautéed breadcrumbs and other types of sautéed bread)
Byena (Hyena)
whools (wheels)
Corinda (veranda)
Crocodile soup (dill soup. Not joking!)
Breadmeat (Savoy cabbage with grated bun and butter)
Unilibry (university library)
Forgettable (in the sense of difficult to hold onto)
Rice eagle (Reich's eagle)
Hogmaday (Hogmanay)
Gratophoph (Photograph; old)
Mitiral water (mineral water)

eightly (lately)
Indida (India rubber)
~~Strak strak~~ Straking match (earlier stroking match)
Mandosquik (perhaps manuscript?) (he insists on hearing a story about one, apparently one that Dora had told him once before.)
Standal (scandal)
The singer (a humming top)
knulled bread (nuggets)
Türkenschwanz Park [*Turk's Tail Park*] (Türkenschanz Park)
Margarrots (carrots)
Rainguleily (regularly)
Tomartoes (tomatoes)
Zunie disease (renal disease)
Niacinthen (December 1923)
Keldel (name for Wolf Heinle—Bern)
Zophe (Zofe June 1925)
Hyptonize (January 1928)

Hosenleder (instead of Lederhosen)
Absicht [*intention*] (conceived as Absatz [*heel*] of a boot)
Baumeißner (instead of Baumeister [*master builder*]. The concierge who was carrying out works in the apartment was called Meißner)
Express dog (This is how he describes[?] himself occasionally. Formed as an analogy with express train)
tograttafaf (to photograph)
Regypt (Egypt)
Taechers (teacher)
Riskling (irises)
Easter egg beetle (this is what he calls the pupa of a beetle)
Fursity (later unifursity)
Melomody (February 1923 melody)
Shellmuck—shellmuckbaby (salamander baby)
Battanemy—Battery (end of 1924)
Varnish out—write out songs on~~t~~ the board (February 1925)
For examspool (e.g.)

[Ms. 1272 recto]

Formulations

Men have to work
What do fishes sing? (on looking at Bertuch[4])
Aunt Pick doeams (probably formed out of "dream" and "do")
Large and mottled mummy (after "big and mottled tiger)

[4] Friedrich Justin Bertuch's 12-volume *Picture-Book for Children* was published in Weimar between 1792 and 1830. It contained one thousand colored and high-quality copperplate illustrations and countless other images, from the eruption of Vesuvius to the patent of an English washing machine. Many animals were illustrated in its pages. It was a book that Benjamin and Dora often showed to Stefan.

What does that say? (on looking at Bertuch)

Good morning—a little mimi (girly)—mummy (very fast, spoken jerkily, a formulation at goodnight time, once he is lying in bed)

Papsize (A game in which he lay in bed with Dora and Dora[?] said: "But Mr Treasure, you wanted to stand up, didn't you, and then when he stood she "capsized" him)

Fiffty Maks a crown (Price description, ~~probably~~ bound up with the idea of being "expensive")

Thirteen (price description, tied up with the idea—not expensive)

The "good miller" and the "bad miller." (After the song [He must be a bad miller] on one[?] sheet[?] often a bird was characterized as a bad and the other as a good miller)

The rocking horse was called Steffe, then, in jest, Aunt Clara, Aunt Ulox[?], later Berta

Losingu almostyou (first used supposedly for the hat belonging to "Mr Treasure,"~~of~~ a wooden doll, coined by Dora. Stefan believed that the words really belonged together, which was apparent in other uses, yet when playing understood them as a joke.

Yesterday is always the time immediately before his last nap, even when it was a midday nap. If, following this, one reminds him of something from the morning, he only understands it by the word "yesterday."

To catch a story. He searches in Dora's bosom, grabs "something" and sticks it into her mouth. She has to swallow it and then tell a story. This is played out in a variety of ways.

Ozzerway rau, not this way (At any type of technical difficulty)

He can help (pronounced: cana help) [Similar also to other uses: He can eat, he may write]

I car nit pleef it (used for a very long period as an expression of extreme happiness, formed according to "I can't believe it.")

Bum he bis, bubba bum, so bum (also too bum) when he begins to cry; dumb he is, abominably dumb, too dumb,

Leave him Emil (Imitating my mother, standing in front of my father, when he has prohibited him from doing something~~)~~ When he was alone at my parents)

Too funny (often with a forced laugh)

It is right, isn't it? (In order to be praised) Also to himself: Quite right

Papa glad

Healthy and sick men (probably first invented by us, Nuremberg figures, whole or in two)

In "All the Birds Returning Again" the rule was as follows: ~~blackbird~~ blackbeard[?], thrush, finch and starlch

Wish you a (~~spy~~?)[?] joyfufl year or dooryear, later always with the comment "Gideon always says: joyous)

[Ms 1272 verso]

He has a peculiar mode of double questioning. Here is one example amongst many: ~~Who~~ ~~With~~Upon looking at a heating device: Now (i.e. at a certain positioning of the screw) is warm? "Yes." But ~~When~~ other way is cold? "Yes, if one turns it the other way it is cold" But when it is this way, it's warm? (This example is [~~x~~] constructed, didn't occur exactly in this way. His questions always return him though to the starting point.)

Curz, Server, Adiu Formulations on leaving the room, until the end of 1921 Often used (curtsey, Server, Adieu)

When two are on, Mr Master complains (refers to the electric light that is not allowed to be on when not in use.)

Always today is my favorite (and similar combinations often appear) I always have my favorite the whole day.

Today I dreamt that Papa is a ... (This was always different, but always completed by inanimate objects: a picture, a pen, a book, an apple. I suppose it is to be thought in relation to the Oedipus Complex [as a peeling[?] of the father. It was the answer to the question what did you dream last night?)

Hope well-behaeff (very old. My mother used to say to him: I hope you were well-behaved)

"I saw that I lived here.—I saw that that is my apartment" (Upon returning home)

If "fiffty Mak" is "too expensive" for me, could we manage to reach an agreement at "eighty Mak?"

The name of the new doll, which he got for his fourth birthday, "Gretl Body."

With stories that begin with the phrase "Once upon a time there were two children," the question he regularly poses is "what is one child called?" and then "what is the other one called?"

Upon going to sleep, when he ~~goes~~ ~~l~~ is lying in bed: Up ~~Wicas~~ Wiasaha—a little mimi ([girly]—Memi—(yes, Mummy is here)—say hello nicely—thousands of times—Tomorrer we'll get up nicely.

The large giant, the medium-sized giant and the really tiny giant—Stefan is the papa and mummy of all three

Later ~~formulations~~ additional formulations upon going to sleep: what should I dream?

A further embellishment: And Mr Roth? And the Chinaman? And Grete? etc.)

He invented a male society comprising above all Mr Gravel, a train driver, like himself, Mr Sievecorpse, Masons, Mr Mode[?] Cellar (Kellner[5]). The last one died of a serious illness. He was older than all the others. How old? Hundred years. Apart from these there are one or two other people whose shared language is "Rogaic." E.g. "Good Night" is "God Nen[?] in it." Mr Mida[?] should be added "he just earns money" as answer to the question of what his job is.

5 Dora's maiden name.

[Ms. 1273 recto]

Sentences prior to 21 November 1921

When he received as a present a picture ~~with a saint on it~~ from Rang[6] upon which amongst other things there was a saint, he named this the kobold.

After Stefan had been undressed he was left alone in the room and he cried. When Dora came in to see him after a little while he said: "Wipe nose and dry tears all by self."

When Dora told him a story about a little mimi (or ~~children~~ small children) and said: "Then they went into a garden and there were lots of Berli podots and then they were very happy," Stefan says: "No, only a little."

On going out one day Stefan was wearing a colorful wool cloth, given to him as a present. When I met him at the door just as he was leaving I took it from him and put it around my neck as a shawl. He shouted out: "Don't give Papa the towel. Stefan needs the towel. Is cold after all."

He asks Dora to draw him a railway train. Dora says he should do it himself. To which he responded (using intervals so that he might discern the effect of his words): "He has not got any time—he has not got any room—he has not got any idea."

Joke: Mr Grete (Grete is his nursemaid)

We were away from the house—this was after several days in which I had pressed very strongly for peace in the apartment because of some work I was doing—he is alone in the kitchen with Grete. He says: "Grete be very quiet. He must do his work now. Very quiet." With that he ascends the dark staircase, opens both doors and goes into his dark room. When Grete comes after him some time later, she sees him standing quite still in the darkness. He says: "Grete do not disturb him. He really has to work."

Once Dora received a young lady as visitor and the next day, when he was asked about the guest, who had even brought a gift for him, he said: "The aunt is baba. A sheared one[?] should come."

To children, who are in a strange garden calling for "mommy," he says, while he is with my mother: "But children what are you thinking, Steffe is still with a mommy."

The lion barks—roars

---

6 Florens Christian Rang, 1864–1924, a writer and theologian.

[Ms. 1273 verso]

When a man at the electric tram stop asked Grete about trams to the zoo Stefan, who overheard, said; "yes, in the zoo is where the apes are."

Morning at breakfast: Papa—you are illuterate—(after a while:) Have you a fiver.

Dora shows him a page in Bertuch with berries on it. Stefan, as usual: "May I eat that, yes?" Dora: Yes Stefan: Little Steffe should eat that. Dora: But you are little Steffe Stefan: No, little Steffe in the book (points to an empty space on the page) should come and eat it.

In the strongly yellow light that accompanies storms the sun's rays reflected on the path. Stefan said: the sun has painted the ground.

He was supposed to have some hot milk, because he had a cough: "The tongue doesn't want it." Then "The tongue doesn't have a cough."

In Breitenstein[7] Dora told him that I was in Heidelberg. "Is that where the red books are?—There where the fishes are?"

After I would not allow him to enter my room he said to Grete: "Papa won't let me go in the room—this Papa."

"As I ~~rn~~ rang a bow wow came. And as I woke up today crying, a dog came too. Now none is coming. Now I am good."

When I went into the room to insist that he be quiet, he says loudly, after I left it again: "The bird there (or: the bear) always comes in the room. The bird should not come in there. It is my room. The room will be spoilt. The whole room spoilt. I also shouldn't be disturbd, I have to work too."

Occasionally my father uses the word "wild boar" [*Wildschwein*]. Thereupon Stefan: Over at our place we always say image boar [*Bildschwein*].

Dora: Do you not like Aunt Mia (the kindergarten teacher) at all. But she is so good. Why do you not like her? Stefan: I don't like her, because I don't like going to kindergarten.

He called the tale of the "seven [*sieben*] ravens," once I had read it to him, the tale of the "lovely [*lieben*] ravens."

---

7 At Breitenstein in Austria there was a sanatorium owned by Dora's aunt. The Benjamins spent periods there.

[Ms. 1274 recto]

Characterizations of letters

The B is Benjamin
R is Benjamin stretching both legs
P is Benjamin on one leg
M is Mummy
S is Steffe
A [Antiqua] A [German handwriting]

For several days (in November 1921) he was addicted to imitating objects, the beating of a clock, the form of a pear, by coiling himself up on the floor.

On the way back home from Aunt Clara's, which he walked with Dora and a man he did not know, he was feeling very sorry for himself: "Poor Steffe. Now the poor Steffe has to walk where it is very dark and the small bell is already hanging in the air poor Steffe still has to walk."

Very old, as he was alone with my parents, [~~X~~] at the midday meal: he doesn't want no tebbles only lesh

Dora sang to him: Alla mukodeia tsching tsching tscheia, he often sang along: Alla nakedeia …

He called condensed milk "white jam."

"Potatoes" [*Kartoffel*] he calls his own little bones [*Knöchel*] and offered them up to be eaten.

[Ms. 1274 verso]

Later Sentences and Games

January 1922
When the uncles sometimes give the aunts a lit cigar the aunts can smoke too.

Me: (responding to the question why am I not writing) Because I am speaking to you now, Stefan. Stefan: One can also speak to small children. But I am now a bit quite bigger.

He sits down on a footstool, after he has been standing for a long time; amongst other explanatory sentences he concludes: am I supposed to tire myself away?

I said, how loud you lot all laughed, my whole ear is laughed full ~~with~~ of headache.

On considering an illustration of a May beetle to Dora: Are May beetles made of chocolate inside too? And when Dora said no: but the bits that they crawl on, they are made of chocolate?

In response to the question about where something that is thrown away ends up my father once answered: in to space. Soon afterwards when she [the] ash of his cigar~~ette~~ ~~app~~ disappeared into the ashtray, he asked: are you putting it into outer space? / From then the ashtray was called "outer space," but by the next day "spacer out."[8]

Incidentally during a conversation with me about the Bertuch: Where did you akshully buy the books, Papa? "In Bern." In which Bern, in Heidelberg? Did you leave your pillow there? (I had left a pillow in Heidelberg in the summer, but there had been no mention of it for months.)

Mama to him: Tell Aunt Dodo that she looks horribly green. He says: Aunt Dodo you look orribly green. Mama: How do you look? Stefan: I look orribly red.

Stories with Rafael Good and Rafael Naughty, Rafael Fatbelly.

He encounters my father while on a walk and sees him without greeting him. Later when asked reproachfully, ~~he~~ ~~says~~ what he meant by not saying good day, he says: But I had to go on my walk.

I noticed something very strange. During Dora's stay in London, on the day after her departure, I tell him that Mum is going to bring him back something very nice. Whereupon he says: a pretzel? I say: No, something even nicer than that. He: An apple? I: No, something much much nicer than that. He: A brick?—It would seem that the most extremely heightened anticipation appears to diminish the capacity to imagine, which descends ever deeper, as if it despairs of ~~fin~~ coming up with a worthy object of this anticipation.

---

8 *Weltenraum*, the word for "outer space" is transposed by Stefan into *Raupenfell*, the word for "larval fur"—the translation here ("spacer out") does not convey this sense, but imitates only the transposition of consonants.

[Ms. 1275 recto]

Dora says that she has brought a banana (from London) and he is allowed to ask for something else that they may buy together. To which he says after a lengthy reflection "Another banana so that there are two." In response Dora: "You can request another thing too, you'll get two bananas." "Then we ought perhaps to buy one or two lemons for next year, for when I am ill again."

He called a pineapple that Dora brought from London a large ~~pineapple~~ strawberry with spikes.

Is there much enough snow?

February 1922
My mother brought him flummery. Later he said to Dora: Mommy brought me flame Marie; why is it called Marie?

Sung: Outside stand two sheep
Father guards the sheep
Mother shakes the little tree
A little dream falls off
If the child is not well-behaved
The black sheep comes and bites it (verbatim)

In one of the fairytales a king is hunting. I asked Stefan if he knows what that means. He says: "When he hunts, he thumps a dog. He thumps the dog with a rod."

"What does Hans Miller (type of ill-mannered boy) say when one gramophies me?"

Stefan entered a room while Dora was crying. He saw tears on her face. He says: "~~The~~ It's raining here in the room.—the little angels must have poured out water up above, to make it rain in the room."

Contremptable low fellow (because people were on strike and there was no electric light) the accursed fellows

Then she went to the mother rav (from ~~Sleepi~~ Cinderella)

[Ms. 1275 verso]

"Sing of the Godthrough." After much persistence it emerges that he meant "There goes the dear Lord God through the forest."

"Papa always has fun in the morning.—Every morning Papa has fun.—This Papa with his fun."

You are the mummy of Papa, aren't you?—So is Papa my childe?—Oh woe, that is what the big people can be. (Some time after he said I was Mommy's son) The papa of you is Walter ≠ (From a discussion with Dora)

Dora shows him the antlions in Bertuch and the edible dormice, which has a carrot in its hand. On another day she points to the dormice and asks what it is called: Carrotlion is the answer.

As Dora is telling Grete that there is nothing for supper in the house, Stefan overhears and says: "It is only the third day and we are so ~~ham~~ poor again."

As Dora enters the room after the afternoon nap, he says: "Somebody disturbed my sleep quite a bit. Someone made hello ~~ever~~ all the time." (Make hello =make a telephone call)

~~give him (a toy~~ [~~x~~] One morning he was supposed to bring a letter to me: in the process he says to Dora: Now I am taking this to owly shiverbeard.

Star often bakes poppy seed cakes for us. He asks Mama, while the moon is in the sky: Is the moon baked? And of Dora: Can one bake a cake from the moon?

Mummy I want to say something in your ear. In her ear: you ape. /

Mummy, I want to say something in your ear. (In her ear:) I am going to marry the princess too.

Mum, today I am the prince, not Steffe. "That's lovely." Mum, I want an orange "But you had one only yesterday." Oh no, oh no, that was not me, that was Steffe. There were none at our house. "Do you think I can buy oranges for all the strange princes?"

[Ms. 1276 recto]

Mum, what have I got in my foot? “Flesh and bones” How do the bones get into my foot? “They grew there” And I ate the flesh.

How when forced to wait for his meal at my parents’ while Dora and Papa have started eating, he says: I suppose someone’s meant to starve here, eh?

I milked Berta (the rocking horse). Berta has a milk[?] (points to the long hairs that hang down at the front) “I milked her there.”

March 1922

When he is tired and wants to go to bed: My mouth keeps on springing open.

On a walk—for no reason at all. When spinach is ~~cooked~~ raw, then it is green leaves and once it is cooked, then it is raealley[?] spinach.

In describing a postcard on which a bit of the sky is colored pink by[?] the sunset. “And it is evening already. The sun there is so swollen.”

He makes a face. “Mummy, is that grisly?” Yes “Grisly is when one rips up the grass.”

We watch the sunset, and he shouts out to me the words: The sky is red and blue calling in his room. He relates (what he has heard) about the angels who have a birthday today. He asks: Does the angel have a birthday today, dear Lord?—Yes—the dear Lord said yes.—But this is rather quiet, perhaps he is ashamed of something.

Mummy, why do you always say saucer [*Untertasse*]; it is a plate isn’t it.—Yes but these plates have a special name because they are always under the cup [*Tasse*].—Yes, but if you take away the cup, then you cannot say saucer anymore.

“Mummy, tell me a story.” Oh, but I don’t feel like it right now. “Oh go on, tell one, I feel like it.” Well then, you tell one? “No—but—there—I have just thrown the feeling into your mouth—now you tell it.”

April 1922

[~~xx~~] As a joke: People—people—that means the humans who hear pealing in their ears.

[Ms. 1276 verso]

"A sadly comic ladder"—"I must climb over there sadly," he said, after my mother replied to his words about having to climb over that it seemed rather sad.

On a linoleum chessboard. "Is that supposed to be the lakes for the chessmen?"

His first apprehensive recognition of necessity was the question: "Is morning fixed to the evening?" I answered it with: no, night comes in between. "Why does morning come?" I allow him to find the answer to his question on his own: "So that the sun comes."

Dora told him the story about the "big, middle-sized and small bears." The next day at breakfast he makes a threatening face at Dora, who responded with: Oh I am so very frightened, it is a big owly giant. He responds to this, saying in Dora's ear: "No it is not the big one, it is the middle-sized giant"

"When I was still a little bird, before I was Steffen, two boys came along, who wanted to thump me, and then my mummy— ~~that w~~ of course that was the bird mum—ranted a lot, and the boys ran away; that was before I was Steffen yet."

Miss Burchard says: The hare tried as hard as he was able, to which he responded with lots of laughter and repeated again and again: "hard as he was able—hard as he was able. That is not able, that is vegetable."

Dora says to him: I am having my breakfast with you today, because you invited me. To which he responds: Well not exactly invited, another time. But I do want to have you. [~~xx~~] He often heard my mother say the first part of the sentence.

May 1922

For him there exists an etymological connection between butterfly and batter, to such an extent that he says that the butterfly batters the flower. He copies this action. But he seems to conceive it as only the slightest contact.

Outside on a walk one day he notices a particularly small man and says: Mum, do you suppose that's a baby-man?

[Ms. 1277 recto]

He talks about how he found a dead mouse in the courtyard. Dora responds: How do you know that? Perhaps it wasn't dead at all. Stefan: "Yes, it was. It was lying there. It wasn't running there any more."

"Mummy, when are we sticking the children's wallpaper?" (a wallpaper on which children are depicted) When we get back from Vienna. "Oh no, when we get back from Vienna we will be different." ~~Why so~~ "If one travels somewhere and comes back again then one is always different."

When my sister sent him a picture postcard, Grete asks him, as per usual, to read it out. To which he replies: I cannot read the card out. I can only read out loud what Papa and Mum write and ~~then~~ [?] the book with the Easter Hare.

"The sun is ill today." Dora: what is wrong with it? "It has lost two rays."

When Dora papsized him: "Don' do it with you dirty foot, I am still fresh."

Live dictation of a letter to me from Vienna:
Warm greetings to you I want to travel home today already I like it very much and I send warm greetings to Aunt Dodo too and also like her very much. Warm greetings I send because I like her very much and Aunt Jula I also like very much and I send greetings to her too. I also greet Grete very thousand times.

June 1922
The radishes strain my tongue so much. I think I have to drink some water.

[lines crossed out]

Papa says to him, when he asks him for sugar: Go straight to Mama, you do not need a go-between—whereupon on another morning he says: Please ~~Pappa~~ Grandpapa a lump of sugar, I want you to go-between~~s~~ Mama and me.

Dora calls "Papa." Stefan: What are you calling ~~P~~ Grandpapa Papa? Dora: Well, who is my Papa then? Stefan: Well, that Papa, the Papa in his room.

When ~~I~~ he heard my mother-in-law calling "Leon," he said to himself: Grandpapa is called Leon—strange.

[Ms. 1277 verso]

Dora is sitting with him. "Mummy I love you very much—Can one say well-behaved to a mum? Yes, I[?] love you very much—you my quite well-behaved mummy."

Dora is lying in bed. He comes in to wish "Good Morning." "You lightweight Mum." Why? You lightweight Mum? "Because you only have a little shirt on."

"Mum, why do people have a head?" You have a think and see if you can answer for yourself? "Well, would it possible to put the eyes and the nose on the neck? "Mum, why do people have hair?" Now, you are asking an awful lot of questions again. "Not everyone can be the same age. ~~Why can't everyone be the same age?~~ Why do people get old?" Silently Dora raises her finger because of all the questions. "Well all these questions

Dora lends him ~~the~~ her dressing gown, which hangs well below his feet, of course, such that he is unable to walk. Then ~~upon~~ he says: "Mummy, the young feet cannot get out of the dressing gowny."

Mummy, if I can't go into the garden, I was so miseryly.

He calls out to little Möller: "Möller." Dora: don't call him Möller. What name should you call him? "Well, Möller Benjamin" No think a bit about it, what does his Mummy call him? "Cleany Hans, so Cleany Hans Möller."

—You shoulds[?] help me[?] to peel the rhubarb.—Grete peels it. "What will we do with the peel?" I don't know. "~~A b~~ Let's make a nice blanket from it, and then you throw it into my bed."

"Grete, will you marry me?" Well, yes, fine "But when a stranger comes along what will you say to him?" Well, I really don't know. "Well, then you will say Steffe has married me."

"All good possibles come from above."

[Ms. 1278 recto]

July 1922
We are in the garden, Dora and I want to return. He has not yet watered the flowers and calls out: The flowers still need their snack!

[From April 1922. Birthday letter to my sister: Best wishes. And once she has had her birthday, so that she doesn't forget it, that she had received best wishes. And that I love her very much. And that she was in Heidelberg and that I love her now, now she is back home. That she should always have the best sleep. And that she has had best birthday.]

He explains: "I dreamt—but not today—the postman had lots of really little babies for money. And he gave us some as a present"—Which postman, the one who brings the letters? "No, the one who sits in the post office, the officer. He gave me some and Mum and Papa and Grete."—How big were they, show me—"I don't have any, I only dreamt it." So, show me how big they were!—"Really really small" shows it using two fingers)—Were they alive?—"Yes, they were quite riell,"—What did he call them?—He thinks for a moment: "Moses." (The questions stem from Dora. He was thrilled that she was so thrilled about his story)

When he was talking about one of the naughty things he had done, Dora said: Well you know, it is not an achievement.—Mummy, what is an achievement?—When one is nice and well-behaved … etc.—Yes Mummy. And what is corn? (Has he heard at some point about sheaf and corn?)

Reading aloud from Bertuch: "Weird fish. Weird fish. They jerk with their teeth and scales a lot, don't they? Don't they? And the tail a lot too. Strangely one was[?] gray one.—Strange butterflies—Strange birds.—Oh flowers just look and it priks terribly just look.—Weird heru[?]"

To me, when he heard Dora on the telephone: We don't always want to say hello to the funny ol' faces. We want to leave the ol' voices, they don interest us.

August 1922
He asks what spiders live off, etc. On another day we (Dora and Stefan) are taking a walk and are plagued a lot by flies. I moan. He says: "Oh, if only we had a spider with us."

"You flies don't bite people. People are not there for biting. They are there for living but no for biting."

Reproachfully Stefan said to Grete, after she had asked him again and again to clear away his things: "Don't expectorate so much from me."

"Mummy, what is expectorate acherly?"

[Ms. 1278 verso]

Letter to me./ Best wishes, come back soon, I am sad because I don't see you anymore. Do you like it a lot in Heidelberg? How do you like it there, whether it is very nice? I am very gladly curious about how it looks there. Papa should bring me something back from Heidelberg. And how is it for him every day, can he sleep badly. Many many many thousands of birds he should bring me, which are not real, are made of cake. Thank you very much for the nice book. I like the nice book very much and the present that he is going to bring back with him. He should drag home lots of nice presents. Lots of best wishes. Thousand times. He should bring a nice little house back. I don't like it here any more. Soon we are traveling to the Baltic and I would like to take Papa with me and Grete. That live in the other red house of the[?] Wagners.

Letter to me from Zingst / Dear Papa! I ~~don't~~ don like it here in the house because Mrs Wunderlich is here. It was very nice on the Baltic. Best wishes, thank you very much for the new book. On the beach it looks very nice, nice mussels, we ate cooked ones but no the shell. He should come back very soon. [Have you written to Mummy that living in the Wagners' house in Berlin? Nonsense? But I don want to.] Thousand times. That there is a spider in the window here. That when he comes back he should please come here. That I played with a girl. That we took books with us. That I had a dream. That I always eat at midday and breakfast. That there is a mirror here. Lots of love.

Letter to me from Zingst / Best wishes. Thousand times. I played—such lovely stars with building blocks—why does he have such a small case—I caught fish very small—seals—that I bathed—and that I plunged myself but not under—he should bring something with him, at most if he has a small case sweets. Among them thousand greetings. I bow.

He comes up from the garden, rings the bell, but has to wait for quite a long time. When Dora then opens the door, he says: "Yes yes that what it is like with stupid people. Yes yes that's what it is like with stupid people. First they are good and then they don't open the door."

To Dora and Grete: "You are my nice funny faces."

September 1922
After going to sleep: Mummy, I still have to ask you ~~a few~~ a lot of words. What is the dear Lord made from? / On another occasion: what is a leaf made from, what is a tree made from, what is a meat made from.

He looks at images of the catacombs in Bertuch. He starts to laugh very loudly and is amused by the strange poses of the skeletons. Mum, look here, is funny isn't it? Later he learns the true meaning of the picture, from Grete, I guess. After this he snuggles up to Dora and says: Mummy, I didn't know that they were already dead—I thought

[Ms. 1279 verso]

that they are still alive the men.—Later: Oh Mum, that is those ones again, those who died already.

Mummy, I am so scared in the toilet. Where you pull [the sound of the water] that afraided me away.

If one eats poisonous things, then one dies. Then one is buried. Some go up to the dear Lord. But so do even some children if they are very well-behaved.

He takes the Chinaman, a rubber doll that I brought him from Heidelberg, with him out onto the street. Dora impresses upon him that he should not let it be taken off him. He comes home again and relates how a boy almost took the doll away from him. Whereupon Dora says: he should only give, and never let things be taken away. Whereupon he: "But Mum don't moan, I didn't take it away from me, it was the other boy."

Close by our house there is building work going on: on the street where the new structure is lie two large piles of bricks. I am approaching the new structure with Stefan and point out to him how quickly it is proceeding. Whereupon he: "But the other one isn't." After long questioning I discover that he thought the piles of bricks for the two new buildings were little houses.

To my mother: Does one do the same thing at the Unilibry as at the Unifursity?

Calling up to Dora's window from the courtyard: You can imagine how good I am. I have specially seen these apples and pears lying in the garden. (With an armful of them)

He wants to speak to Dora and Grete and cannot, because Dora is telling Grete what to get at the market. Whereupon he says: Don't, you undo the good behavior all the time. Don't undo the good behavior all the time. (Very angry that his patience is constantly disappointed) You always take the naughty out again[?].

October 1922
After hearing the story of the [✱] Flood he sings a song about it. It begins: When I was not yet on the worlte at all / My heart was already dead / My heart was already dead / And the beach began to swim forwards / And all the mountains and valleys were gone / And then the fire was gone too and the fairground screamed [spoken as commentary:] you see this is because the men were away.—After he has sung this, Dora requests that he repeat it. Whereupon: Mummy, those were not songs for you. They were only for little children. Mummy, I have got a lot more songs in my mouth, I will sing you all of them, tomorrow. (All of this was while he was sitting in bed.)

[Ms. 1279 verso]

Expressions of affection: "ultra mummy" instead of wonderful mummy.—One day when he meets Dora on the stairs, he says: "You happy monkey."

November 1922
He goes outside with Grete. She points in the direction of the Gutkinds' home and says, now he should go over to Pupps[?](the Gutkinds' little girl) and into nursery school (where for a short time previously he was very unhappy). He tells Grete how nice it is in the [✱] new nursery school as well and refuses to go to Pupps[?]. Finally he says: But you Know, I am not going to go there, but when I am big I will send my children there and then I will go there with them.

He repeats a song that he heard at nursery school: "…outside it is wafting foamily cold."

January 1923
He hears that an old lady (in Breitenstein) has broken her arm. "But Mummy, it is not broken at all, because it is still hanging there."

Asked if he gets along well with another child, and is being well-behaved, he says, since earlier there had been talk of how badly behaved they both were: Two ill-behaved children together are always well-behaved.

February 1923
He said quite unprompted: "Is Mister Miacca still alive?" And when Dora said yes: "When will we finally be rid of him?"

Furthermore he asked what it means when on some images people have napkin rings above their heads (presumably halos)

(December 1922) Report from his grandmother in Vienna: After the evening meal he reminded me of the chocolate. I said he could have it; I stick to my word; there are people who do not do that, but Grandpapa and I do not belong to them. He asks how people do that, not sticking to their word. I say: Well, they promise something that they then do not stick to. He: Yes, for example, they promise to go on the mountain and then do not do it.—I had indeed promised him that Papa would go on the famous mountain with him, if the weather allowed it.

Letter to Dora: Dear Mummy, lots of love. Dear Mummy, what kind of cake are you baking? I love you very much. Aunt Jetty gave me a piece of chocolate as a present. It was Hanukkah. I got a town and sweets and a clown. Lots of love Your little lamp

In Vienna, while eating, his grandmother asks him several times what he would like next. He says: "Now wait a bit; I can't pull it out of my head, can I."

[Ms. 1280 recto]

March 1923
Dear Mummy! I love you very much. Come home again soon. What is happening in Vienna? How are you? How are you, Pappa? And how is Grete? Say hello to Papa and Mommy and Dodo and Georg and Ida [my parents' maid.] I am well, no, poorly because I have not seen you for so long. I love you very much. Frieda—I have to think about it, I don't know what it is at the moment. Frieda is always here only one time did she go to sewing school. I just received an apple from Aunt Rosa, it is so big I will have to munch on it all night. I am sleeping in Peter's room now and Peter has gone away. I send you lots of kisses. I love you very much. Steffen

Mum, why do I actually always feel so tummily when little Ernst goes over my face with his clawses[?]—What do you mean by tummily?—Here in my tummy. [January 1923]

August 1923
We encounter an ice-cream van while out walking. He discusses the difference between [x̶] ice for eating and "winter ice" and says: "winter ice is caught in winter."

September 1923
He sees a box on my writing desk we [with?] bookmarks. Asks what it is. I show him their use in a book in which there are several. In response he says, after a short while: "Isn't it because you were there, that bit interests you and you cannot [x̶] finish reading it."

October 1923
He sees a man in a picture book standing morosely in front of a table. "What is he worried about? Because he is not married?"

He is rolling about on the carpet and Dora hears him say to himself: "That I don't know that. If only I knew that. Well, one day I'll know it." Then he sees Dora. Pause. "Mummy, does one know everything." "Yes, later (once one is with the dear Lord) one knows everything" "Well, then I will know it too." Pause. "What will you know then?" "Well, nothing." "Well, what did you mean about then you would know it." "Well, why I am such a coward." "But who said that you were a coward?" "Well, I can see it for myself, when I can't go after the other children when they pester me and Grete said it too."

I show him a new style of building for factories. He says: "How does the house see. It is totally unwindowed."

November 1923
"There are beautiful witches too" he says, as I seek to convince him of the ugliness of a depicted figure by indicating that it is a witch.

December 1923
The word "rush" [*Rausch*] appeared in a fairytale and [I] asked him if he knew what it meant. "Yes, when someone has drunk a lot of wine and then it rustles inside."

I read Stefan a fairytale in which a naughty goblin appears as the enemy of some dwarves. ~~He seems still~~ Apparently he doesn't quite understand it and I ask him: Whose enemy is the naughty goblin? Then he tries to deduce the object of enmity from its naughtiness and says: His parents.

[Ms. 1280 verso]

Someone was speaking of how "Mr Lehmann has his birthday at Christmas." Stefan is of the opinion that he only celebrates Christmas. I ask him when his birthday is. "Easter" I tell him the date and: why on the eleventh of April. "Because I had on the fifth." No. "Because I will be eleven years old."

He sees some material with stripes. "Mummy, that is just like your strip-pynied dress."

January 1924

Dora gives him some carob bread. He feels its surface and says: actually this is not like bread. It should be called chocolate-banana.

In a letter that he dictates to Dora for her mother in Vienna, he says while dictating: Mum, don't write to her, she should send parcels. Perhaps she'll send one just like that.

February 1924

He was invited over to Bubi Rothshild and later recounts: "When I was invited a girl said to me I should eat something. But I said: No thank you. But I was still hungry. But isn't it right, one shouldn't stuff oneself?" Dora: "Who said that to you?" He: "Well, nobody. Sometimes the dear Lord gives you something in your head, not only people."—(After a pause)—Isn't that right, Mummy, the dear Lord gave Adam and Eve a mind in their heads? And we get it then from them.—Mummy, do blackamoors also come from Adam and Eve?

March 1924

He complains about Dora going out so much. Dora: "One has to attend to all manner of things before embarking on a journey." He: "Ah, so you mean it doesn't matter, because we are not separated the whole time on the journey if we don't see each other beforehand."

"Mummy do you love me more than a flower?" Yes. "I love you more than a flower too; I love you even more than a green bush."

"The priormeval 'people'[?]" i.e. Prehistoric people.

Stern gave Dora a picture. Stefan asks: "Mummy what shall we give Uncle Stern back for the picture?" Dora: "Well, perhaps you would like to do a picture for him?" "But Mummy, picture for picture, that is not on." (He usually likes painting very much, so it was not an excuse.)

"I am practicing songs, then Mummy writes them down and then they will be printed and we'll get money."

He asks how one gets the hens to always lay hard and soft eggs, just as one needs them.

[Ms. 1281 recto]

A conversation over the way[?]. While eating he asks (probably a sly way to bring the discussion round to such things, whether the dead Lord is [eating] his lunch. "No." "I suppose that is the difference between Heaven and Earth then?"—In Heaven there is no eating.—"What is in it for me once the soul ~~comes~~ is in ~~the~~ Heaven, when I am dead. The soul has to come down then when it wants to eat."

November 1924

We are riding on the electric tram. He ~~asks whether the c~~ surmises that the conductor has to learn the street names in advance in order to call them out and imagines that they do this by writing them out. (Just as he learns at school by transcribing.)

He sometimes calls the lines in the fable "roams" instead of "rows."

In response to the question "what happened in school," he took to answering for several days "ice"—and then the reply. "whether nice or horrible, it is of no interest to me …"

[Addendum from earlier: He sees a small girl (mimi) with a satchel (bagschool) walking along the street. But mimi, no take the books. They belong to Papa. (All books belong to Papa—said or "thought")]

December 1924

We saw Snow White at the children's theater. At the end Snow White forgives the evil queen. After a few weeks he comes back to it again and explains it in the following way: it is not possible to do that bit with the red-hot iron shoes. Therefore—because it is not possible to take real ones either—Snow White ~~he~~ has to forgive the stepmother. (Subsequently I find out that he heard it from Dora.)

March 1925

He wants to do something "weird" in bed. I: "The weirdest thing one can do in bed is sleep.—No, think. E.g. think of different varieties of apple."

~~In response to the question~~ He is fantasizing about what he would wish for himself if he could wish for anything in the world. "That all of the whole ol' money is removed from the world, so that you (Dora) don't have to go to the office any more—and can read out loud to me all day long."

"Mummy, all children love their mother more than their father—?—because one loves more the one who brings one up."

June 1925
"Cheerful things" is what he calls certain apparatuses in the gym that he likes a lot: ladders and bars, as opposed to running in circles, ~~st~~ ropes.

[Ms. 1281 verso]

February 1925
Dora says to him that if she were a Catholic she could celebrate today, because it was her saint's day. But Jews do not have saints.—Stefan: Well, what about Saint Moses?

December 1925
After returning from my journey I ask Stefan where they are with their religious education. Conversation about biblical history and why it does not extend until today. Finally he says: "when Joseph is in Egypt and marries the clergywoman or whatever she is called, such a genteel lady."

I am reading a fairytale: Seafarers have got lost and do not know any longer where morning and evening are. I ask him what that means: "Well, the trees are so dense there, they simply couldn't see anything any more, and they were completely lost." "Trees in the middle of the ocean? Where do the trees come from then?" "Well they have reached the bank."

He is absorbed by the infinity of numbers.—I am talking with him about grumbling and say, in reference to this: "Everything must have a limit." "Everything does not have to have a limit. For example one can always count higher." "Well yes, counting is an exception, but everything else has a limit." "No everything does not have a limit. The Earth doesn't have a limit." "How come? The Earth does have limits." "No, one can always go round and round it, again and again" (referring to its spherical form). "Well: in any case grumbling has a limit." "Grumbling has no limit either. One can always say something more: Out Out Out Out Out for as long as one wants."

Stefan speaks of "comical words" "Prince is a word with a star tied around it." (That evening after multiple questions in bed he mentions a "serpent," which [~~x~~] sometimes still has a crown—the explanation is: "a 'serpent crest'[?]."

At the table Stefan says that in every single book it is always the case that the people one loves come off well. I say: "In your books that is always the case—later on for grown-ups there are books where that is not the case." In response he laughs out loud and says: "Yes, a lover is killed!" (By "lover" he means, as it transpired, someone who is loved (by the reader) and the sentence "a lover is killed" he had read to his great amusement a few days previously on the cover of the *Profile.*[9]

"Stomach fright" for severe fright. (Similarly: "Shudderhorror")

January 1926

He comes to me asking where my slippers are, not the small ones (those are his own) but "the fathers" of these. (Dora had said to him that he should ask after the "parents" of his slippers.

[Ms. 1282 recto]

Stefan holds colorful shiny paper against the light ~~thereby~~, while shouting out over and over again: "German illusions"

Stefan distinguishes words "that one never hears about" from the others "sprained—one doesn't hear about that one either. Well, those are more illnesses."—"~~empul~~" Compulsion that comes from compel" (As an example of a word that one hears) Naughty—that is half and half, not exactly heard and not exactly unheard. (In the same manner he presents: well-behaved, change)— (according to Dora's findings) words that clearly betoken things that are not easy to paraphrase (sausage) are "German."

When Papa is asked if he knows what happens in all of the stories. Papa knows all of the stories in the whole world. "But Mummy knows all the fairytales too" Well, I mean knowing everything in the stories. That is magical. A magical Papa. Someone who has a magical Papa is a Sunday child.

He is called Tilly[?] and he has another father. Soon he is flying to him in England.

---

[9] *Der Querschnitt* was a magazine of "art and culture," which appeared between 1921 and 1936, edited by Alfred Flechtheim and H. v. Wedderkop in Berlin.

God Mummy—it is such a pity that I am not a Sunday child.— "Well you were born on a Thursday, that is very nice too."—God Mummy couldn't you have brought me into the world three days later—you could have pushed me back in again—Isn't that possible then?

February 1926
He asks what a "pampire" (for vampire) is.

"My stomach is grinning"—Expression for when he is looking forward to something.

Mummy, the cat is laughing. It is really laughing. But I don't know why it is laughing. It is laughing even when I don't say anything funny. But perhaps cat jokes are different.

March 1926
For a long time he got into the habit of always asking: "Mummy, who do you prefer: me or a piece of chocolate flake (or a spoon, or ~~a~~ ticket, or a lion etc.) To which the answer: a chocolate flake, because I can suck on it (or something equivalent) To which he says: you can suck on me too (etc) Dora: Well, then I prefer you.

He is talking about the ~~prefaces in the~~ notes (or prefaces) in the fairytale books, where the fairytale motives are itemized and says, that he reads them too. "They are almost lots of ~~fairy~~ little fairytales again all at once."

He is lying in bed, pulls his pyjamas up. I ask: why? "It is modern, you know. … One has to see the stomach, the navel, at all times, because then one knows what holds one together." ("It is modern, you know" has been one of his turns of phrase for a while.)

[Ms. 1282 verso]

"Drink water by the light of the moons
imagine, it would be champagnackwine" (old, still recited)

He has some tinfoil in his hand, on one side it is silver, on the other gold. Lies in bed and asks me which I prefer. I say: the golden side. He says: Me too, one can sleep better with that.

August 1926

From the improvised songs that came into fashion for a while: "Skeleton dance is the order of the day / In the forest, in the forest, in the forest the skeletons are clacking … They have no flesh on their chests any more … (And then in the middle of a wild pantomimic dance:) the carpet won't get any better from this (after that it continues as before: the whole is a development of the quotation "And the skeleton fails, crush'd to atoms" from the ballad by Goethe,[10] that Dora used to read to him at the time.—In addition there were also "stork songs.")

Games from around this time in the garden with Möller: Limited Company. Kempinski[11]

As I am going away I bid farewell to Stefan, who is about to have a bath, with the words: have lots of fun in the bath. He responds: "have lots of joy in the town."

While at the table he asks whether the ~~female bear ar~~ female bear also suffers pain when she brings her young into the world, and in response to the answer "yes," why? Because they have not been in Paradise.

He lets it be known that he is writing a novel "The chree[?] Spheres."

October 1926

He is writing a novel called "The Room" in instalments that appear each morning and evening. The "novel" are drawings, the text on the page messages about the newspaper, the caption on one of them "I suppose you understand that one can call this novel."

Letter to Vienna from 9 October: "Dear Mama! Berlin, 9 October Now as I am writing to yoou, there was such a storm that the trees fell over. The birds in the cage were cheeping engagefully and then suddenly the sun threw a ray away, but thenn there was a storm against. Hopefully yoou are well. Afterwards the birds snuggled each other. Thenn one ate, so ~~n~~ ~~deintl~~ daintily. Once again best regards [stamp] [stamp] 9. 1926 (on the back drawings of bird[s], of stamps and other things.

After his bath Stefan is ranting in bed. He has a picture book with which he is larking around. He had written something down (at the front, maybe earlier): "It is very thin, but one can get fat from cleverness." I take it away from him and want to turn off the lights. "One doesn't read at night." He~~:~~ ~~"but otherwise~~ wants to have it back: "Otherwise the darkness will read it and will remain dark for ever." "Book to book, book of books."

[10] From Goethe's poem "Der Totentanz" [1815]. This line is from the English version "Dance of Death," translated by Edgar Alfred Bowring.

[11] A Berlin restaurant chain.

[Ms. 1283 recto]

November 1926

He shows me a sheet on which are stuck various words clipped out of newspapers, printed namely on yellow paper (the newspaper was yellow). It reads: "Stefan's efficiency—beauty." I say: "A messed-up beauty." (The ~~letters~~ words were cut out poorly.) He: "Here one sees just how beautiful people can become through yellowness—like the Chinese."

He said to Dora: "Mummy, now I am thinking about gruesomeness"[12] "Well, may the devil claim you." "Oh, but now I am thinking about 'greensomeness' or 'whitesomeness'".

February 1927

"Twinslight"—instead of twilight

Shortly beforehand~~, some~~, I heard the formulation "laterly" (He has been saying "earlierly" instead of "early" forever)

He was ~~the~~ at the Pestalozzi celebration. I ask him about the various performances, and finally also whether there had not been any music there. He says: "yes, a singer." But she pulled so many funny faces. "She hardly ever showed herself in her true form."

March 1927

Dora was talking with him one morning and told him about words that he used to pronounce incorrectly, when he was little. E.g., he always said "gratophoph" instead of "photograph." He says: "I suppose I mixed it up with 'philosopher.'"

I ring home. Stefan comes to the telephone. I say: "Can I talk to Mummy?" Stefan: Mummy is outside. She is showing someone out. (It was Hans Wiszwianski[?]) I ask: "Who is that then?" "A man." "Who?" "A strange bandit with whom she is secretly courting.

He comes home from school. I ask him what happened. He talks of a woman who they saw from the Spreewald area "with a kinda tablecloth behind her."

Dora overhears him saying to the cat: "Yes you are nice, you are concrete too. But Pazzi is abstract, no one wants him." (Pazzi is a singing teacher who they dislike extremely, and who lately, just like "famous Böhme" is a permanent feature in his reports of school.)

[12] The word is *Grausamkeiten*. Its first syllable *grau* is the word for gray. Stefan coins other versions using *grün*, green, and *weiß*, white.

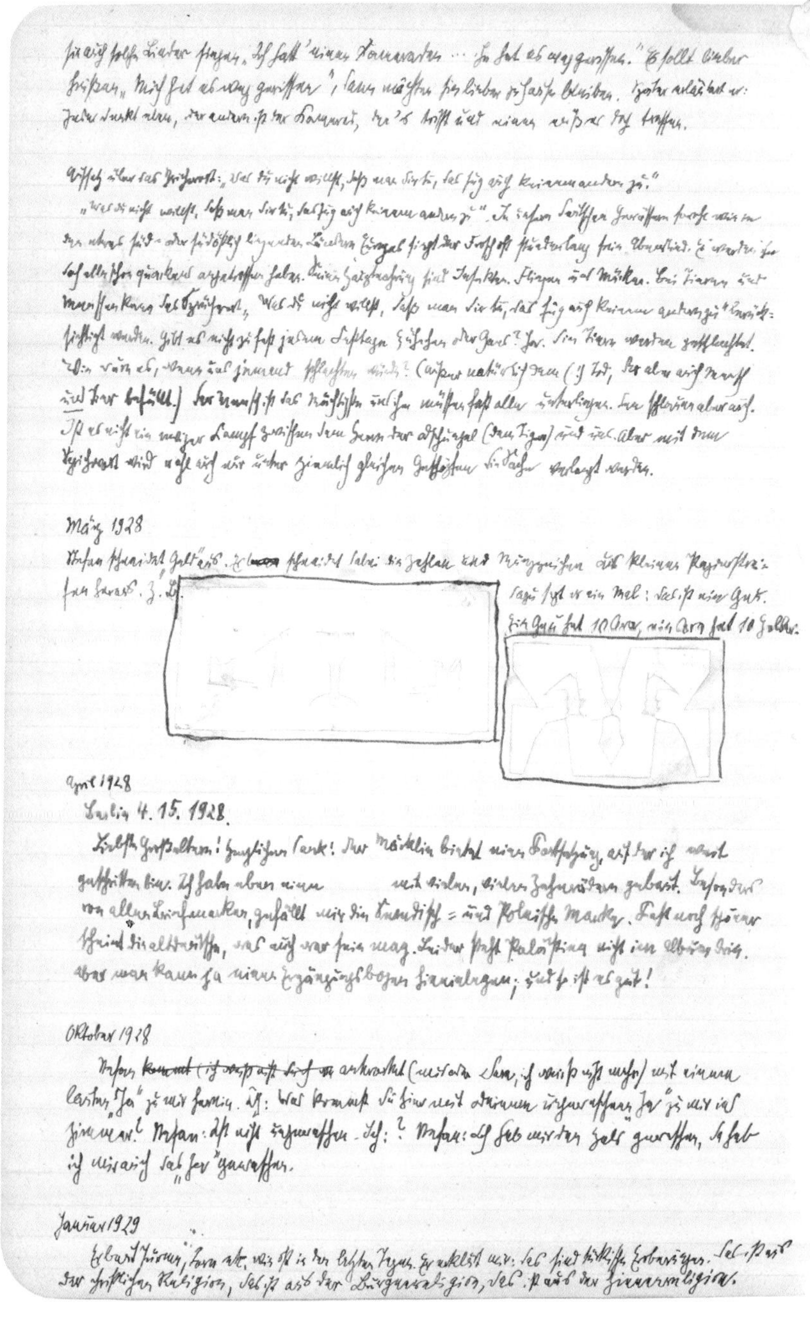

Fig. 5.3

October 1927
He has built a town in the garden, "Substancnick on the Substance"

January 1928
Conversation with Dora about war. Dora says: Perhaps everyone would be against war if they only thought about how it hits everyone and how they too will die, but they only ever think: it won't happen to me, it'll happen to somebody else: Stefan: That is why they have

Fig. 5.3 [Ms. 1283 verso]

to sing those songs as well "I had a chum … it carried him away." It would be better if it went "It carried me away," then they might prefer to stay at home. Later he elucidated: Everyone thinks that the other person is the chum who is hit by it and yet it has to hit someone.

Essay on the proverb: "Do unto others as you would have done to you."
"Do unto others as you would have done to you."
In our German waters just as in those of the countries lying to the south or southeast of Europe the frog sings its evening song often for hour after hour. Everyone has come across him croaking. His main source of food is insects, flies and bugs. The proverb "Do unto others as you would have done to you" can be considered in relation to animals and people. Is there not on almost every day of celebration chicken or goose? Yes, animals are slaughtered. How would it be if somebody slaughtered us? (Except, of course, for (!) death which happens to both person <u>and</u> animal.) Man is the most powerful and almost everything must succumb to him. The wily too indeed. Is it not an eternal struggle between the Lord of the Jungle (the tiger) and us. But with the proverb it seems that the matter is required only between quite similar creations.

March 1928
Stefan cuts out money. To do this he clips out the figures and mint-marks from little strips of paper. E.g. [strips of paper stuck in]
Once he pointed out: that is a Geu. A Geu has 10 Ara, an Ara has 10 Halfs[?]

April 1928
Berlin, 4. 15. 1928.
Dearest Grandparents! Many thanks! Märklin[13] offer an extension, which I have got quite far with. I have just built a   with many, many gears. Out of all the stamps the ones I like especially are the Swedish and Polish stamps. The old German ones seem almost even nicer, which may be

[13] German toy company, best known for model railways.

März 1929

Selbstverfertigte Briefmarken

QUAMBUSCH
POSTAGE
POSTES
POST

11 April 1929

März 1932

Fig. 5.4

tru too. Unfortunately Palestine is not in the album. But it is possible to include a supplementary leaf, so that is all right!

October 1928
Stefan ~~enters (I don't know through w~~ answers (me or Dora, I can't remember) with a loud "yes" as he enters my room. I say: What are you doing coming in my room with your unwashed "yes"? Stefan: It is not unwashed. I: ? Stefan: I washed my neck, and so I also washed my "yes" at the same time.

January 1929
He is building towers and gates, etc. which he has done a lot recently. He explains what they are: These are Turkish conquests. That is from the Christian religion. That is from the castle religion. That is from the battlement religion.

Fig. 5.4 [Ms. 1284]

March 1929
All through the winter the game "Mr Quambusch." After lunch. Quambusch. The name of a correspondent. "Mr Quambusch, Mr Quambusch"—with these words Stefan leaps around the room. I chase him and he finishes by fleeing under the grand piano where he continues his maneuver with badinages.

Homemade stamps
[four stamps glued in]

11 April 1929
Stefan received a stamp album for his eleventh birthday. That evening he said: "The word 'album' is the only one that signifies for me a flight, a flight into the wonderful, what one otherwise only dreams of."

March 1932
During a chess game with him, Dora, impatient for his move: "Do it, one could wait the soul to leave one's body." Stefan: "This is not a waiting room for souls."

6
Daintiest Quarters
Notebooks

> I carry the blue book with me everywhere and speak of nothing else. And I am not the only one—other people too beam with pleasure when they see it. I have discovered that it has the same colours as a certain pretty Chinese porcelain: its blue glaze is in the leather, its white in the paper and its green in the stitching. Others compare it to shoes from Turkistan. I am sure that there is nothing else of this kind as pretty in the whole of Paris, despite the fact that, for all its timelessness and unlocatedness, it is also quite modern and Parisian.
>
> To Alfred Cohn, July 21, 1927, *GB* III, p. 273

> He owned many tiny notebooks, not only for taking notes, but also for writing down the titles of all the books he read. Yet another one was reserved for excerpts from his readings, destined later to become epigraphs.
>
> Jean Selz, "Benjamin on Ibiza," in Selz, p. 359

Notebooks are part of the fundamental equipment of writers, artists, architects, scientists, in short, all intellectuals who devise things—thoughts, images—that they need to record and register. Notebooks are handy traveling companions, places for the safekeeping of drafts. They provide storage space for ideas and data. When necessary they can release sheets to be passed on or inserted into another context. They make plain their owners' modes of thinking and working. Some are famous: Lichtenberg's waste books, the octavo notebooks in which Goethe conceived *Poetry and Truth*, Kafka's quarto copybooks, Tucholsky's Q diaries, Thomas Mann's notebooks, the black Efalin books with Brecht's *Fatzer* fragment, Proust's *Carnets* or Joyce's *Finnegans Wake* notebooks at Buffalo.

Benjamin's notebooks are a special case. Their owner devoted an unusually great amount of attention to them. Indeed, he promoted a cult around them. First and foremost this applied to the high value that he assigned to their features (format, cover, binding, paper, etc.). But it was also true of their mode of usage and their wandering possession, both of which were not without extravagant traits. Once it is known that Benjamin called *One-Way Street* a "notebook," because he did not think that the label "book of aphorisms" was appropriate, it is clear that there is nothing incidental here.

Six notebooks and three notepads are preserved in Walter Benjamin's archive. A seventh notebook, bound in vellum, is now situated amongst Gershom Scholem's bequest in Jerusalem. In addition there are countless notes on torn-out sheets whose physical qualities often provide pointers for dating or the context of their composition. At least one "blue octavo notebook," one "Soennecken lecture notebook" and a "long parchment book" are missing. The "sizable notebook with flexible parchment binding," which is now in Jerusalem, was especially prized by Benjamin, and he wrote of it: "Using it has produced in me a shameful weakness for this extremely thin, transparent, yet excellent stationery, which I am unfortunately unable to find anyplace around here" (*Correspondence*, p. 345). The chamois-colored paper of a notebook bound in cardboard, with notes, drafts of critiques and diary entries from the years 1929–1934, is thicker and has—crosswise and longwise—a fine line structure (figs 6.3 and 6.4).

The almost magical quality that they possessed for their owner is not only due to their choice materials, but also relates to a particular relationship of exchange: Some notebooks were presents from Benjamin's school friend Alfred Cohn (1892–1954), who worked as a salesman in Berlin, Mannheim, and Barcelona and had bookbinding skills. In January 1929 Benjamin submitted a proposal to Cohn: "The fabulous parchment notebook that I received from you has suddenly been put to intensive use and I cannot contemplate the prospect of soon having to write homeless thoughts again. So I had the following thought: If you can, make me another book just like it and, in exchange, I will give you the one I have written in, which holds just about all of the drafts that I have completed recently" (*GB* III, p. 433). In this way the notes accrued an addressee, a potential reader, whom the author could obligate to not only store the notebook, in which there was a lot of unpublished material, but also, at the same time, to allow him access to it at any time.

Gratitude to the supplier of the means of production was conceptualized by the producer in a complex of images that accorded with his concern for the welfare of his treasured product. On January 2, 1933 he appealed to Cohn—with echoes of the phrase "homeless thoughts": "Perhaps you don't know how nice it is to see the changing and disparate thoughts of so many years always hospitably accommodated in the daintiest and cleanest quarters, which you have assigned them" (*GB* IV, p. 153). The user keeps the notebooks neatly—there are no blots. And these are temporary resting places; he would have had to call printings "houses."

Benjamin always utilized several notebooks in parallel. Alongside the booklets in which he wrote his diary, described his travels, fixed his ideas, drafted texts and letters and composed literature, he kept up the recording of entries in a little book that was a *Catalogue of Items Read*. Jean Selz observed such a variety of uses at work. And he must also have seen a booklet that contained a "collection of epigraphs." Amongst them were the following: " 'Just as every town signifies a giant play room to a Gulliver, even the most scientific book contains its author's playthings.' / Else Lasker-Schüler / Concert Berlin / 1932" or " 'Attendre, c'est la vie' / Victor Hugo." Ironically, coming from a contrasting direction, that is to say starting from the end, the collector added another function to the notebook, in compiling a *Catalogue of Curious Book Titles*. These sound as if they are derived from the high spirits of the University of Muri but are actually not contrived: "Mü[l]ler, A.W.: The Sacrosanct Foreskin of Christ in the Cult and Theology of the Papish Church Berlin 1907," "Whether Animals Are Sathan? Examined in Writing and Reasonn and answered by J.F.B., an Evangelical Theologo Bremen 1740" or "F.J. Egenter: Secret Tragedies With a Sequel The Infallible Lpz 1873 [A small volume of banal lyric poems]."

The amount that Benjamin's minimal handwriting could accommodate in the notebooks is astonishing. The parchment notebook in Scholem's papers alone contains on its sixty-three pages the drafts or complete transcriptions of over twenty works, including the early Hölderlin essay, the *Surrealism* essay and the review of the premiere of Brecht's play *The Mother*.

"Avoid haphazard writing materials," recommends Benjamin in *The Writer's Technique in Thirteen Theses*. The notebooks show that the theses epitomize his own mode of work. "Let no thought pass incognito, and keep your notebook as strictly as the authorities keep their register of aliens" (*SW* I, p. 458). However, this is not to be taken completely literally, for, in practice, Benjamin crisscrossed his notebooks with writing, as he told Cohn (*Correspondence*, p. 345). The entries begin on different parts of the page and follow various directions. Texts are interrupted and continued several pages later. Entries are obliterated, mostly crossed out, as a sign that passages have been transferred to another manuscript.

Benjamin once characterized notepads as a "technical thesaurus" (*GB* III, p. 274). The archiving function of the notebooks encouraged him to write. He was fueled by the ambition to fill them and, in view of the intended recipient, it was not a matter of indifference for him what their contents were. At the same time the notebooks exerted a certain disciplinary pressure. To begin a new one was quite a challenge.

The notebooks are a medium that connects author and work. They are stages where thinking and writing take place, quarries, fields for experimentation, on which thoughts can be gathered, structured, discarded, formed anew—creatively and sometimes chaotically. The notebooks hold up a mirror to the author's face. In it Benjamin's preferences and peculiarities can be discerned. He worked on several texts simultaneously. He had a weakness for small forms, quotations, and aphoristic diminutions. And he did not want to carry out his work in enclosed conditions, sealed off from reality. Rather he loved to write while on the move, on the street, in the café, on his travels—wherever he happened to find himself. Could he have found a more faithful companion for all that than his notebooks?

Figures

6.1 Notebook Ms. 673. Leather cover (1927/1929).

6.2 "For *One-Way Street*" and "Reviews" (c. 1928/1929)—Entries in notebook Ms 673, one double page.
Jottings in a notebook from 1928/1929.

Under the heading "For *One-Way Street*" can be found keywords from Benjamin's book, which appeared in Rowohlt's imprint in 1928. It seems as if there may also be some ideas for a sequel listed. These include: "Child drags a horsey along," "How a 'modern' person avoids death." "Waiting," "Children's collecting."

Under the rubric "Reviews" there is a list of authors and titles of books reviewed by Benjamin (Bibesco, Brion, Fiesel, Holitscher, Kommerell, Lenin, Sostschenko, Yorck von Wartenburg; *The German in the Landscape, Adrienne Mesurat, Secret Berlin, Primitive Forms in Art*, amongst others). Other names of authors, titles, and keywords are pointers to future reviews or reading (Daudet, Gracián, Lessing, Quint; Worringer "India," "Africa," "Chinese Novel," amongst other things).

6.3. *Julien Green* (1929)—Manuscript in notebook Ms. 674, three sides; shown here, page 1. Compare *GS* II.1, pp. 328–30.

6.4. Postcard from Gershom Scholem with poem "Greetings from Angelus" (1921), glued into notebook Ms. 674. Compare Scholem/Adorno, *The Correspondence of Walter Benjamin*, Chicago, University of Chicago Press 1994, pp. 184–5.

6.5. Notebook Ms. 672. Leather cover (1932).

6.6. *Humor* (1917/1918)—Manuscript in a notepad, two sides; shown here, page 1. Compare *GS* VI, p. 130.

6.7 *Berlin Chronicle* (1932) with dedication "For my dear Stefan" and the crossed-out dedication "Written for four of my dear friends / Sascha Gerhard / Asja Lacis / and Fritz Heinle"—Manuscript in notebook Ms. 672, 59 sides; shown here, dedication page and page 1. Compare *SW* 2:2, pp. 595–6.

6.8 *Spain 1932*—Manuscript in notebook Ms. 672, nineteen sides; shown here, page 1. Compare *SW* 2:2, pp. 638–9.

6.9 Organization of *Ibizan Sequence*—Manuscript in a notepad, one side. Compare *GS* IV.2, p. 1002.

Fig. 6.1

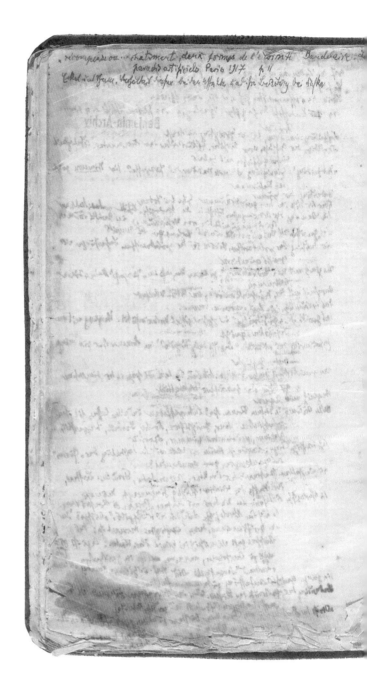

Fig. 6.2

Thomas von Aquin

Proust

Memoiren

Mysterien

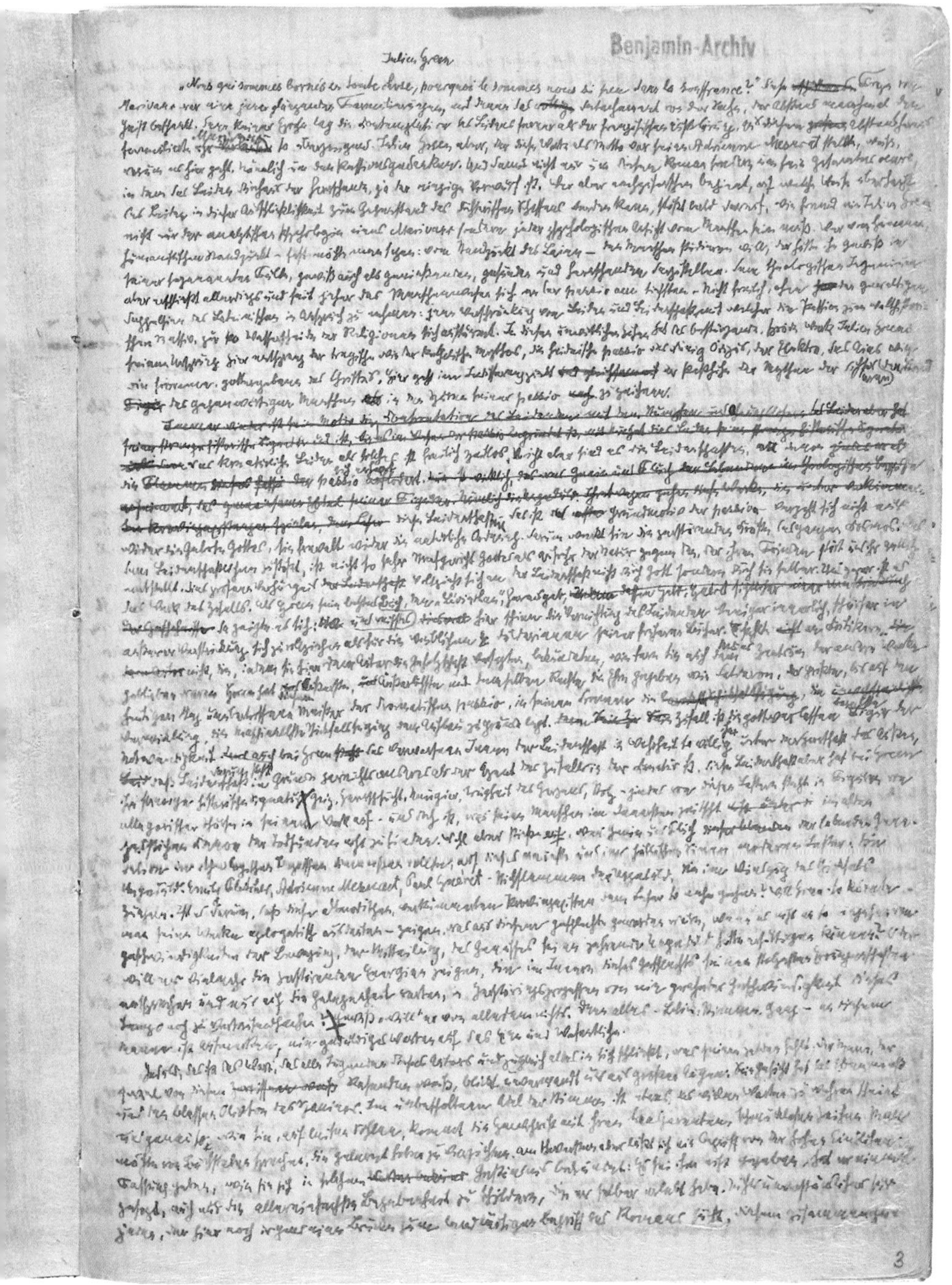

Julien Green

Fig. 6.3

[1] There are some crossings-out and symbols on the manuscript that have not been communicated here.

[2] In the published version, Benjamin corrected inaccuracies in this citation from Marivaux's *La vie de Marianne*: "Nous qui sommes bornées en tout, comment le sommes-nous si

Fig. 6.3

Julien Green[1]

"Nous qui sommes bornés en toute chose, pourquoi le sommes nous si peu dans la souffrance?"[2] This question by Marivaux was one of those lucid formulations with which detachment or distance from the matter sometimes bestows the intellect. For no epoch lies further from the contemplation of suffering than the French Enlightenment. It is from such a distance that Marivaux coined so convincing a phrase. But Julien Green, who placed these words as a motto at the beginning of his *Adrienne Mesurat*, knows what is at stake here. It is a question of passion. Not only in this novel, but in his work as a whole, for across his oeuvre suffering is, to all intents and purposes, the dominant, if not the sole reproach. But anyone who begins to look into how suffering can become so exclusively the object of poetic creation soon comes up against Julien Green's distance from not only the analytical psychology of a Marivaux, but also from any sort of psychological speculation about people. Anyone who sets out to study man from a human or humanist perspective—one is tempted to say the perspective of a layperson—would definitely have to depict him as a so-called rounded human being, that is to say as a person who enjoys life, is healthy and active. But for the theological genius, the human being reveals himself most profoundly and since time immemorial in *passio*. Of course this is not to be taken on without the double meaning inherent in the Latin: that entanglement of suffering and passion, with which passion mounts up as a world-historical massif, as a watershed between the religions. The disconcerting, sparse work of Julien Green has its origin in these inhospitable heights. From these sprang tragic myth as much as Catholic myth, the heathen passio of Oedipus Rex, of Electra, of Aia, just as did the pious God-given one of Christ. Here, at the point of indifference, the poet scales the summit of myth in order to chart the state of contemporary man in the vestiges of his passio.

Creaturely suffering as such is, of course, timeless. But the passions on which passio nourishes itself are not. This passion—that is the basic motif of passion—does not only offend against the command of God; it also commits an outrage against the natural order. That is why it rouses the destructive forces of the whole cosmos. What befalls the passionate is not so much divine judgment as the revolt of nature against those who disturb its peace and disfigure its face. This profane fate is not meted out on passion through God but through itself. Indeed, it is the work of chance. It made an appearance when Green published his last and most mature book, *Leviathan*: here the destruction of the suffering person takes place less internally, sharper in its external entanglement than for the silent female sufferers of his earlier books. And it did not lack critics, who, by denying the author their allegiance, evinced how far they had remained from the center of the other works too. Green honored this externality, this most extrinsic aspect with the same rights as Calderon, the greatest master of dramatic passio, unmatched until the current day, in whose plays the most Baroque entanglement, the most mechanical providential guidance lie at the base of the construction. Chance is the godforsaken figure of necessity. That is why for Green the discarded innerness of passion is, in all truthfulness, so completely under the domination of the external that passion is fundamentally nothing other than the agent of chance for the creature. This passion, though, has a strict historical signature in Green. Greed, imperiousness, indolence of the heart, pride—in this work each of his vices stands out in figures of allegorical incisiveness, and yet the thing that flogs his people in their most inner being is not to be found in the old Christian canon of the Deadly Sins. More likely whoever might wish to adumbrate the genius and curse of the living in theological concepts would stumble upon the latest and, in a hellish sense, most modern vice: impatience. Emily Fletcher, Adrienne Mesurat, Paul Guéret—darting flames of impatience who flicker in the draft of fate. Is this the reason why these old-fashioned, atrophied provincial existences still manage to affect the reader? Does Green wish to show—this is how one might explain his work apologetically—what would have happened to this generation if it had not been able to satiate its wasting impatience on such massive accelerations of movement, of communication, of pleasure? Or would he rather show the destructive energies that correspond to the proudest achievements in the interior of this generation and which only await the opportunity to multiply a thousandfold in destructive processes that accelerate this tempo to unsuspected speeds? Certainly he "wants" none of all of this. For everything—look, voice, gait—about this man is alertness, the attitude of a man patiently waiting for the one, essential thing.

Patience, that is the word that contains within itself all the virtues of this author and, at the same time, everything that is lacking in his heroes. The man who knows so much about these frenzied people looks steadfastly and with wide eyes. His face has the symmetry and pale olive tone of a Spaniard. In the irreproachable nobility of his voice there is something that appears to resist many words, and, equally, his handwriting arrives on light soles with its transparent, unornamented characters. One would like to speak of letters that have learnt to renounce. The hardest thing is to conceptualize the childlike attitude that announces itself in such a confession: he once said that he had not been given the task of depicting only the simplest events, experienced by him himself. There is nothing more incomprehensible for someone who is searching for some sort of bridge to the commonly accepted concept of the novel, this cobbled

---

peu lorsqu'il s'agit de souffrir?" (GS II.1 p. 328). The sentiment in both is as follows: Why is it that we who are limited in so many respects find hardly any limits when it is a question of suffering?

Dr. G. SCHOLEM

JERUSALEM
Mea Schearim
P. O. B. 36

Gruß vom Angelus — zum 15. Juli 1921

Ich hänge edel an der Wand
und schaue niemand an,
ich bin vom Himmel her gesandt
ich bin ein Engelsmann

Der Mensch in meinem Raum ist gut
und interessiert mich nicht
ich stehe in des Höchsten Hut
und brauche kein Gesicht

Der ich entstammen, jene Welt
ist maßvoll tief und klar:
was mich im Grund zusammenhält
erscheint hier wunderbar

In meinem Herzen steht die Stadt
in die mich Gott geschickt
Der Engel der dies Siegel hat
wird nicht von ihr berückt

Mein Flügel ist zum Schwung bereit
ich kehrte gern zurück
denn blieb' ich auch lebendige Zeit
ich hätte wenig Glück

Mein Auge ist ganz schwarz und voll
mein Blick wird niemals leer
ich weiß, was ich verkünden soll
und weiß noch vieles mehr

Ich bin ein unsymbolisch Ding
bedeute was ich bin
du drehst umsonst den Zauberring:
Ich habe keinen Sinn.

Fig. 6.4

Fig. 6.4

Greetings from Angelus

(To Walter on 15 July, 1921)

I hang nobly on the wall
Looking at nobody at all.
I have been from heaven sent,
A man of angelic descent.

The human within me is good
And does not interest me
I stand in the care of the highest
And do not need a face

From whence I come, that world
Is measured, deep, and clear.
What keeps me together in one piece
Is a wonder, it would appear.

In my heart stands the town
Whence God has sent me
The angel who bears this seal
Does not fall under its spell.

My wing is ready to beat,
I am all for turning back.
For even staying in timeless time
Would not grant me much fortune.

My eye is darkest black and full,
My gaze is never blank.
I know what I am to announce
And many other things.

———

I am an unsymbolic thing
My meaning is what I am.
You turn the magic ring in vain.
I have no sense.

Fig. 6.5

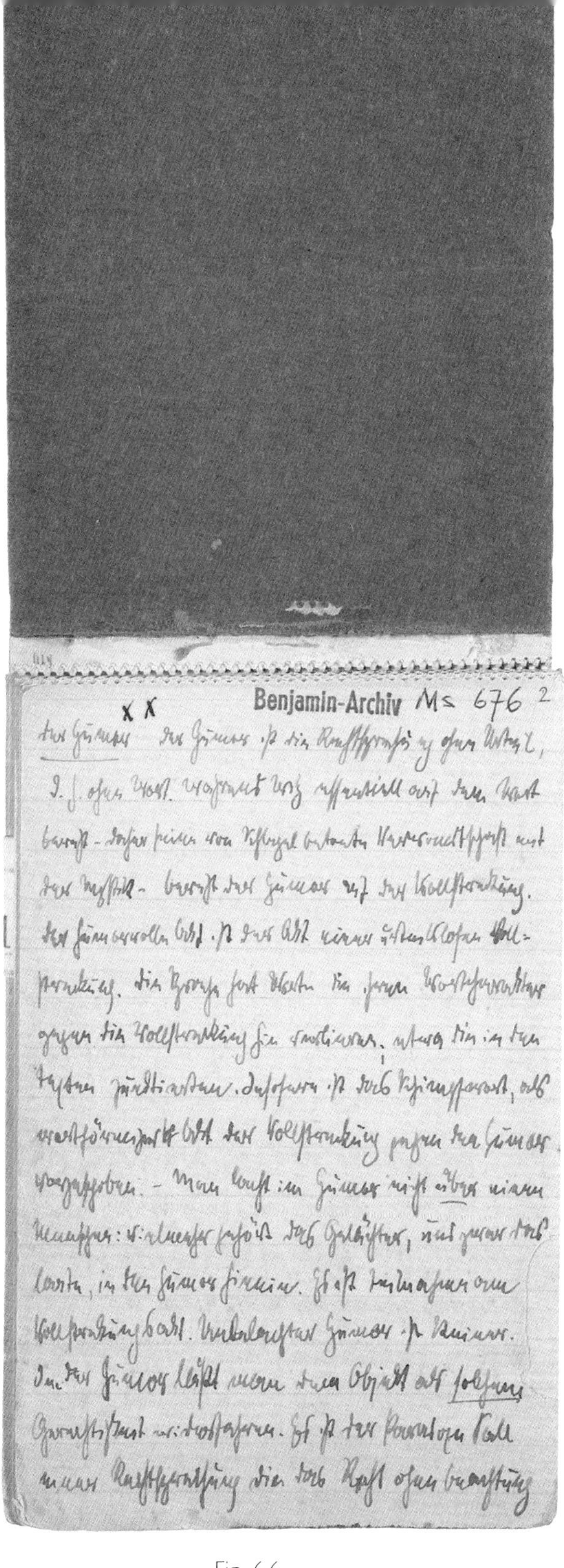

Fig. 6.6

Fig. 6.6 (previous page)

Humor

Humor is jurisdiction without judgment, i.e. without a word. While the joke rests essentially on the word—and that is the reason for its relationship to mysticism, as emphasized by Schlegel—humor rests on enforcement. The humorous act is the act of enforcement without judgment. Language has words that lose their character as words in enforcement; for example those that appear as dotted in texts. Such is the swearword, as a word-forming act of enforcement advanced against humor—In humor one does not laugh *about* a person: rather laughter, indeed loud laughter, belongs as a part of humor. It is participation in the act of enforcement. Humor without laughter is none. In humor one allows the object as *such* to be served with justice. It is the paradoxical case of a jurisdiction that enforces right wordlessly without attention

Fig. 6.7 (see below, pp. 166–7)

A Berlin Chronicle

For my dear Stefan

Now let me call back those who introduced me to the city. For although the child, in his solitary games, grows up in closest proximity to the city, he needs and seeks guides to its wider expanses, and the first of these—for a son of wealthy middle-class parents like me—are sure to have been nursemaids. With them I went to the Zoo—although I recall it only from much later, with blaring military bands and "Scandal Avenue" (as the adherents of Jugendstil [Art Nouveau] dubbed this promenade)—or, if not to the Zoo, to the Tiergarten. I believe the first "street" I thus discovered that no longer had anything habitable or hospitable about it, emanating forlornness between the shopfronts and even danger at the crossings, was Schillstrasse; I like to imagine that it has altered less than others in the West End and that it could even now accommodate a scene rising irresistibly from the mist: the saying of the life of "little brother." The way to the Tiergarten led over Herkules Bridge, whose gently sloping embankment must have been the first hillside the child encountered—accentuated by the fine stone flanks of the lion rising above. At the end of Bendlerstrasse, however, began the labyrinth, not without its Ariadne: the maze surrounding Frederick William III and Queen Louise, who, rising sheer from the flower beds on their illustrated, Empire-style plinths, seemed as if petrified by the runes that a little rivulet inscribed in the sand. Rather than the figures, my eyes sought the plinths, since the events taking place on them, if less clear in their ramifications, were closer in space. But that a particular significance attaches to this Hohenzollern labyrinth I find confirmed even now by the utterly unconcerned, banal appearance of the forecourt on Tiergartenstrasse, where nothing suggests that you stand but a few yards from the strangest place in the city. At that time, it is true, it must have corresponded more than closely to what was waiting behind it, for here, or not far away, were the haunts of that Ariadne in whose proximity I learned for the first time (and was never entirely to forget) something that was to make instantly comprehensible a word that, since I was scarcely three, I cannot have known: love. Here the nursemaid supervenes,

Fig. 6.8 (see below, p. 168)

Spain, 1932

The first images worth pondering in San Antonio: the interiors that can be glimpsed through open doors whose bead curtains have been gathered to one side. Defying the shadows, the gleaming white of the walls stands out. And in front of the wall, to the rear, there are usually two to four chairs in a strict symmetrical arrangement. Much can be gleaned from them as they sit there, unpretentious in form but with strikingly beautiful wickerwork, all highly presentable. No collector could hang expensive rugs or pictures on his hallway walls with greater pride than the farmer who puts out his chairs in the otherwise bare room. Moreover, they are not just chairs. They change their function instantly when a sombrero is hung on the back of one of them. And in this new arrangement the straw hat appears no less precious than the chair. And it will no doubt generally be the case that in our well-furnished rooms, equipped with every conceivable comfort, there will be no place for what is truly precious, because there is no room for utensils. Chairs and clothes, locks and rugs, swords and planes can all be precious. And the true secret of their value is the sobriety, the austerity, of the living space they inhabit. It means that they do not simply occupy, visibly, the space they belong in, but have the scope to perform a variety of unforeseen functions which enables them constantly to surprise us anew. This is what makes them precious and elevates them above the level of a common object.

A dream from the first or second night of my stay in Ibiza. I went home late—it was not actually my house, but rather a splendid apartment house in which, in my dream, I had put up the Seligmanns. Suddenly, close to the building's entrance, a woman came out of a side street toward me, and as she passed she whispered, as quickly as she was walking, "I'm going to tea! I'm going to tea!" I did not yield to the temptation to follow her but instead went into the Seligmanns' apartment, where an unpleasant scene took place, in the course of which their son pulled me by the nose. Protesting vigorously, I slammed the door behind me. Scarcely was I outside again than the same woman darted up to me from the same side street, with the same words, and this time I followed her. To my disappointment,

Fig. 6.7

Fig. 6.8

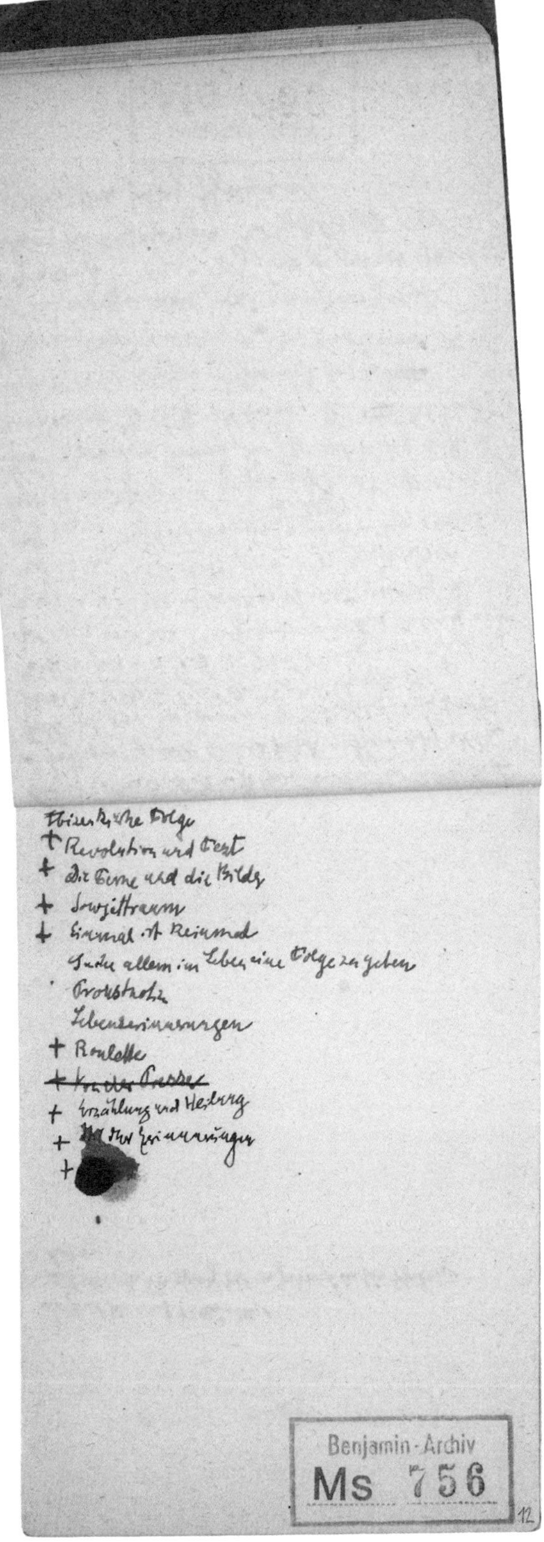
Ibizenkische Folge
Die Ferne und die Bilder
Einmal ist Keinmal
Suche allem im Leben eine Folge zu geben
Lebenserinnerungen
Roulette
Erzählung und Heilung
Benjamin-Archiv
Ms 756
12

Fig. 6.9

Fig. 6.9 (previous page)

Ibizan Sequence[3]

Revolution and festival
Distance and images
Soviet dream
Once is as good as never
Attempt to give everything in life a consequence
Proust note
Memoirs
Roulette
~~On the press~~
Narrative and healing
Style of recollections

[3] These headings do not correspond to those found in the published piece titled *Ibizan Sequence* (*SW* 2:2, pp. 587–94). However, these headings do correspond to short pieces that appeared in other contexts subsequently. For example, "Distance and Images" appeared in *Short Shadows (II)*, published in the *Kölnische Zeitung* in February 1933 (See *SW* 2:2, pp. 700–1); "Narrative and Healing" was published in the *Frankfurter Zeitung* on November 15, 1933; "Once Is as Good as Never" appeared in a Swiss magazine called *Der öffentliche Dienst* in 1934.

7

Travel Scenes

Picture Postcards

> Don't take offence: my speciality is precisely such antiquarian postcards.
>
> *GB* III, p. 82

> There are people who think they find the key to their destinies in heredity, others in horoscopes, others again in education. For my part, I believe that I would gain numerous insights into my later life from my collection of picture postcards, if I were to leaf through it again today. The main contributor to this collection was my maternal grandmother, a decidedly enterprising lady, from whom I believe I have inherited two things: my delight in giving presents and my love of travel. If it is unclear what the Christmas holidays—which cannot be thought of without the Berlin of my childhood—meant for the first of these passions, it is certain that none of my boys' adventure books kindled my love of travel as did the postcards with which she supplied me in abundance from her far-flung travels. And because the longing we feel for a place determines it as much as does its outward image, I shall say something about these postcards.
>
> *SW* 2:2, pp. 620–1

Buying, writing, sending, receiving, reading, and collecting picture postcards featured in Walter Benjamin's life from childhood into his adult years. He enjoyed all the uses of a medium that was barely as old as he. The first polychrome picture postcard, manufactured according to a photographic template, appeared three years after his birth. Such postcards were not simply a novelty: they were also cheap enough to be purchased by masses of people. Bringing home images of a trip to Italy or sending a tableau of one's home town to friends and relations was something previously restricted to the wealthy. With the invention of the picture postcard it was possible for those of lesser means to show to other people places and things that they themselves had seen. Just two months after their introduction more than two million pictorial postcards had been bought. And ever more new cards were produced; within a short period, virtually every locality, every village, many railway stations, hotels and restaurants had their own picture postcards.

But picture postcards were not only bought and sent en masse. They were also quick to become items that inflamed the passions of collectors, and Benjamin too fell victim. Picture postcards from his grandmother—a "decidedly enterprising lady," whose wide-flung seafaring and camel rides filled Walter the child with awe—formed the cadre of his collection and remained for him a source of fascination. Losing himself in the postcards' world of images, he soon undertook dream-journeys to "Tabarz, Brindisi, Madonna di Campiglio" and across the world's oceans with the "bows of the 'Westerland' slicing high through the waves" (*SW* 2:2, p. 621). He hoarded his picture postcards like a valuable treasure, stored them in three collector's albums, alongside other valuables, in a small "locker hidden beneath the seat" by the window, his favorite spot (*SW* 3, p. 399). Picture postcards were his first great collecting passion. Later on, in his notes and texts, Benjamin concerned himself with the theoretical aspects of collecting. For him collecting is "a form of practical memory" (*AP*, p. 205) and a "primal phenomenon of study" (*AP*, p. 210).

When did Benjamin begin to write and send postcards himself? The earliest indication is in a letter to his school friend Herbert Blumenthal. On July 15, 1910, his eighteenth birthday, Benjamin wrote to him, while on holiday with his family in Vaduz: "I haven't yet received a single line from you in response to my many postcards" (*Correspondence*, p. 3). For Benjamin, these written cards were not only greetings from afar. He requested their return from the recipient once back home again. Nine days later he wrote from St Moritz: "At any rate, I hope you are holding on to the other ones, if not for you, then as a memento for me" (*GB* I, p. 18). These cards became part of his illustrated memory as well as a starting point for his literary efforts. In 1911 he went on his final family holiday. On this occasion too he sent cards and letters and kept a travel diary. But something had changed. The diary, up until now a private travel journal with precise details written up every day, was to become a literary compendium, composed only in retrospect using letters, notes, and postcards. He described the change to his friend Herbert Blumenthal: "And then there are an abundance of impressions and thoughts, which ought to be captured quickly or polished and spun out, and which belong in a diary. But nothing has come of it. Simply because of their abundance and my lack of time. What I have written to date is bad, but to be sure there are few more difficult tasks for a writer than a diary; I have learnt from this attempt and have planned a very different arrangement for next year. I have to go now. Hold on to my letters please. Perhaps I might like to borrow them off you some time in the future in order to reconstruct a diary" (*GB* I, p. 42).

As announced, he did indeed devise a rather novel form for the diary *My Travels in Italy Whitsun 1912*. "The journey will emerge only from the diary that I am about to write. In it I hope what occurs is the development of the whole essence, that calm, self-evident synthesis, which a sentimental journey requires and which constitutes its essence. This seems all the more necessary to me since no individual experiences ever absolutely forcefully shaped the impression of this whole trip. Nature and art equally culminated everywhere in what Goethe calls 'solidity.' And no adventure, no desire for adventure on the part of the soul presented a potent or charming enough backdrop" (*GS* VI, p. 252). This type of travelogue was later developed in a series of masterly little "travel scenes"—such as *Moscow, San Gimignano* or *Naples*—which were published in various newspapers and magazines.

Over the course of the years the medium of the picture postcard itself became a focus of his philosophical interests. In 1924/1925 he planned a publication that was intended to include an essay on the "Aesthetics of the Picture Postcard" (compare *GS* VI, p. 694). It would appear that this publishing plan collapsed, but his interest in a written confrontation with the phenomenon of the picture postcard remained, as can be discerned in a letter to Siegfried Kracauer in June 1926: "If you pursue further the skewed bits of the petty-bourgeois stage of dreams and desires, then I think you will come across wonderful discoveries and perhaps we will meet each other at a point which I have been gauging with all my energy for a year without being able to hit it in the center: the picture postcard. You may perhaps one day write that salvation of the stamp collection for which I have been waiting for so long without wanting to chance it" (*GB* III, p. 177). Benjamin did actually "chance" the "salvation of the stamp collection" in the wonderful text "Stamp Shop," which appeared in the *Frankfurter Zeitung* on August 9, 1927 and was published in *One-Way Street* in 1928.

From 1924 onwards Benjamin spent most of his life traveling. He traveled across Spain and Italy, visited Riga, Paris, Marseille and Monaco, Moscow, Toulon, Nice, Corsica and he went on a cruise to Norway, Finland, and the Arctic Circle. Time after time he was drawn to Paris, where he would, as he told Gershom Scholem, have gladly settled, "because he found that city's atmosphere so much to his liking" (Scholem, *Friendship*, p. 158). In all of these places he went on a search for special postcards; so, for example, in Moscow: "It was also today that I discovered some fabulous postcards, the kind I had long been looking for, old white elephants from the czarist days, primarily colored pictures on pressed cardboard, also views of Siberia" (*Moscow Diary*, p. 76).

In summer 1929 he made a week-long trip to the Tuscan town San Gimignano and on the journey back to Berlin he visited Volterra and Siena. A number of the postcards in the bequest stem from this sojourn.

In April 1932 he boarded a ship in Hamburg and sailed via Barcelona to the island of Ibiza, which was in those days a little-known place, far away from the beaten track of tourism. He described the beauty of the island in "Ibizan Sequence," a series of short meditations that was published in the *Frankfurter Zeitung* on June 4, 1932.

In March 1933 he set off on a second journey to Ibiza. On this occasion, however, he did not undertake the trip for pleasure. He did not travel voluntarily. When he visited Ibiza in 1932 he stayed there for a few months, and then at the end of his visit traveled back to Berlin as usual, back to his native land, back to his home. But in 1933 he was compelled to leave Germany. As a Jew and a left-wing critic, his life was in severe danger. Anti-Semitic attacks were commonplace in the German Reich, even before 1933, but with the assumption of power by the National Socialists the disenfranchisement and persecution of the Jewish population became state policy. His second sojourn on the island was spent as a refugee, a stateless person, who did not know what the future would bring, nor how and where, and from what he was supposed to live. He had been expelled from his home, forced to leave behind his carefully administrated archive, his books, and his collections. Many of his writings, materials, and notes were saved with the help of friends, but it seems that most of his picture postcards were lost. His bequest holds just a few picture postcards from Italy, which he presumably bought during his final trip to Tuscany, and also a few cards from the islands of Ibiza and Mallorca, which he probably acquired in order to send them to others or as mementos.

In 1932, while on Ibiza as a visitor, Benjamin wrote "Berlin Chronicle." In this piece too there are reminiscences about his postcard collection: "It was a noisy, cheerful evening, but all the more silent was the journey there, through a snow-covered, unknown Berlin spreading about me in the gaslight. It stood in the same relation to the city I knew as that most jealously guarded of my postcards, the depiction of the Halle Gate in pale blue on a darker blue background. The Belle-Allianceplatz was to be seen, with the houses that frame it; the full moon was in the sky. From the moon and the windows in the facades, however, the top layer of card had been removed; their contrasting white disrupted the picture, and one had to hold it against a lamp or a candle to see, by the light of windows and a lunar surface parading in exactly the same illumination, the whole scene regain its composure" (*SW* 2:2, p. 626). Perhaps he suspected at that moment already that he would soon be separated from Halle Gate as well as from the most jealously guarded items in his postcard collection. Perhaps he had an inkling that he would not be able to return to Berlin again, that he, the passionate traveler Benjamin, would soon transform into a homeless refugee.

San Gimignano

In memory of Hugo von Hofmannsthal

To find words for what one has before one's eyes—how difficult that can be. But once they come they batter with tiny hammers against reality, until they have pressed a picture from it as from a copper plate. "In the evening the women congregate at the fountain by the town gate in order to fetch water in large jugs"—only once I had found these words did the image emerge with hard dents and deep shadows out of what had been experienced all too bedazzlingly. What did I know previously of the flat white pastures, which wake before the town walls each afternoon with their flamelets? How tightly must the thirteen towers have managed heretofore, and how considerately did each take up his place from now on, and between them there was still a lot of room.

If one arrives from far away the town is suddenly as noiseless as if one had stepped through a door into landscape. It does not give the impression that one could ever manage to come any closer. But should one succeed, then one falls into its lap and cannot find oneself again for all the humming of grills and children's cries.

Over the course of many centuries its walls consolidated themselves ever more thickly; barely a house is without the traces of large rounded arches over its narrow gate. The openings, in which now dirty linen cloths blow gently as a protection against insects, were once bronze doors. The remains of the old stone ornamentation have been left poking godforsaken from the masonry, which lends it a heraldic air. If one enters through the Porta San Giovanni, one feels as if one is in a courtyard, rather than on the street. Even the squares are courtyards, and one feels secure on all of them. What one often encounters in the towns of the south is nowhere more tangible than here; that, in order to get what one needs for life, one must first make the effort to visualize it, because the line of these arches and battlements, the shadows and the flight of the doves and crows make one forget one's needs. It is difficult to escape from this exaggerated present, in the morning to have evening before one and in the night the day.

Everywhere where it is possible to stand it is also possible to sit. Not only children but women too take up their place on the threshold, their bodies close to the floor and soil, its customs, and perhaps its gods. The chair in front of the house door is in itself an emblem of the town's renovations. Only the men ever make use of the crass seating opportunities at the cafés.

I have never previously seen sunrise and moonrise in my window like this. When I lie on my bed at night or in the afternoon there is only sky. I begin habitually to wake shortly before sunrise. Then I await the sun's ascent from behind the mountains. There is one first brief moment when it is no bigger than a stone, a tiny glowing stone on the ridge of the mountain. What

Goethe said of the moon: "Your edge gleaming as a star"—has never been thought of the sun. But it is not a star but a stone. Early man must have possessed the ability to harbor this stone as a talisman and thereby to turn the hours to good account.

I look at the town from the wall. The land does not vaunt its building and settlements. There is a lot there but it is screened and shaded. The courtyards, which were built by nothing but need, are more elegant than any manor house set in its landscape, not only in terms of the outlines but also in each tone of the bricks and window glass. But the wall, on which I lean, shares the secret of the olive tree, whose crown opens itself to the sky as a hard brittle wreath with a thousand cracks (*GS* IV.1, pp. 364–6).

Figures

7.1 San Gimignano—Panorama dal Poggio.

7.2 San Gimignano—Palace of the Pesciolini family and the twin towers of the Salvucci family.

7.3 San Gimignano—Tower of the Cortesi (also known as Devil) behind the Piazza della Cisterna.

7.4 San Gimignano—Piazza Ugo Nomi with towers.

7.5 San Gimignano—Tabernacle of Saint Fina (Lorenzo di Niccolò di Pietro Gerini, around 1400).

7.6 San Gimignano—The bishop Saint Gimignano holding the model of the town (Taddeo di Bartolo, around 1400).

7.7 San Gimignano—Saint Augustine as a child with his grammar teacher in Tagaste (Benozzo Gozzoli, around 1463).

7.8 San Gimignano—Church of Saint Agostino, Virgin on the Throne and Saint Michael (Lippo Memmi, around 1400).

7.9 San Gimignano—Church of Saint Agostino, Altarpiece *The Birth of the Virgin* (Bartolo di Fredi, around 1440).

S. Gimignano - Palazzo Pesciolini
e le due Torri Salvucci (XIV sec.)

Figs 7.1 and 7.2

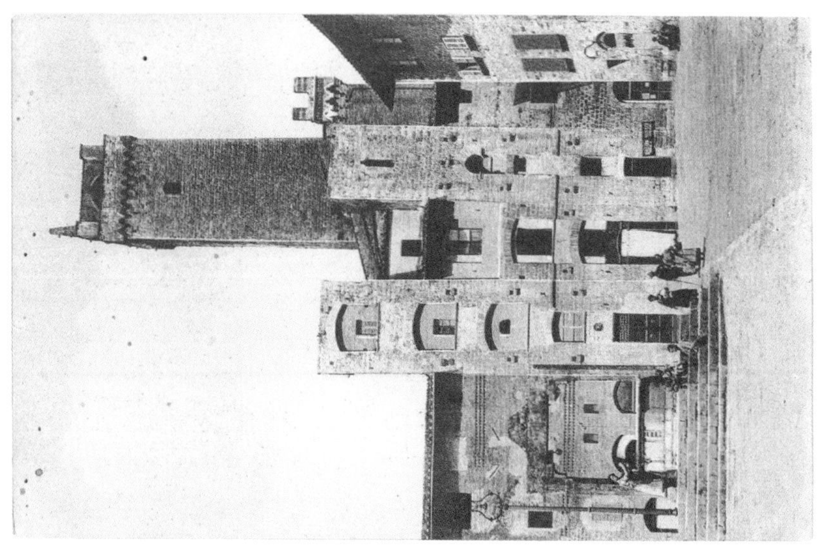

Figs 7.3 and 7.4

Figs 7.5 and 7.6

S. GIMIGNANO - Chiesa di S. Agostino - S. Agostino fanciullo dal maestro di grammatica in Tagaste; Gozzoli.
1262

S. GIMIGNANO - Chiesa di S. Agostino - La Vergine nel trono e S. Michele; Lippo Memmi.
1292

Figs 7.7 and 7.8

S. GIMIGNANO - Chiesa di S. Agostino - La Natività della Vergine; Bartolo di Fredi.
1291

Fig. 7.9

To Gershom Scholem, Volterra, July 27, 1929

Dear Gerhard

Say what you like: all in all, my letters are not all that infrequent, and rarely brief. And what I took the liberty to say to you about the state of my European correspondence should only have shown the virtues of my international correspondence to better advantage. One of these virtues is how tirelessly I attempt to present you with rare and changing dates. At least in this sense, even the letter now before you may demand your attention. For it comes from a center of Etruscan culture, let us say from its limbo, to the extent that I have atoned for thirty-seven years of being ignorant of these things with a three-hour visit to a museum. From Volterra. Unknown, and not without reason; even praised in song by D'Annunzio without suffering any damage; extremely grand, situated in the middle of a kind of snowless African Engadine—the huge wastelands and bald mountains of its environs are that clear (*Correspondence*, pp. 353–4).

7.10 Volterra—Octagonal baptistery.

7.11 Volterra—Chiesa di S. Giusto.

7.12 Volterra—Palazzo del Priori (thirteenth century).

7.13 Volterra—Porta Fiorentina.

7.14 Volterra—Porta S. Francesco.

7.15 Volterra—Collegio Comunale and Chiesa di S. Michele.

Volterra - Battistero o Chiesa di S. Giovanni - Costruzione del VII secolo

Figs 7.10 and 7.11

Figs 7.12 and 7.13

Figs 7.14 and 7.15

Siena [...] but the whisky-cathedral (Black and White) of Siena is an original choice (*GS* IV.2, p. 1023).

Ritual teaches us: the church did not build itself up by overcoming the love between men and women but rather homosexual love. That the priests do not sleep with the choir boys is the miracle of the mass (cathedral at Siena July 28, 1929) (*GS* VI, p. 204).

7.16 Siena—Cathedral.

7.17 Siena—Mosaic in the cathedral, The Seven Ages of Man.

Siena - Cattedrale
L'interno, visto dal lato destro dell'altare maggiore

Figs 7.16 and 7.17

The Wall

I had been living for a few months in a rocky eyrie on Spanish soil. I often resolved to set out into the environs one day, as it was bordered by a ring of severe ridges and dark pinewoods. In between lay hidden villages; most were named after saints, who might well have been able to inhabit this paradisiacal region. But it was summer; the heat allowed me to postpone my resolve from day to day and I even wished to save myself from the cherished promenade to Windmill Hill, which I could see from my window. And so I stuck to the usual meanders through the narrow, shady alleyways, in whose network one was never able to find the same hub more than once. During my wanders one afternoon I came across a general stores, where postcards could be bought. In any case some were displayed in the window and amongst their number was a photo of a town wall. Many such walls have been preserved in numerous places in this corner of the land, but I had never seen one quite like this. The photograph had captured all of its magic: the wall swung through the landscape like a voice, like a hymn singing across the centuries of its duration. I made a promise to myself that I would not buy the card before I had seen with my own eyes the wall that was depicted on it. I told no one of my resolve and I was all the more able to refrain from doing so for the card led me with its signature "S. Vinez." To be sure I did not know of a St Vinez. But did I know any more of St Fabiano, a holy Roman, or Symphorio, after whom other market towns nearby were named? That my guidebook did not include the name did not necessarily mean anything. Farmers had occupied the region and mariners had made their markings on it, and yet both had different names for the same places. And so I set about consulting an old map and, when that did not advance my quest at all, I got hold of a navigational map. Soon this research began to intrigue me and it would have been a blot on my reputation to seek help or advice from a third party at such an advanced stage in the matter. I had just spent another hour poring over my maps, when an acquaintance, a local, invited me on an evening walk. He wanted to take me to the hill just outside the town, from where the windmills that had long been still had so often greeted me above the tops of the pine trees. Once we had managed to reach the top it began to turn dark, and we halted in order to await the moon, upon whose first ray we made our way home again. We stepped out of the little pine forest. There in the moonlight, near and unmistakable, stood the wall, whose image had accompanied me for days, and in its custody was the town, to which we were returning home. I did not say a word, but soon parted from my friend.—The next afternoon I stumbled suddenly upon my general stores. The picture postcard was still hanging in the window. But above the door I read on a sign, which I had missed before, in red letters "Sebastiano Vinez." The painter had included a sugarloaf and bread

(*GS* IV.2, pp. 755f).

7.18 Ibiza—La Carroza.

7.19 Ibiza—Windmill (photo Domingo Viñets).

7.20 Ibiza—View of the town (photo Domingo Viñets).

7.21 Ibiza—Museum (photo Domingo Viñets).

7.22 Ibiza—Gothic window (photo Domingo Viñets).

7.23 Ibiza—Es Vedra island (photo Domingo Viñets).

7.24 Palma de Mallorca—View from the lighthouse to Bellver castle.

7.25 Palma de Mallorca—View of the harbor and La Seu cathedral.

7.26 Palma de Mallorca—View of La Seu cathedral.

7.27 Palma de Mallorca—Harbor.

7.28 Palma de Mallorca—La Seu cathedral.

Figs 7.18 and 7.19

IBIZA (BALEARES) - 33
Vista de la ciudad
Vue de la ville
View of the town
FOTO VIÑETS

Figs 7.20 and 7.21

Figs 7.22 and 7.23

Figs 7.24 and 7.25

Figs 7.26 and 7.27

Fig. 7.28

8

A Bow Being Bent

Composing, Building, Weaving

> The overall conception of the "Baudelaire"—which now only exists as a draft, of course—shows the philosophical bow being bent to the greatest extent possible.
>
> *Correspondence*, p. 602

> The work is the death mask of its conception.
>
> *SW* I, p. 459

> Reflection in art goes through the intellectual as a medium to construction.
>
> *GS* VI, p. 117

In "Caution: Steps," a piece in *One-Way Street*, Walter Benjamin writes: "Work on good prose has three steps: a musical phase when it is composed, an architectonic one when it is built, and a textile one when it is woven" (*SW* I, p. 455). To grasp this model as one describing his own mode of work would, however, be to underestimate the variety at work in his thinking and writing. Benjamin's writing was not schematic, rather it was dependent on the particular scope of individual texts and the significance that he accorded them. In addition, the phases of production should not be defined as discrete; they exhibit fluid transitions, and one is often able to recognize anticipations of the next stage or regressions to the previous one. On several occasions even the proofs of pieces that have already been published evidence traces of reworking. Benjamin did not regard them as finished pieces, and so they remained open to further revision.

The "Notes on 'Objective Mendacity' I," a preliminary study for the planned but unwritten *Work on the Lie*, bring to light a dynamic occurring within the spatial limits of a single sheet of notes (figs 8.1 and 8.2). Out of the flow of his first thoughts and ideas, which Benjamin jots down on the paper associatively, arises "Attempt at a Layout," which remains in fragment form; this is followed by bibliographic references, questions, quotations that have still to be utilized, as well as notes that are written both as keywords and in detailed form, by means of which Benjamin sought to locate the thematic emphases of the projected work.

The processual nature of Benjamin's writing reveals itself in a quite different manner in "Layouts of Perception." The manuscript (fig. 8.3) registers reflections on the theme of perception, which Benjamin compiles with no particular application in mind. Different shades of ink and a change in the style of the handwriting lead to the suspicion that the notes were written down at different times. That Benjamin continued to evaluate them appears proven by the markings on the left-hand margin of the sheet—as well as by a glance at *One-Way Street*, which includes several of the notations, in part word for word, in part modified.

Similarities in his writing procedures can be discerned in the more substantial essayistic works: in their conceptual figuration "nothing may be forced and [...] nothing may be allowed to slide" (*Correspondence*, p. 570). This specific mode of work can be seen in exemplary form in relation to the Kafka essay of 1934. An abundance of preliminary studies have been handed down amongst Benjamin's papers, a proof of Benjamin's many years of engagement with Kafka's writings.

In the essay from 1934 he attempted to interpret Franz Kafka's work in relation to the stress ratio of politics and mysticism. The conceptual configuration of this relationship is precipitated in an intensive laboring on the material; countless plans, layouts, and drafts in keyword form are evidence of his fumbling around for an adequate form of representation. He reported on the difficulties to Scholem in October 1934: "It remains to be seen whether I will ever be able to arch the bow so that the arrow zings into flight. But whereas my other works tended to find their termination rather quickly, at the point where I took leave of them, I won't be through with this one for a while. The image of the bow suggests why: I am confronted with two ends at once, the political and the mystical" (*Correspondence*, p. 458).

First of all, Benjamin began by jotting down his initial thoughts and reflections, and, through a perusal of his own and others' work, he assembled motifs, excerpts, and quotations for evaluation: he generated a record of ideas and a stockroom at one and the same time. Frequently notes of varying origin and form are found on one page, which Benjamin then, in a second step, sorted according to themes and carefully copied out. In this way he compiles on one sheet the "Motifs" in Kafka's works in ten points (fig. 8.4).

Another sheet likewise lists motifs in the essays but in tabular form and, in a subsequent inspection, these are allocated alphabetic classifications—in similar fashion to the synopsis of *The Arcades Project*. The resultant ordering of the motifs—without denoting their classifications and, in part, deviating from the previous characterization—is registered once again on the bottom right of the sheet and modified. At the top of the right-hand column Benjamin counterposed the first "motifs" with "leitmotifs" (fig. 8.5).

A further manuscript, in which thoughts and quotations are collated, stems from a file of earlier notes. Passages that are crossed out here are evidence not of the scrapping of material but of the transposition of a thought into the next phase of work or its adoption in the completed text (fig. 8.6).

Benjamin allocated the accumulated material to thematically related groups, out of which subsequently resulted plans and layouts—and finally the complete outline of the work. Such schematization is apparent in the manuscript on *The World of Forms in Kafka*, which makes visible Benjamin's efforts to bundle ideas and motifs, in order to achieve clear groupings and an adequate structure (fig. 8.7). The headings "Potemkin Story", "Story by Hamsun" and "Hasidic Fairytale about the Beggar," form the centers of the diagram, and various groups of motifs are ascribed to these. They correspond in the completed essay to the sections "Potemkin," "The Little Hunchback"—which begins with the "Story by Hamsun'—and "Sancho Panza," at whose start there is the "Hasidic Fairytale about the Beggar." The second part of the later essay—"A Childhood Photograph"—corresponds here to the keywords that are still under the heading "Kafka's World Theater." At the foot of the page and on its reverse side "reserve motifs" are listed, which presumably Benjamin had yet to integrate into the text.

Alongside this work *on* the sheet Benjamin also used a very different technique: work *with* the sheet. He cut it crosswise into units which each represent one motif or building block of text. In the case of the Kafka material this resulted in about eighty manuscript strips in total (fig. 8.8). The complexity of Benjamin's editing procedures is revealed in this process: presumably, as a consequence of previous collations and groupings of ideas, individual motifs are formulated and written out randomly on a sheet of paper. Using colored symbols on the clear edge of the sheet, these are then pooled into units, which are placed in a sequence indicated by the number of signs. After this—if necessary—the sheets are cut up, in order to make the placing of the units in the planned order physically possible. Figure 8.9 shows a sheet where the sequence in which it has been written down largely corresponds to the text as it is intended (markings: five, later corrected as four—six, seven blue circles), such that only the lower quarter of the sheet has been cut off; the following passage (eight circles), which should presumably be inserted here, clearly stems from another sheet (fig. 8.8). In addition, some of the other single strips allow the reconstruction of a further stage of processing. To create a new ordering Benjamin introduced further color symbols—this time directly on what he had written—which are then enumerated.

After a rough draft of the essay had been constructed with the aid of the manuscript strips, Benjamin had a first typewritten version made, which he then sent to friends such as Gershom Scholem, Werner Kraft, and Theodor W. Adorno. He also discussed it with Bertolt Brecht during his stay in Denmark. Their reactions, as well as his own further work on materials, were collated in a "dossier containing suggestions others have made, as well as my own reflections" (*Correspondence*, p. 469). This stock of material or archive, which contains forty-four entries—together with its corresponding elements (fig. 8.10)—provides an essential basis for further revisions of the essay (fig. 8.11). The suggestions made by others and his own reflections are taken into account partially in the publication, in the *Jüdische Rundschau*, of two parts of the essay in December 1934. But Benjamin did not regard the essay even at this point as completed; he did not want to conclude his work on it. Rather he had "already decided to tackle this project again in considerable depth by the time of its 'last' completion" (*Correspondence*, p. 462). Benjamin began a revision of the essay at the start of 1935, but despite various bids, a new version never actually appeared.

Arranging the polar aspects of his thought and shaping them in language was similarly Benjamin's aim in his work on *The Arcades Project*. In his acknowledgment of Adorno's critique of its first *Exposé* of 1935, he adopts the imagery of the bending bow once again, and simultaneously reveals the source from whence he hoped to draw the energy for shooting the arrow: "These two drafts are in a polar relationship to each other. They represent the thesis and antithesis of the work. Therefore, 'number 2' is for me anything but a conclusion. Its necessity is based on the fact that the insights contained in 'number 1' permitted no direct figuration—unless it were an inadmissible 'poetic' one. Thus the subtitle, long since abandoned, in the first draft, 'A Dialectical Fairy Play.' / I now have gotten hold of both ends of the bow—but still do not have the strength to arc it. I can get this strength only through long training, of which my work with source materials represents only one element among others. [...] What other elements does this training include? Constructive ones. If W[iesengrund Adorno] has reservations about the division of the chapters, he has hit the mark. The organization lacks the constructive moment" (*Correspondence*, pp. 506–7).

For Benjamin, the dialectical rigor and transparent form of the layout of his essay on *Goethe's Elective Affinities* represented an ideal (fig. 8.12). He referred repeatedly to its exemplary nature. The layout records the organization of the essay right down to the conceptual branching of individual passages. It is transcribed with a calligraphic virtuosity, free of corrections or additions; even its image as writing appears thoroughly composed. It does not point to something still to be woven, but rather something already constructed. It is to be read less as a draft, and more as a table of contents and an architectural model.

Figures

8.1 and 8.2 "Notes on 'Objective Mendacity'" *I* (1922/1923). Sketch for an unrealized project on lies—Manuscript, two sides. Compare *GS* VI, pp. 60–2.

8.3 "Layouts of Perception". Early notes on *One-Way Street*—Manuscript, one side. Compare *GS* IV.2, p. 938.

8.4 "Motifs". Notes on *Franz Kafka* (1934)—Manuscript, one side. Compare *GS* II.3, p. 1206f.

8.5 "Motifs/Leitmotifs". Notes on *Franz Kafka* (1934)—Manuscript, one side. Compare *GS* II.3, p. 1209.

8.6 Notes on *Franz Kafka* (up to 1931)—Manuscript, one side. Compare *GS* II.3, p. 1198f.

8.7 "The World of Forms in Kafka / Reserve Motifs" (1934). Early schematization of the essay—Manuscript, two sides; shown here, page 1. Compare *GS* II.3, pp. 1207f.

8.8 Preliminary works for *Franz Kafka* (1934)—Manuscript, five strips. Compare *GS* II.3, pp. 1222–45.

8.9 "A Childhood Photograph IV". Notes for *Franz Kafka* (1934)—Manuscript, one side. Compare *GS* II.3, p. 1230.

8.10 Letter from Werner Kraft to Walter Benjamin, September 16, 1934—Manuscript on two double sheets, eight sides; shown here, pages 2 and 3; with marginalia by Walter Benjamin. Compare *GS* II.3, pp. 1167f.

8.11 "On 'Kafka'-Revision"—"Dossier containing suggestions others have made, as well as my own reflections"—Manuscript, seven sides; shown here, page 1. Compare *GS* II.3, p. 1248f.

8.12 "On *Elective Affinities*. Layout" (c. between 1921 and 1923)—Manuscript, one side. Compare *GS* I.3, pp. 835–7.

8.13 and 8.14 Early sketch for the planned conclusion of *The Origin of German Tragic Drama* on the back of a return reminder from the Berlin State Library, dated April 10, 1924—Manuscript, one side; with reverse side. Compare *GS* 1.3, p. 920.

8.15 *Fragments of the General Layout*. Layout for the exposé *Paris, Capital of the Nineteenth Century* (1935)—Manuscript, one side. Compare AP, pp. 915–6.

8.16 "The Flâneur and the Mass". Grouping of motifs for *Charles Baudelaire. A Lyric Poet in the Era of High Capitalism*—Manuscript, one side.

The motifs, underlined in different colors and allocated a square symbol, are as follows: "Physiognomic phantasmagoria," "detectif novel," "depiction of the mass," "journalism," "crowd in Hugo," "crowd as veil," "social causes."

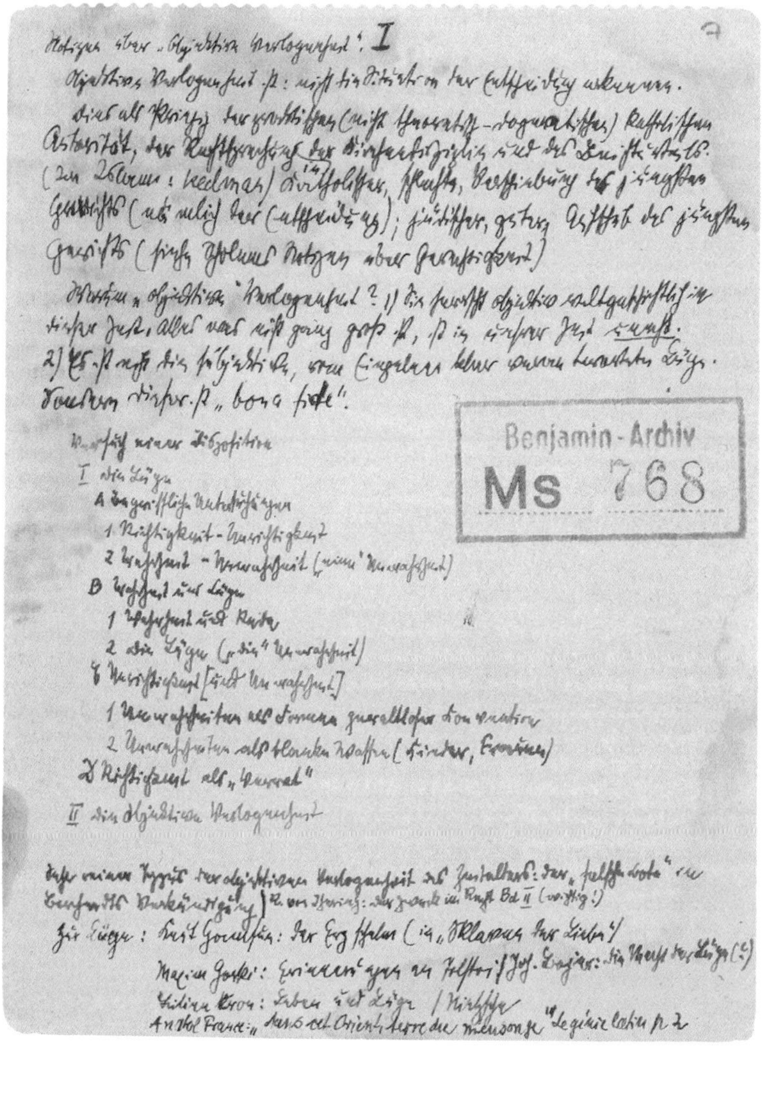

Fig. 8.1

Fig. 8.1 Notes on "Objective Mendacity" 1

Objective mendacity means: not to recognize the situation of decision.

This as a principle of practical (not theoretical-dogmatic) Catholic authority, the jurisdiction in church discipline and in the judgment of confession. (In Islam: kedman) Catholic, bad, postponement of the Last Judgment (namely the decision); Jewish, good, adjournment of the Last Judgment (see Scholem's Notes on Justice)

Why "objective" mendacity? 1) It rules objectively in world-historical terms in our time. Everything that is not quite great is *ingenuine* in our times. 2) It is not subjective, a lie whose responsibility is clearly that of an individual. Rather this is "bona fide."

Attempt at a layout

I The lie
- A Conceptual investigations
  - 1 Correctness—incorrectness
  - 2 Truth—Untruth ("an" untruth)
- B Truth and lie
  - 1 Truth and speech
  - 2 The lie ("the" untruth)
- C Incorrectness (and untruth)
  - 1 Untruths as forms of non-violent convention
  - 2 Untruths as pure weapons (children, women)
- D Correctness as "betrayal"

II The objective mendacity

Very pure type of objective mendacity of the epoch: the "false envoy" in Borchardt's Promulgation

On the lie: Knut Hamsun: The arch-rogue (in *Slaves of Love*)
Maxim Gorky: Reminiscences of Tolstoy / Joh. Bojer: The Power of the Lie (?)
Liliencron: Life and Lie / Nietzsche
Anatole France: "dans cet Orient, terre du mensonge" Le genie latin p. 2

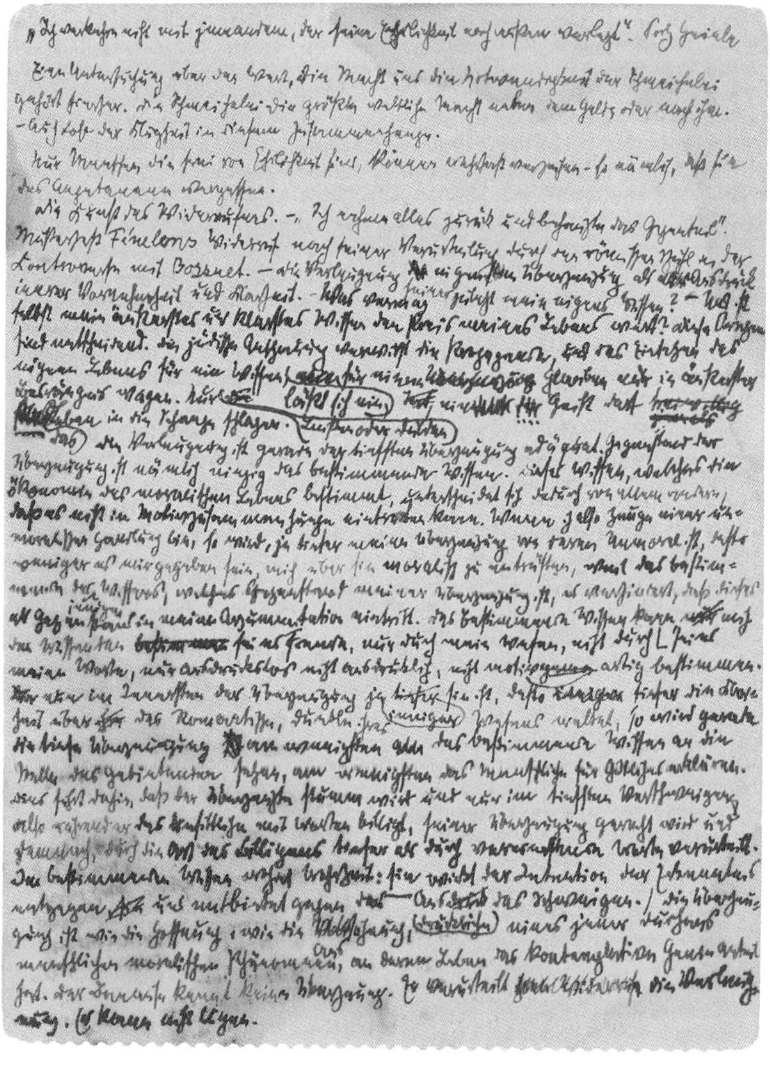

Fig. 8.2

Fig. 8.2

R. von Ihering: Purpose in Law Vol. II (important!)

"I will not consort with someone who wears his honesty externally." Fritz Heinle

An investigation of the value, power, and necessity of flattery belongs here. Flattery the greatest worldly power next to money or after it.—Also in this connection, praise of cleverness.

Only people who are free of honesty can truly forgive—such, namely, that they forget what has been done.

The art of abrogation.—"I take everything back and maintain the opposite." Exemplary—Fénelon's abrogation after his condemnation by the Roman Holy See in the controversy with Bossuet.—The renunciation of one's own most held conviction as expression of inner refinement and clarity.—Of what in the end is my own knowledge capable?—And is even my most outermost and clearest knowledge worth the price of my life? These questions are decisive. The Jewish conception rejects propaganda, and the staking of one's own life for knowledge is never dared, and for a belief only in the most extreme affliction. Only expiation or sufferance, never the intellect may put life on the line.

Renunciation is quite adequate for the deepest conviction. Object of conviction is namely solely the knowledge that determines. This knowledge, which determines the economy of the moral life, distinguishes itself from everything else by not entering into a relation with motives. If, then, I am the witness of an immoral act, then, the deeper my conviction is that it is immoral, the less am I in a position to be morally indignant, because the determining thing about such knowledge, which is the object of my conviction, prevents it from entering into my argumentation as an object. Determining knowledge cannot determine me the knower, whether [through] strangers, or through my own being, through my words, rather it can determine only without expression, not expressly, not in terms of motives. Given that, at the very heart of conviction, the more internal it is, the deeper clarity presides over the Romantic, the darkness of its being, then precisely deep conviction is least likely to situate determining knowledge in the place of the imperious, least likely to explain the human as divine. This leads to a situation where the one who has conviction is dumb and is only true to his conviction in deepest silence, that is while he endorses the immoral with words. Accordingly he condemns through this type of endorsement more deeply than through reproachful words. Truth resides in determining knowledge: it counteracts the intention of perception and offers silence in the place of the expressive. / Conviction is like hope, like reconciliation, one of those thoroughly human moral phenomena, in whose life contemplative genius plays a part. The philistine knows no conviction. He condemns renunciation. He cannot lie.

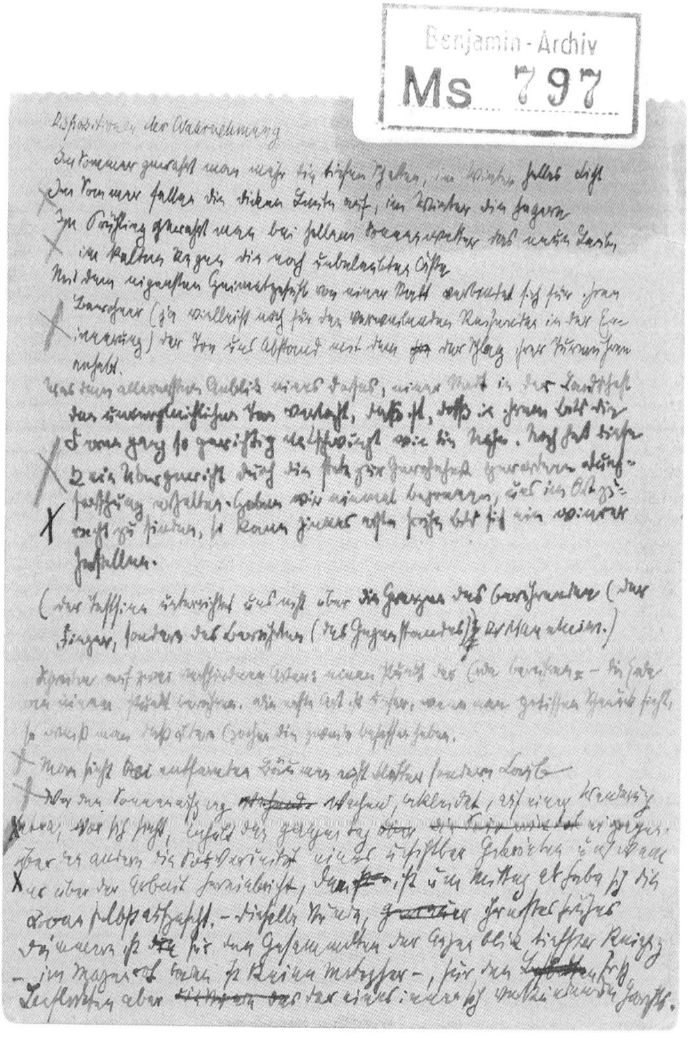

Fig. 8.3

Fig. 8.3

Layouts of Perception

In summer, one notices more the deep shadows, in winter the bright light.
In summer, fat people are conspicuous, in winter the thin are.
In spring, attention is caught, in bright sunshine, by the young foliage, in cold rain, by the still leafless branches.
Inhabitants' most intimate sense of home in a town (indeed maybe also in the memory of the traveler who stays there a while) is connected with the sound and intermittence that the beat of its town clocks marks out.
What lends an incomparable tone to the very first view of a village or a town in the landscape is the fact that in one's image of it distance resonates just as importantly as nearness. This latter still has not yet gained preponderance through the constant exploration that has become habit. Once we begin to find our way around the place, that earliest picture can never be restored.

(The sense of touch does not teach us about the limits of what touches (the finger) but the touched (the object) Dr Mannheim.)

Treading in two different ways: to touch one point of the earth—to touch the earth at one point. The first type is ours. When one sees Gothic decoration, one knows that older epochs possessed the second form.

On distant trees one sees not leaves but foliage.

He, who, awake and dressed, perhaps while hiking, witnesses the sunrise, preserves all day before others the serenity of one invisibly crowned, and he who sees daybreak while working feels at midday as if he himself has placed the crown upon his head.—This same hour, its first early dawning is a moment of deep cleansing for those who are gathered—to bathe in the dawn's red is not a metaphor—for the freshly blemished, though, it is a judgment that announces itself internally.

Motive

„der Schlag ans Hoftor" (Bau)

1) „Ich bin mit Recht verantwortlich für alle Schläge gegen Türen" (Betrachtung)

der [illegible] läuft über den schmalen Teppich seines Zimmers „wie in einer Rennbahn". (Betrachtung)

2) Die Rennbahn in dem Roman „Amerika"
„Zum Nachdenken für Herrenreiter" (Betrachtung)

Das gespenstische Kind im „Unglücklichsein" (Betrachtung)
3) die Kinder bei Titorelli (Prozess) bei Gracchus (Bau)

4) „die anderen mit Einblick auffangen" – ein Ausdruck für „[illegible]." (Betrachtung)

die Ritzen in den Brettern des Affen-Käfigs
5) die Ritzen in der Tür Titorellis (Prozess)

Der [illegible] kann den Kopf über dem [illegible] halten (Verwandlung)
6) die Galeriebesucher stoßen mit dem Kopf an die Decke (Prozess)

die Dorfjungen [illegible] (Bau)
7) die [illegible] (Landarzt)
Leni mit ihrer Schwimmhaut (Prozess)

Der Kaufmann erklärt: „gehe ich auf Wellen, klappere mit den Fingern beider Hände" (Betrachtung)
8) Beim Kranken [illegible] auf die „[illegible], die nur ihre weißen Flügel bewegten" (Prozess)

9) die beiden Gehilfen, die zum Fenster hereinsehen (Schloss)
die beiden Pferde, die [illegible] (Landarzt)

die Dohlen, die gegen den Himmel [illegible] (Bau)
10) die Dohlen, welche ums Schloss fliegen (Schloss)

Fig. 8.4

Fig. 8.4

Motifs

1) "The Knock at the Gate" (*Great Wall*)
"I am quite rightfully responsible for all knocks on doors" (*Contemplation*[1])
The writer runs across the narrow carpet of his room "as in a racetrack." (*Contemplation*)
2) The racetrack in the novel *America*
Reflections for Gentlemen-Jockeys (*Contemplation*)
3) A ghostly child in "Unhappiness" (*Contemplation*)
The children at Titorelli's (*Trial*) at Gracchus's (*Great Wall*)
4) "To behold an other with the look of an animal"—an expression for last grave-like rest." (*Contemplation*)
5) The cracks in the boards of the ape's cage [*Report to an acad.*]
The crack in Titorelli's door (*Trial*)
The bug unable to lift his head under the sofa (*Metamorphosis*)
6) The visitors to the gallery knock their heads against the ceiling (*Trial*)
7) The crossbreed of a lamb and a kitten (*Great Wall*)
Odradek's spool (*Country Doctor*)
Leni with her webbed hand (*Trial*)
The salesman explains that he "walks as if on waves, clattering with
8) the fingers of both hands." (*Contemplation*)
When Huld is ill the author indicates how he is "flapping his hands about like short wings." (*Trial*)
9) The two assistants who look in through the window (*Castle*)
The two horses who do the same (*Country Doctor*)
The crows who tackle heaven (*Great Wall*)
10) The crows who fly around the castle (*Castle*)

[1] *Betrachtung—Contemplation*—was a collection of Kafka's short prose writings from 1913.

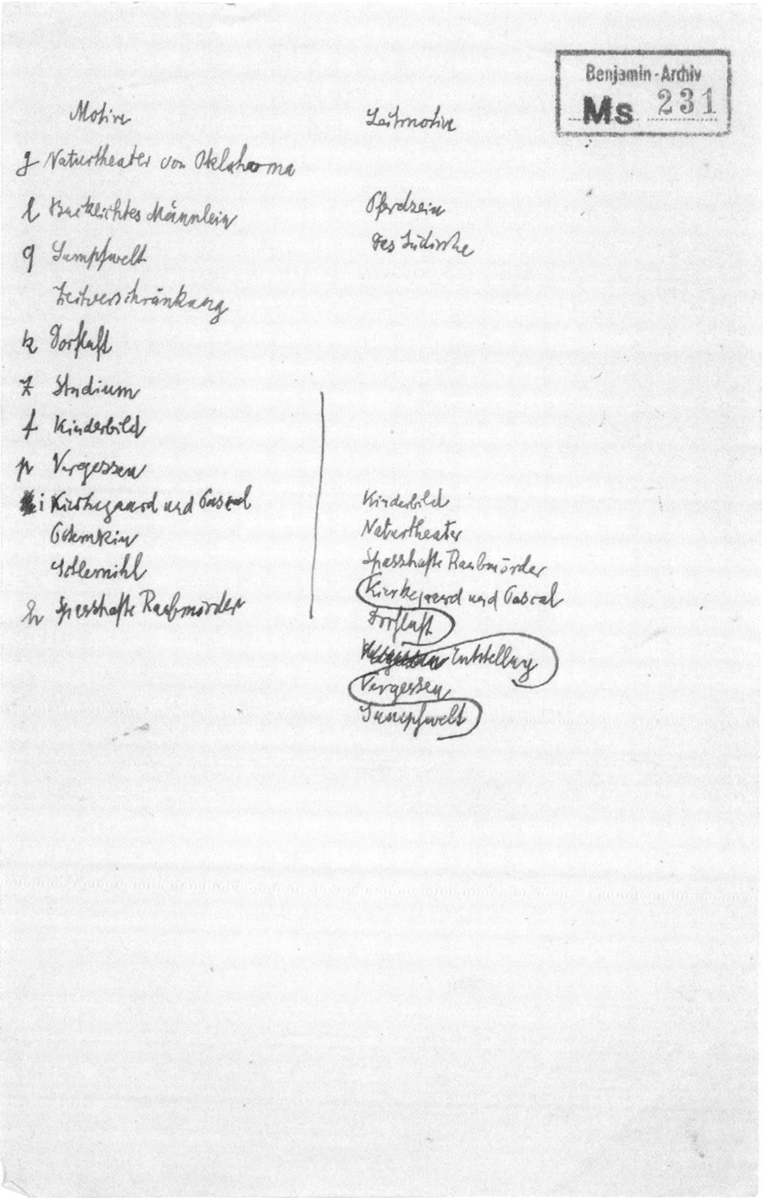
Benjamin-Archiv
Ms 231

Motive

g Naturtheater von Oklahoma
l Bucklichtes Männlein
q Sumpfwelt
Zeitverschränkung
k Dorfluft
z Studium
f Kinderbild
p Vergessen
i Kierkegaard und Pascal
Potemkin
Schlemihl
h Spasshafte Raubmörder

Leitmotive

Pferdsein
Das Jüdische

Kinderbild
Naturtheater
Spasshafte Raubmörder
Kierkegaard und Pascal
Dorfluft
~~V…~~ Entstellung
Vergessen
Sumpfwelt

Fig. 8.5

Fig. 8.5

	Motifs	*Leitmotifs*
g	Nature theater of Oklahoma	Being a horse
l	Little hunchback	Jewishness
q	Swamp world	
	Restriction of time	
k	Village air	
z	Study	
f	A childhood photograph	
p	Forgetting	
i	Kierkegaard and Pascal	A childhood photograph
	Potemkin	Nature theater
	Schlemihl, the unlucky devil[2]	Facetious robbers and murderers
h	Facetious robbers and murderers	Kierkegaard and Pascal
		Village air
		~~Forgetting~~ Disfiguration
		Forgetting
		Swamp world

[2] *Schlemihl*, from the Yiddish word *Schlemiel*, meaning a bungler, is a reference to Peter Schlemihl, who appeared in a story by Adelbert von Chamisso: he entered into a silly bargain with the devil who obtained his soul.

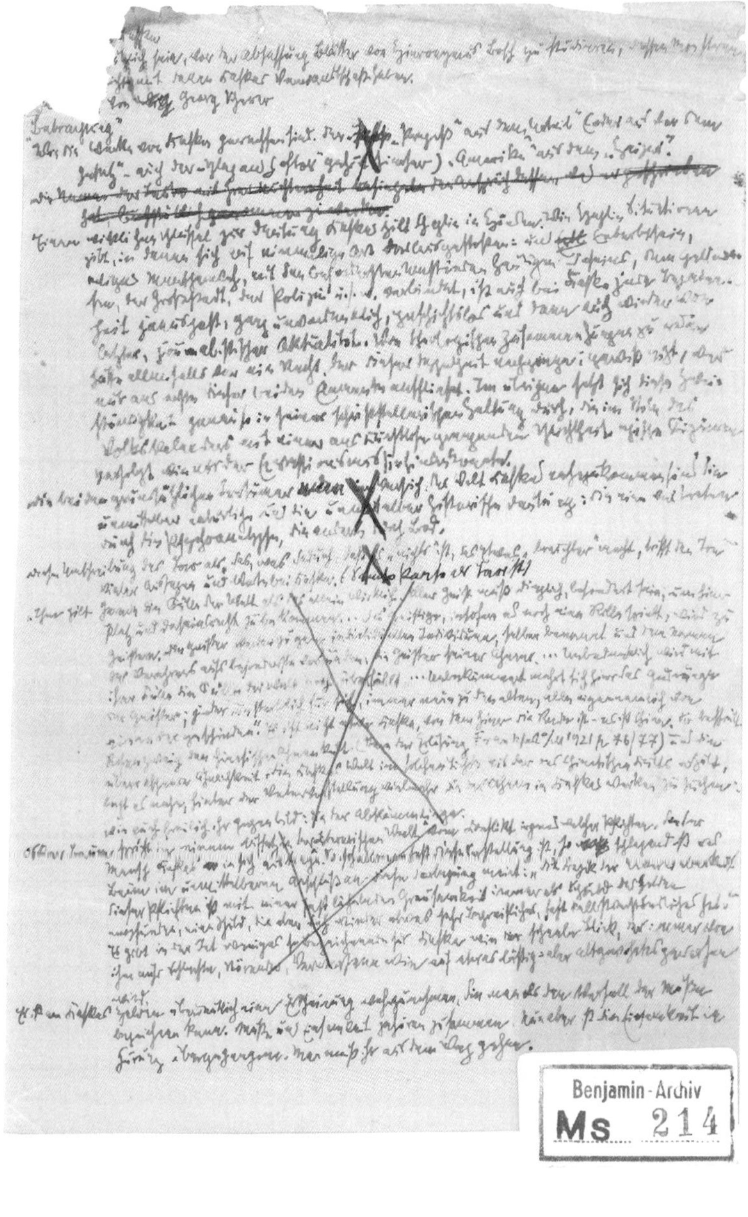

Fig. 8.6

Fig. 8.6

Kafka
[...] be useful to study pages by Hieronymus Bosch before composition, whose monsters
[...]ly bears some relationship to those of Kafka.
[...] by Georg Scherer

Contemplation
How Kafka's works grew. *The Trial* out of *The Judgement* (or out of *Before the Law—The Knock at the Gate* belongs here) *America* out of *The Stoker.*}
~~The names of the people with [...] sobriety seals the claim of someone who wants what he has written to be taken literally~~
Chaplin holds in his hands a genuine key to the interpretation of Kafka. Just as occurs in Chaplin's situations, in which, in a quite unparalleled way, rejected and disinherited existence, eternal human agony combines with the particular circumstances of contemporary being, the monetary system, the city, the police, etc., so too in Kafka every event is Janus-faced, completely immemorial, without history and yet, at the same time, possessing the latest, journalistic topicality. In any case one would be justified in speaking of the theological context if one pursued this doubledness; but certainly not if one only adopted the first of these two elements. Incidentally this double layering is likewise present in his writerly demeanor, which, in the style of the popular almanac, pursues epic characters with a simplicity that borders on artlessness, such as only Expressionism could detect.

The two fundamentally erroneous attempts to approach Kafka's world are the directly natural and the indirectly historical interpretations: one is represented in psychoanalysis and the other by Brod.

This rewriting of the Tao as "that nothing which alone makes it possible for a 'something' to be 'useful,'" hits the tone of many statements and words in Kafka. (Sancho Panza as Taoist)

"Here the very fullness of the world is considered the only reality. All spirit must be concrete, particularized, in order to have its place and *raison d'être*. The spiritual, if it plays a role at all, turns into spirits. These spirits become definite individuals, with names and a very special connection with the name of the worshipper ... Unhesitatingly, the fullness of the world is filled to overflowing with their fullness ... Unconcernedly, the crowd of spirits is swelled ... New ones are constantly added to the old ones, and each is distinguished from the others by its own name." All this refers not to Kafka, but to—China. This is how Rosenzweig described the Chinese ancestor cult (*Star of Redemption*, Frankfurt am Main, 1921, pp. 76–7) and the surprising similarity that the world of Kafka shares with that of the Chinese cult in such a light suggests one search in Kafka's work behind the idea of the father for the ancestors: as well as of course their counter-image: that of the descendants.
Oskar Baum in an essay in the *Literary World* speaks about a conflict of duties that affects the person in Kafka's world. As schematic as this idea is, what Baum opines directly following this analysis is striking: "The tragedy of the incompatibility of these duties is always experienced, with an almost simpering cruelty, as the guilt of the hero, a guilt that has, though, something understandable, almost self-evident about it." Indeed there is little else so characteristic in Kafka than the askance look, which is always cast by him onto something bad, disturbing, depraved as if on something troublesome but known of old.
Kafka's heroes display a blatantly obvious trait that might be described as the decline of leisure. Leisure and loneliness belong together. But now loneliness has transformed into disquiet. One should avoid it.

Die Gestaltenwelt Kafkas

Potemkingeschichte | Die Väter, die Ermüdeten, die Oberen / Prozess

Die Frauen, die zu allem zu haben sind / Der Schoss der Familie /

Die Monstra / Die Tiere / Die Vermittler und Botengänger: Gehilfen

Hoffnung für wen? Landarzt

Kafkas Welttheater

Kinderbild / Wunsch Indianer zu werden / Erfüllung in Oklahoma /

Das Gestische / Vieldeutigkeit / Verzicht auf Rationalisierbarkeit / Pirandello

Vorläufer des Naturtheaters / Engel, Teufel

Theologische Interpretation Dorfluft / Laotse / Das Körperdorf /

Nachbarschaft des Dorfes / Kafkas Ratlosigkeit / Brod Schoeps Rang Haas /

Geschichte von Hamsun | ~~[illegible]~~ Theologie unanständig /

Kein Gott

Die hetärische Welt

Keine Liebe / Leni, die Frauen Kafkas / Moorboden der Erfahrung / Schuld

Die Oberen auf dem Weg in die Tiefe / Die Welt des Gerichts / Das Vergessen

Das bucklige Männlein

Die Tiere / Ihre Gesten / Der blonde Eckbert / Odradek / Das bucklichte Männlein

Entstellung in der Zeit

Chassidisches Bettlermärchen | Schlaflose Flucht in die Vergangenheit, aus der er sich ein Hemd holt / Studium: schlaflose Flucht in die Vergangenheit / Die Nimmermüden: Narren und Gerechte / Die Schnelligkeit: das Studium als Flucht / Leben – eine Flucht in die Vergangenheit

Der freie Reiter, das freie Pferd

~~[illegible]~~ Rossmann / Der neue Advokat / Sancho Pansa

Reserve-Motive

~~Die kleinen Kinder~~

Nahrung, Feste, Wachen

Der Bau

Der Schlemihl

Die Musik

~~[illegible]~~

Lesebuchstil

~~[illegible]~~

Das Schweigen

Der Stein

Bestandteil eines Monuments

+ Gebäude

+ Taoismus und Hämmern

Fig. 8.7

Fig. 8.7

The World of Forms in Kafka

Potemkin Story The fathers, the tired, the upper ones / *Trial*
Women who are ready for anything / The lap of the family / The monstra / The animals /The mediator and ghost of a messenger: assistants
Hope for whom?

Kafka's world theater
A childhood photograph / wish to be a Red Indian / Fulfillment in Oklahoma / integrity
The gestural / ambiguity / renunciation of rationalizability / Pirandello
Precursors of nature theater / angel, devil

Theological Interpretation
Village air / Lao-tze / the body of the village / night side of the village / Kafka's perplexity / Brod Schoeps Rang Haas

Hamsun Story theology improper / no God

The heteric world
No love / Leni, Kafka's women / swampy soil of experience / thighs
The upper ones on the way to the depths / The world of the court / Forgetting

Little Hunchback
The animals / Their gestures / Blond Eckbert / Odradek / The little hunchback

Distortion in time

Hasidic Beggar Tale
Sleepless flight into the past, from whence he fetches himself a shirt / Study: sleepless flight into the past / Those who never get tired: fools and the righteous / Speed: study as life of flight—a flight into the past

The free rider, the free horse
Roßmann / The new advocate / Sancho Panza

Reserve Motifs
So many children
Nutrition, fasting, waking
Construction
Schlemihl, unlucky devil
Music
~~Folie d'interprétation~~
style of a primer
~~the testament~~
Silence
Appearance

Components of a monument
+Original sin
+Taoism and hammers

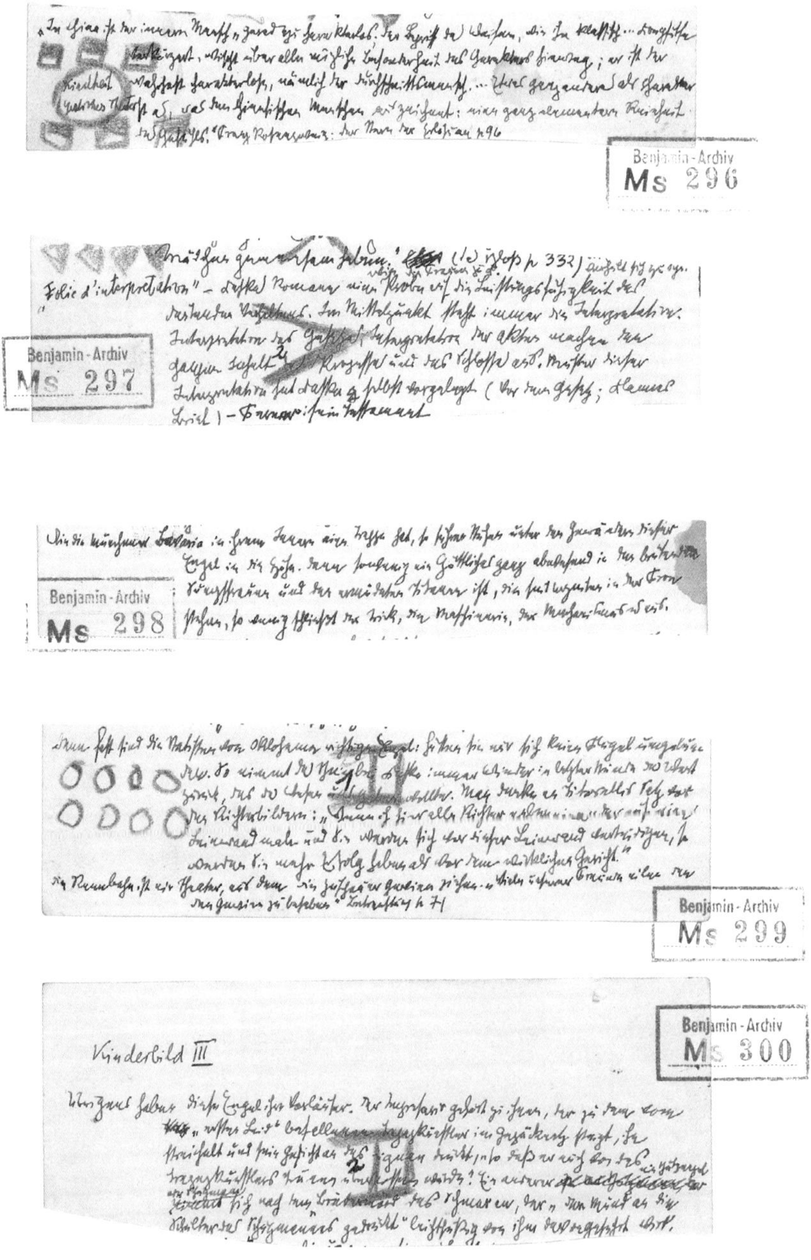
Benjamin-Archiv Ms 296
Benjamin-Archiv Ms 297
Benjamin-Archiv Ms 298
Benjamin-Archiv Ms 299
Kinderbild III
Benjamin-Archiv Ms 300

Fig. 8.8

Fig. 8.8

In China the inner person is "devoid of individual character, as it were. The idea of the wise man, of which Confucius … is the classic incarnation, blurs any individuality of character; he is the truly characterless man—namely the average man … What distinguishes a Chinese is something quite different from character: a very elemental purity of feeling" (Franz Rosenzweig: *The Star of Redemption*, p. 96).

[on margin: Childhood Gestic theater]

"Folie d'interprétation"—Kafka's novels a test of the effectiveness of the interpreting attitude. Interpretation is always at its core. Interpretation of the law, interpretation of the files comprise the whole contents of *The Trial* and *The Castle*. Kafka himself set out an example of this interpretation (Before the Law; Klamm's letter)—In addition: his testament.

Just as the people of Munich have a stairway to Bavaria in their insides, so too steps under the robes of this angel lead into the heights. For just as a divine presence is not entirely absent in the brooding bog women and the exhausted Titans, who having been doing drudgery since primeval times, the trick, the machinery, the mechanism likewise does not exclude it.

For the extras of Oklahoma are almost proper angels: but for the fact that their wings are tied on. And in this way appearance in Kafka always at the last hour takes back the word that the substance wished to give us. One is reminded of Titorelli's line in front of the portraits of the judge: "If I painted all the judges next to each other here on canvas, and you were trying to defend yourself in front of it, you'd have more success with them than you'd ever have with the real court."

The racetrack is a theater from which the spectators draw profit. "Lots of our friends rush to pick up their profit" (*Contemplation*, p. 71).

Childhood Photograph III
Incidentally, these angels have forerunners. One of them is the impresario who climbs up on the luggage rack next to the trapeze artist beset by his "first sorrow," caresses him, and presses his face against his, "so that he was bathed by the trapeze artist's tears." Another, a guardian angel or guardian of the law, takes care of Schmar the murderer following the "fratricide" and leads him away, stepping lightly with Schmar's "mouth pressed against the policeman's shoulder."

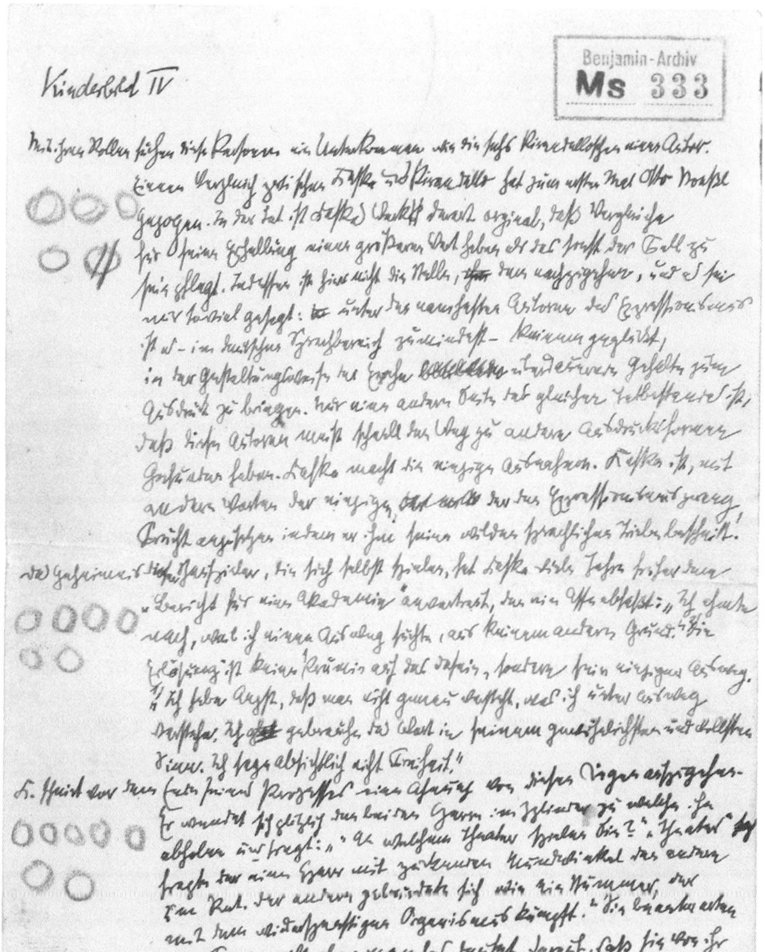

Kinderbild IV

Fig. 8.9

Fig. 8.9

A Childhood Photograph IV

With their roles, these people look for a position in the Nature Theater in the same way that Pirandello's six characters seek an author. The first person to draw a comparison between Kafka and Pirandello was Otto Stoessl. Indeed Kafka's work is so original that comparisons have greater value for its illumination than might otherwise be the case. But here is not the place to follow that up, and it will suffice to say: amongst the well-known authors of Expressionism—in the German-language realm at least—none has been successful at bringing to expression in their mode of composition the enduring aspects of the epoch. And one other aspect of the same state of affairs is that most of these authors found their way to other modes of expression fairly quickly. Kafka is the sole exception. Kafka is, in other words[,] the only one who compelled Expressionism to bear fruit, by pruning it according to his wild linguistic drives.

The secret of those actors who play themselves was entrusted many years ago by Kafka to his "Report to an Academy," written by an ape: "I imitated people because I was looking for a way out, and for no other reason." "I fear that perhaps you do not quite understand what I mean by 'way out.' I use the expression in its fullest and most popular sense—I deliberately do not use the word 'freedom.' " Salvation is not a premium on existence, but the last way out.

Before the end of his trial, K. seems to have an intimation of these things. He suddenly turns to the two gentlemen wearing top hats who have come for him and asks them: "What theater are you playing at?" "Theater?" asked one, the corners of his mouth twitching as he looked for advice to the other, who acted as if he were a mute struggling to overcome a stubborn disability.' The men do not answer this question, but there is much to indicate that it hit home.[3]

[3] See *SW* 2:2, pp. 804–5.

1) hier zu erwarten hat und was nicht.
Darstellungsform In diesem Sinne habe ich unabhängig
von <u>meinen</u> Einwänden gewisse Bedenken
gegen die Form des Aufsatzes. Sie ist my-
stisch, fast esoterisch. Gerade Brecht, in
dessen Nachbarschaft Sie doch im Augenblick nicht nur zufällig wohnen,
müßte Ihnen, wenn anders Sie nicht selber
nach ihr streben, was ich keineswegs
leugne, die <u>Verständlichkeit</u> in einem
neuen Licht zeigen. Mir wenigstens würde
es als sehr reizvoll erscheinen, den Auf-
satz noch einmal als nüchternen Lehrvor-
trag aller jener Ideen zu schreiben, die
wesentlich in ihm enthalten sind und
dann auch unter Weglassung sämtlicher
Gleichnisse wie Potemkin usw. Können und
wollen Sie dies nicht, so habe ich auch dafür Verständnis und werde Ihnen nicht
mein eigenes Stilideal, das ich ja keineswegs
realisiere, aufdrängen versuchen. – Darüber
habe ich allerdings keinen Zweifel, daß für

2) Sie das Kafka'sche Werk identisch ist mit
tiefere Schicht einer gleichsam phänomenalen Oberschicht
und daß Sie nur indem Sie sich's streng
versagen, eine tiefere Sinnschicht anzuerken-
nen, Ihren eigenen Standpunkt zu halten
vermögen. Dies ist folgerichtig. Wenn ich aber
Ihrem Standpunkt so weit wie nur möglich
entgegenzukommen suche, so würde ich sagen
müssen, Ihr Standpunkt sei <u>auch</u> in dem
Werk enthalten, aber nur durch einen künst-
lichen Abstraktionsvorgang sichtbar zu machen, wie dies z. B. in der Phänomenologie
vielfach geschieht. Konkret sieht das für mich
nun so aus. Alles was Sie über Gestus, Theater
usw sagen, taste ich am wenigsten an. Es
wird in Ihrem Verfahren überzeugend deutlich.
Vaterproblem Wenn Sie aber gleich im ersten Kapitel den
Zusammenhang zwischen Beamten- und Vater-
tum im Schmutz erhärten wollen und dafür
das Beispiel des Vaters in der „Verwandlung"
und seine schmutzige Uniform usw heranzie-
hen, so stimmt das eben <u>nur</u> phänomenal,

Fig. 8.10

Fig. 8.10

[Marginalia in Benjamin's hand*:* *1) Form of exposition*]

what he can expect here and what not.

In this sense, independently of *my* objections I have certain thoughts about the form of the essay.

It is mystical, almost esoteric. Brecht of all people, in whose neighborhood you are, after all, not coincidently living at the moment, could well demonstrate for you *comprehensibility* in a new light, if you are unable to strive for it another way, which I am not denying may occur. For me, at least, a stimulating task would be to write the essay once again as a sober lecture for students, detailing all the ideas that are essentially contained in it and leaving out all the analogies such as Potemkin. I do understand if you cannot and do not wish to do this, and would not attempt to impose on you my own stylistic ideal, which I by no means manage to attain myself.—But there is one thing I do not doubt: for you Kafka's work is identical to a phenomenal upper layer, as it were, and it is only in strictly denying yourself the recognition of a deeper level of meaning that you are able to maintain your own standpoint.

[Marginalia in Benjamin's hand: *2) deeper level*]

This is logical. But if I try to accommodate your standpoint as far as possible, then I have to say, your standpoint is *also* contained in the work, but is only made visible through an artificial process of abstraction, as occurs, for example, frequently in phenomenology. This is how it seems to me concretely: everything that you say about gesture, theater, etc., I will leave largely alone. Your procedures make it convincingly clear. But when right away in the first chapter you want to substantiate the connection between officials and fatherhood in terms of filth and to this end use the example of the father in *Metamorphosis* and his dirty uniform etc., then that is *only* true phenomenally

[Marginalia in Benjamin's hand: *Father problem*]

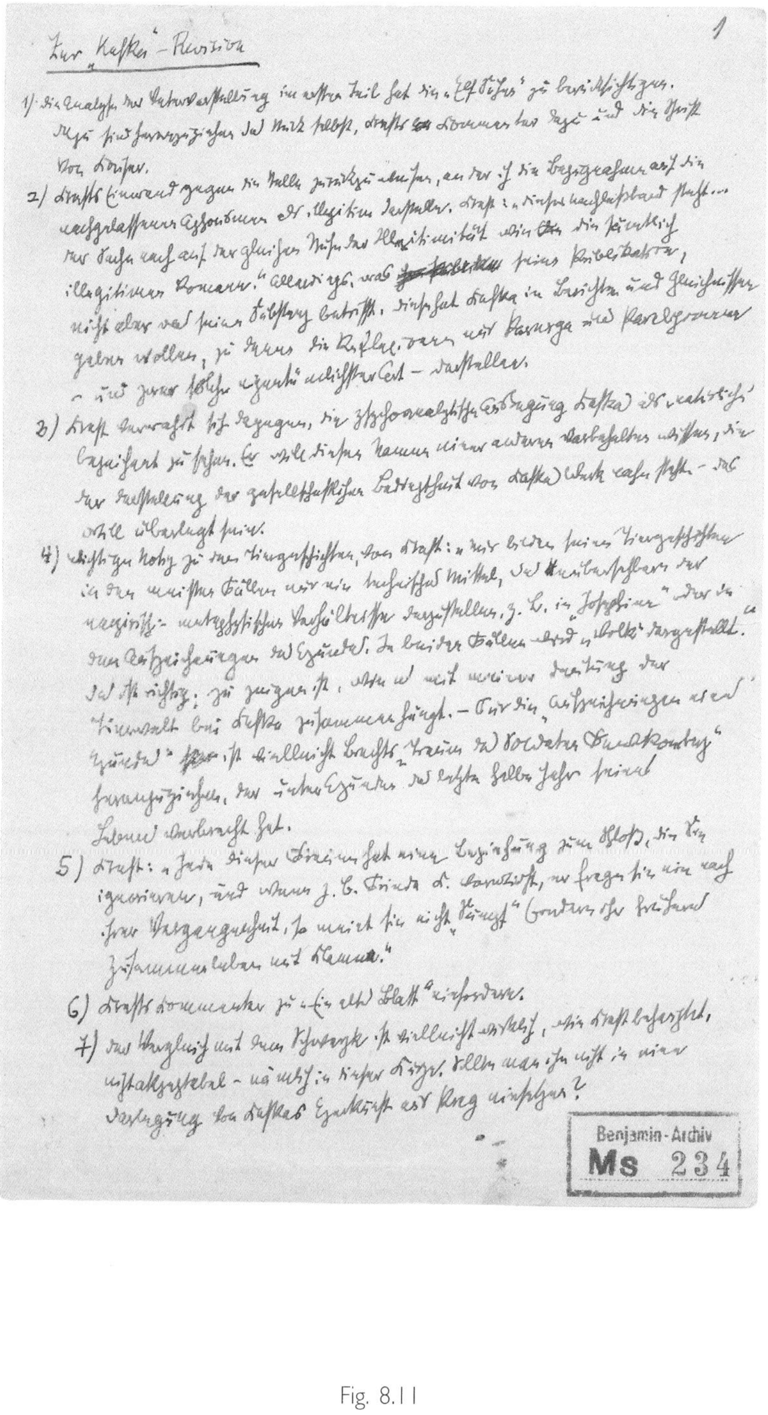

Zur „Kafka"-Revision 1

1) [illegible]

2) [illegible]

3) [illegible]

4) [illegible]

5) [illegible]

6) [illegible]

7) [illegible]

Fig. 8.11

Fig. 8.11

On "Kafka"—Revision

1) The analysis of the idea of the father in the first part needs to take account of the *Eleven Sons.* For this draw on the play itself, Kraft's commentary on it, and the piece by Kaiser.
2) Fend off Kraft's objection to the bit where I present the reference to the posthumous reflections as illegitimate. Kraft: "This posthumous volume stands . . . . accordingly on the same level of illegitimacy as all the illegitimate novels." Certainly in terms of publication, but not in terms of substance. Kafka wanted to mediate this in reports and parables, in relation to which the reflections are simply parerga and paralipomena—indeed a most peculiar type of same.
3) Kraft repudiates the characterization of the psychoanalytical exposition of Kafka as "natural." He wants to see this label reserved for another approach, which is closer to the representation of the social conditionality of Kafka's world—to be considered.
4) Important note on the animal stories, by Kraft: "For me his animal stories are in most cases simply a technical means to represent the inestimable aspects of empirical-metaphysical relations, e.g. in *Josefine* or in the notations of a dog. In both cases 'the folk' is represented." That is correct: need to show how this connects with my interpretation of the animal world in Kafka.—For *Investigations of a Dog* draw instead on Brecht's *Dream of Fewkoombey the Soldier,*[4] who spent the last six months of his life amongst dogs.
5) Kraft: "Each of these women has a relationship to the castle, which you ignore, and when, for example, Frieda reproaches K. for never asking her about her past, she does not mean the 'swamp' but her earlier life together with Klamm."
6) Request Kraft's commentary on *An Old Manuscript*
7) The comparison with Schweik is perhaps truly, as Kraft maintains, unacceptable—that is because it is too short. Should it be placed within an exposition of Kafka's derivation from Prague?

[4] In Brecht's *Threepenny Novel.*

Zu den Wahlverwandtschaften

Disposition

Erster Teil: Das Mythische als Thesis

I Kritik und Kommentar
A Wahrheitsgehalt und Sachgehalt
B Sachgehalte in der Aufklärung

II Die Bedeutung der mythischen Welt in den Wahlverwandtschaften
A Die Ehe als mythische Rechtsordnung
1 Die Ehe in der Aufklärung
2 Die Ehe in den Wahlverwandtschaften
B Die mythische Naturordnung
1 Das Tellurische
2 Das Wasser
3 Die Menschen
C Das Schicksal
1 Die Namen
2 Die Todessymbolik
3 Das schuldhafte Leben
4 Das Haus
5 Das Opfer

III Die Bedeutung der mythischen Welt für Goethe
A nach seinen Werken
1 Die zeitgenössische Kritik der Wahlverwandtschaften
2 Die Fabel von der Entsagung
B nach seinem Leben
1 Der Olympier oder die mythischen Lebensformen des Künstlers
a Das Verhältnis zur Kritik
b Das Verhältnis zur Natur
2 Die Angst oder die mythischen Lebensformen im Dasein des Menschen
a Das Dämonische
b Die Todesangst
c Die Lebensangst

Zweiter Teil: Die Erlösung als Antithesis

I Kritik und Biographik
A Die traditionelle Auffassung
1 Die Analyse der Werke
2 Die Darstellung von Wesen und Werk
B Die heroisierende Auffassung

II Gundolfs „Goethe"
A methodische Entkräftung
1 Der Dichter in der hergebrachten Sphäre
a als Heros
b als Schöpfer
2 Das Leben als Werk
3 Mythos und Wahrheit
B sachliche Entkräftung: Der alte Goethe

III Die Novelle
A Ihre Notwendigkeit in der Komposition
1 Die Romanform der Wahlverwandtschaften
2 Die Form ihrer Novelle
B Ihre sachliche Bedeutung
1 Die Korrespondenzen im Einzelnen
2 Die Korrespondenzen im Ganzen

Dritter Teil: Die Hoffnung als Synthesis

I Kritik und Philosophie

II Die Schönheit als Schein
A Die Jungfräulichkeit
B Die Unschuld
1 im Wesen
2 im Leben
C Die Schönheit
1 Das Galatea-Motiv
2 Die Erschütterung
3 Das Ausdruckslose
4 Der schöne Schein

III Der Schein der Versöhnung
A Auflösung und Rührung
1 Harmonie und Frieden
2 Leidenschaft und Neigung
a Ottilie, Luciane, das Mädchen in der Novelle
b die liebenden Paare [Novelle
c die Ehe in dem Roman
d die Trilogie der Leidenschaft
B Die Erlösung
1 Die Erschütterung
a der versöhnende Schein
b die Hülle der Schönheit
c die Enthüllung
2 Die Hoffnung

Fig. 8.12

Fig. 8.12

On *Elective Affinities.*

Layout

First part: The mythic as thesis
- I Critique and commentary
  - A Truth content and material content
  - B Material content in the Enlightenment
- II The significance of the mythic world in *Elective Affinities*
  - A Marriage as mythic legal order
    - 1 Marriage in the Enlightenment
    - 2 Marriage in *Elective Affinities*
  - B The mythic natural order
    - 1 The telluric
    - 2 Water
    - 3 The human being
  - C Fate
    - 1 Names
    - 2 Symbolism of death
    - 3 Guilty life
    - 4 The house
    - 5 Sacrifice
- III The significance of the mythic world for Goethe
  - A After his words
    - 1 Contemporary criticism of *Elective Affinities*
    - 2 The fable of renunciation
  - B After his life
    - 1 The Olympian or the mythic life forms of the artist
      - a The relationship to criticism
      - b The relationship to nature
    - 2 Fear or the mythic life forms in the existence of humanity
      - a The daemonic
      - b Fear of death
      - c Fear of life

Second part: Redemption as antithesis
- I Criticism and biography
  - A Traditional conception
    - 1 The analysis of the works
    - 2 Representation of essence and work
  - B The heroizing conception
- II Gundolf's "Goethe"
  - A Methodological enfeeblement
    - 1 The poet influenced by Stefan George
      - a As hero
      - b As creator
    - 2 Life as work
    - 3 Myth and truth
  - B Material enfeeblement The old Goethe
- III The novella
  - A Its compositional necessity
    - 1 The form of the novel in *Elective Affinities*
    - 2 The form of its novella
  - B Its material meaning
    - 1 Correspondences in detail
    - 2 Correspondences across the whole

Third part: Hope as synthesis
- I Criticism and philosophy
- II Beauty as semblance
  - A Virginity
  - B Innocence
    - 1 In dying
    - 2 In life
  - C Beauty
    - 1 The Helen motif
    - 2 Conjuration
    - 3 The expressionless
    - 4 Beautiful semblance
- III The semblance of reconciliation
  - A Conciliation and affection
    - 1 Harmony and peace
    - 2 Passion and inclination
      - a Ottilie, Luciane, the girl in the novella
      - b The loving couples
      - c Marriage in the novel
      - d The trilogy of passion
  - B Redemption
    - 1 Shock
      - a Extinguished semblance
      - b Veiling of beauty
      - c Nakedness
    - 2 Hope

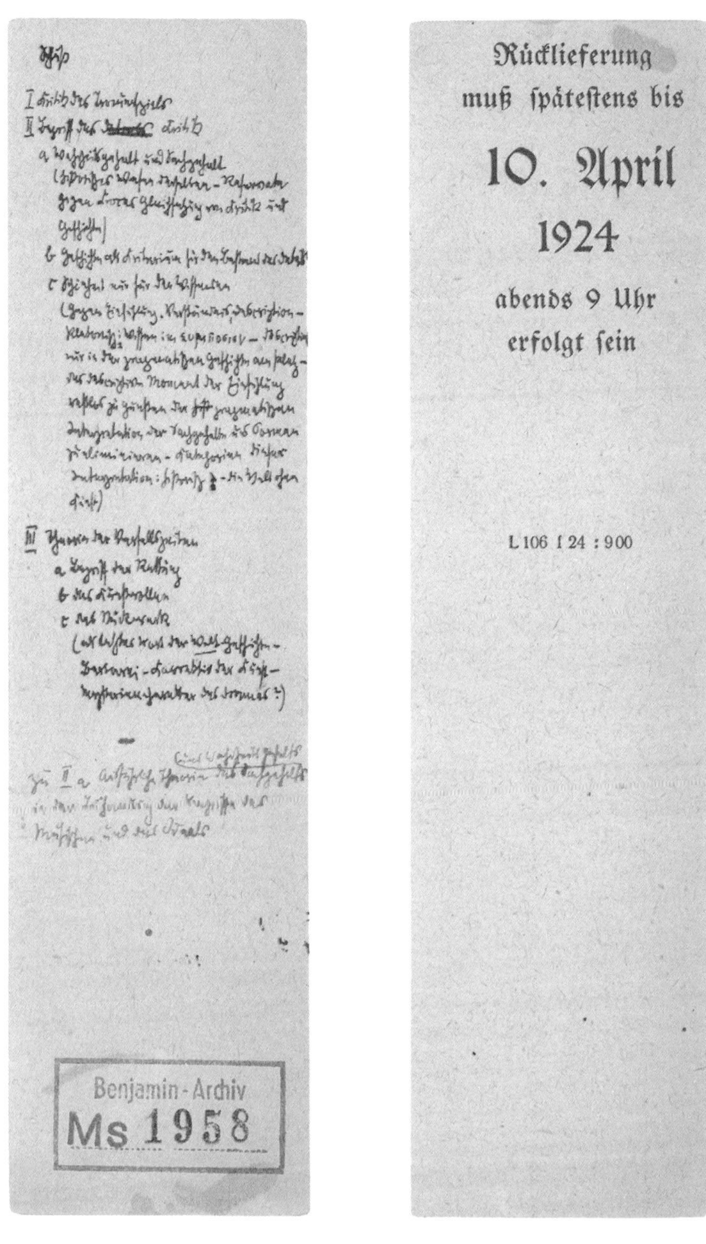
Benjamin-Archiv
Ms 1958
Rücklieferung
muß spätestens bis
10. April
1924
abends 9 Uhr
erfolgt sein
L 106 I 24 : 900

Figs 8.13 and 8.14

Fig. 8.13

Conclusion

I Critique of tragic drama
II Concept of criticism
  a Truth content and material content
   (historical essence of the same—reservations against Croce's equivalence of criticism and history)
  b History as a criterion for the inventory of details
  c Beauty only for those who know
   (Against empathy, understanding, description—Platonic: knowledge in σνμποσιον —Description has a place only in pragmatic history—completely eliminate the descriptive moment of empathy in favor of the pragmatic interpretation of material content and forms—categories of this interpretation: historical: the world without art)
III Theory of Epochs of Decay
  a Concept of salvation
  b Artistic volition
  c Unfinished work
   (as last word of world history—barbarism—corrective of art—mystery character of the drama?)

On IIa detailed theory of material content and truth content in the treatment of concepts of the muse and the ideal

Fig. 8.14

Return must be effected at the latest by
April 10, 1924,
9 o'clock in the evening

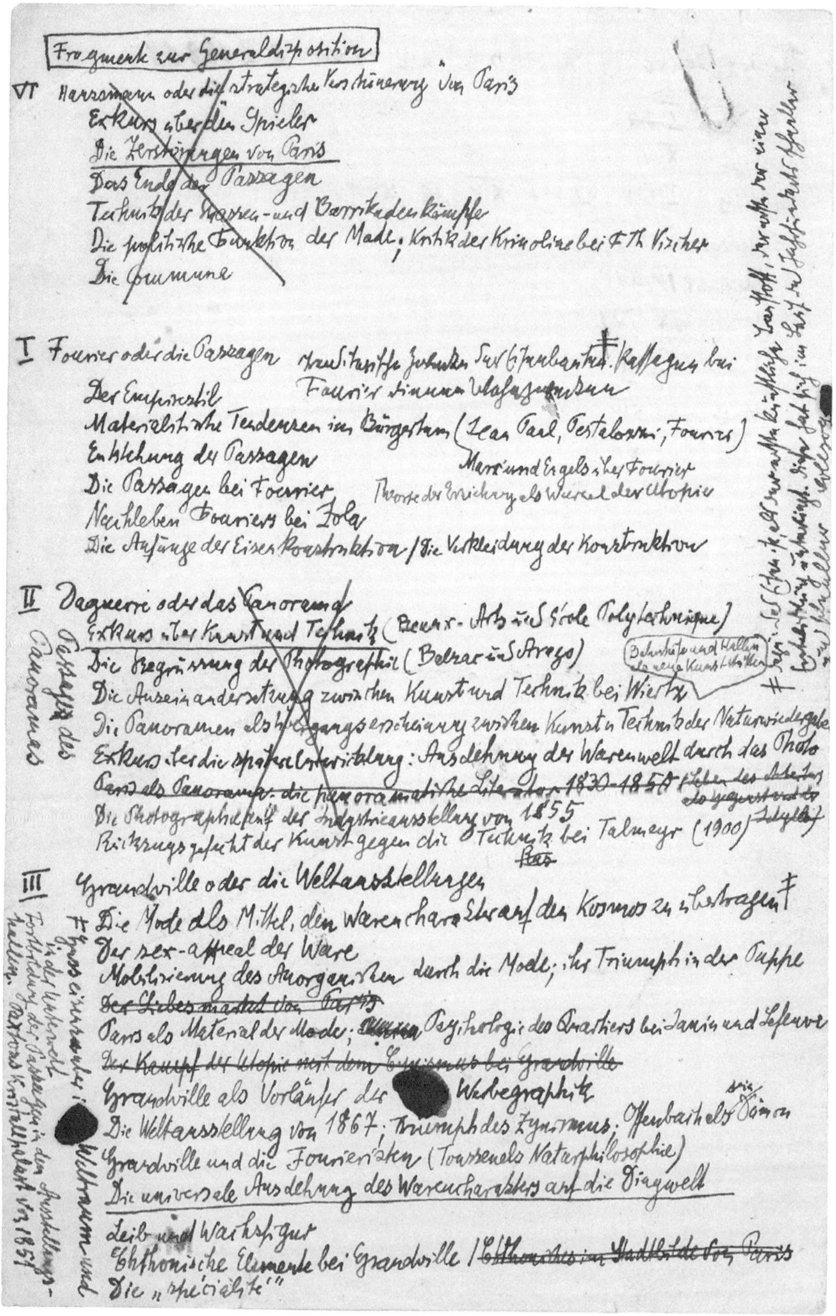

Fragment zur Generaldisposition

VI Haussmann oder die strategische Verschönerung von Paris
Exkurs über den Spieler
Die Zerstörungen von Paris
Das Ende der Passagen
Technik der Straßen- und Barrikadenkämpfe
Die politische Funktion der Mode; Kritik der Krinoline bei F. Th. Vischer
Die Commune

I Fourier oder die Passagen — Architektonische Schulen der Eisenbahnhalle. Passagen bei Fourier Wandelgänge
Der Empirestil
Materialistische Tendenzen im Bürgertum (Jean Paul, Pestalozzi, Fourier)
Entstehung der Passagen — Marx und Engels über Fourier
Die Passagen bei Fourier — Theorie der Erziehung als Wurzel der Utopie
Nachleben Fouriers bei Zola
Die Anfänge der Eisenkonstruktion / Die Verkleidung der Konstruktion

II Daguerre oder das Panorama
Exkurs über Kunst und Technik (Bauar-Arb. an d. École Polytechnique)
Die Begründung der Photographie (Bekrar an Arago)
Die Auseinandersetzung zwischen Kunst und Technik bei Wiertz
Die Panoramen als Übergangserscheinung zwischen Kunst u Technik der Naturwiedergabe
Exkurs über die Spezialunterteilung: Ausdehnung der Warenwelt durch das Photo
~~Paris als Panorama: die panoramatische Literatur 1830–1850~~
Die Photographie auf der Industrieausstellung von 1855
Rückzugsgefecht der Kunst gegen die Technik bei Talmeyr (1900)

(Bahnhöfe und Hallen als neue Kunststätten)

(left margin: Technik des Panoramas)

III Grandville oder die Weltausstellungen
Die Mode als Mittel, den Warencharakter auf den Kosmos zu übertragen
Der sex-appeal der Ware
Mobilisierung des Anorganischen durch die Mode; ihr Triumph in der Puppe
~~Der Liebesmarkt von Paris~~
Paris als Material der Mode; Psychologie des Quartiers bei Janin und Lefeuve
~~Der Kampf der Utopie mit dem Zynismus bei Grandville~~
Grandville als Vorläufer der Werbegraphik
Die Weltausstellung von 1867; Triumph des Zynismus; Offenbach als Dämon
Grandville und die Fourieristen (Toussenels Naturphilosophie)
Die universelle Ausdehnung des Warencharakters auf die Dingwelt
Leib und Wachsfigur
Chthonische Elemente bei Grandville / ~~Chthonisches im Stadtbilde von Paris~~
Die „spécialité"

(left margin: Fortbildung der Passagen in den Ausstellungshallen. Kristallpalast von 1851; Fassade als Unterwelt — Weltraum und)

(right margin: ‡ Ausstellungen, Kritik des Kosmos ... Fortschrittsglaube ...)

Fig. 8.15

Fig. 8.15

Fragments of the general layout

VI {Haussmann, or the "Strategic Embellishment" of Paris
- Excursus on the gambler
- *The demolitions of Paris*
- The end of the arcades
- Technique of street- and barricade-fighting
- The political function of fashion; critique of crinoline in F. Th. Vischer The Commune}

I Fourier, or the Arcades
- Transitory aims of constructions in iron.
- Moreover: iron, as the first artificial building material, is the first to undergo a development. This proceeded more and more rapidly in the course of the century. Arcades in Fourier are designed for dwelling.
- The Empire style
- Materialist tendencies in the bourgeoisie (Jean Paul, Pestalozzi; Fourier)
- Rise of the arcades
- The arcades in Fourier
- Fourier's afterlife in Zola
- Marx and Engels on Fourier
- Theory of education as root of utopia
- The beginnings of iron construction/The disguising of construction

II {Daguerre, or the Panorama

Passage des Panoramas
- Excursus on art <and> technology (Beaux-Arts and Ecole Polytechnique)
- The welcoming of photography (Balzac and Arago)
- The confrontation between art and technology in Wiertz Railroad stations and halls as new sites for art
- The panoramas as transitional phenomenon between art and the technique of reproducing nature
- Excursus on the later development: extension of the commodity world through the photo
- {Paris as panorama; the panoramic literature, 1830–1850
- (Life of the worker as subject of an idyll)}
- Photography at the industrial exhibition of 1855
- Rear-guard action by art against technology, in Talmeyr (1900)}

III Grandville, or the World Exhibitions
- Fashion as means of communicating commodity character to the cosmos
- Magic of cast iron in outer space and in the underworld
- Further development of the arcades in the exhibition halls; Paxton's Crystal Palace of 1851
- The sex appeal of the commodity
- Mobilization of the inorganic through fashion; its triumph in the doll
- [The love market of Paris]
- Paris as material of fashion; psychology of the *quartier* in Janin and Lefeuve
- {The battle between utopia and cynicism in Grandville}
- Grandville as precursor of advertising graphics
- The world exhibition of 1867; triumph of cynicism; Offenbach as its demon
- Grandville and the Fourierists (Toussenel's philosophy of nature)
- *The universal extension of commodity character to the world of things*
- Body and wax figure
- Chthonic elements in Grandville / {Chthonic elements in the image of Paris}
- The *spécialité*

416

Fig. 8.16

9
Constellations
Graphic Forms

> One day he invited Valéry to be the first to see the manuscript of "Coup de dés." "Take a look at it and tell me whether I have gone mad!" (This book is known from the posthumous edition of 1914. A quarto volume of a few pages. Words are distributed across the pages in changing typefaces, separated by quite considerable and irregular distances.) Mallarmé, whose rigorous immersion in the midst of the crystalline construction of his manifestly traditional writing beheld the true image of the future, has here processed the graphic tension of the advertisement, for the first time (as a pure poet), in the actual image that the writing forms.
>
> *GS* IV.1, p. 480

Benjamin often applied much care to the graphic form, the physical arrangement, of his manuscripts. While he worked extremely carefully on the structure and layout of his essays and books, equally important to him were the proportions and the architecture of the page. Part of the writing's sense of form involved the need to create something for the eye to do. Topographical relationships, spatial organization, optical alignments and divisions are not only apparent on the drafts and the pages that include calligraphic elements. Countless scraps and sheets in the bequest are evidence of a sensibility attuned to graphic elements, spatial dimensions, and design. Such deployment of graphic figurativeness is one of the characteristics of Benjamin's writing.

He referred repeatedly to Stéphane Mallarmé, whose *Coup de dés* dispersed the conventional line-based print image with its undeviating presentation. Black on a white background, distributed sparingly across the book's pages, the words of the poem appear in constellations rich with tensions: Mallarmé's idea was that of a negative image of the stars. "Arrested Auditor of Books" in *One-Way Street* (*SW* I, p. 456) points out correspondences between Mallarmé's procedures and emergent forms of advertising: a striking vision of visual versification.

Many of Benjamin's manuscripts transgress linear norms, loosening up writing's sense of direction—some bring words and groups of words into figural relations. A handwritten manuscript with themes relating to *Charles Baudelaire* (fig. 9.1) configures eight groups; each one of them is allocated a position in the arrangement, set askew from the others. Spatial correlation, proximity of arrangement and writing's orientation generate relationships. Thus four thematic blocks ("Baudelaire's literary reception," "Baudelaire's relationship to his own work," "Ferment of after-effects" and "Approaches to the reception raisonnée") are connected through a shared orientation in the writing.—An arrangement of keywords for the essay "On the Image of Proust" (fig. 9.2) might also be regarded as a constellation. Here the thematic groups are boxed and relationships are established by connecting lines.

The efforts to organize the motifs of the essay on "Karl Kraus" are reflected in some complex layout sketches. One of these stabs at finding a structure (fig. 9.3) forms a polycentric mesh: proliferating shapes made of dashes, lines, squares, letters, words, and numbers. Amongst the "Motifs in the Third Part" five are picked out as central: "Eros," "Actors," "Justice," "Poetry," and "Monster." These five keywords each gather three or four more around themselves, of which some are connected in their spanning across groups. Benjamin drew a box around the keywords and indicated the central ones by shading. Such a shape can only be adequately reproduced in facsimile form.

An experiment with the drug mescaline, carried out under the medical supervision of his friend Fritz Fränkel on May 22, 1934, gave rise to a shape with rolling lines drawn in freehand (fig. 9.4), which played around with the words of lullabies—sleep, little child, sleep; sleep, my kiddikin, go off to sleep. The variety of the writing's orientation and the curves that consume the space, the loops, the snaking and spiraling figures endow what is written with an ornamental character. Internally the form of an embryo, configured by the boundary line, suggests the writing is on its way back to drawing.

The figure of the ellipse appears in a number of contexts in Benjamin's work. It is not simply to be understood rhetorically. "Kafka's work," he writes, "is an ellipse with foci that lie far apart and are determined on the one hand by mystical experience (which is above all the experience of tradition) and on the other by the experience of the modern city dweller" (*Correspondence*, p. 563). The ellipses correspond to the widely flung foci of Benjamin's thinking: materialism and theology. As figure for such tension-ridden divergence, this dialectical thinker chose the ellipse. In an elliptical diagram for "Karl Kraus" "Eros" and "Language," "mere mind," and "mere sexuality" are braced dialectically (fig. 9.7).

In a number of cases Benjamin also used coordinate planes. "The diagrams of coordinates have eleven concepts optimally: four for the outer points of the axes, four for the fields, two for the axes, one for the crossing point" (*GS* VII.2, p. 764). The "Wind Rose of Success," which Benjamin sketched for Marietta Noeggerath on Ibiza (fig. 9.8), is constructed from four axes, captioned at each end, from which arise contiguous directions. The diagrammatic figures for the essay on "Karl Kraus" (fig. 9.6) bear similarities to wind roses. Visual models, sketches, and diagrams figure predominantly in Benjamin's preliminary studies: his efforts to orient writing and thought.

Figures

9.1 Themes for *Charles Baudelaire*—Manuscript, one side.

9.2 Keywords on Proust (1929)—Manuscript, one side. Compare *GS* II.3, p. 1060.

9.3 Layout sketch for the essay on *Karl Kraus* (1930). *Motifs in the Third Part*—Manuscript, one side.

9.4 Lullaby Drawing (May 22, 1934)—one side. Compare *On Hashish*, p. 90.[1]

9.5 Plan for *Anthropology*—one side. Compare *GS* VI, p. 64.

9.6 Notes and diagrams for *Karl Kraus* (1930)—Manuscript, one side.

9.7 Plan for *Karl Kraus* (1930)—Manuscript in notebook Ms. 674. Compare *GS* II.3, pp. 1091–4.

9.8 The "Wind Rose of Success." Extract missing the note on the bottom right-hand corner: "For Marietta Noeggerath / San Antonio / May 17, 1932 / Walter Benjamin"—Manuscript, Jörg Leinweber Collection; one side.[2]

---

[1] The translation is different here.

[2] See also *SW* 2:2 p. 590 for a different translation of the text in the context of "Ibizan Sequence".

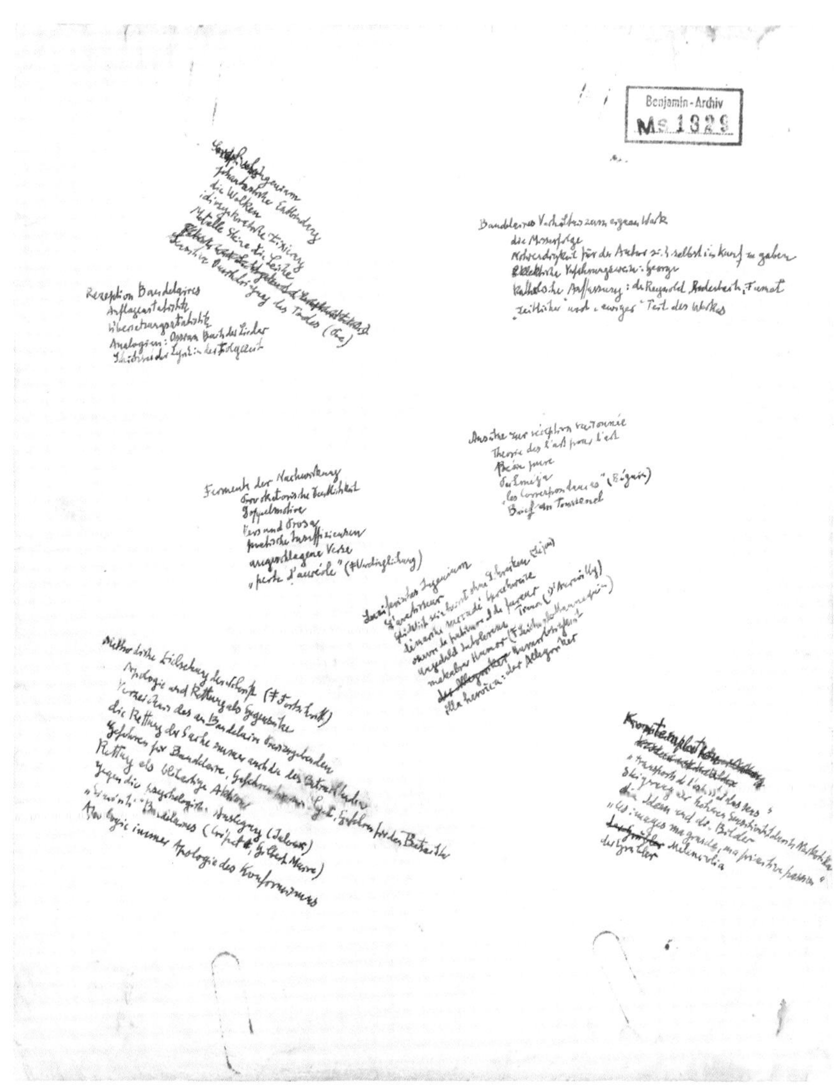

Fig. 9.1

Fig. 9.1

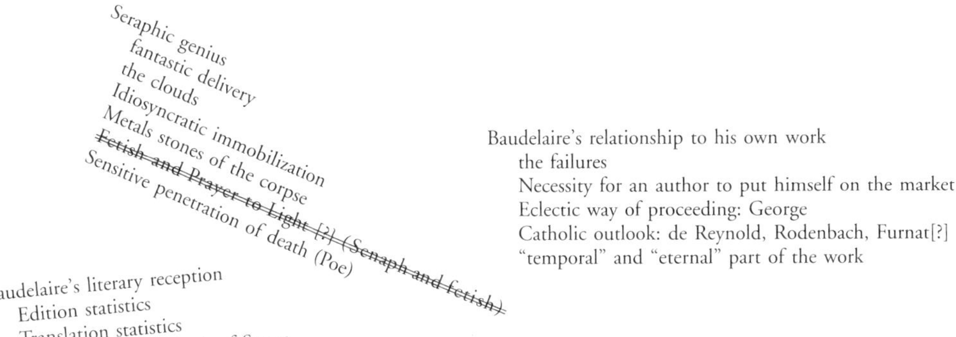

Seraphic genius
fantastic delivery
the clouds
Idiosyncratic immobilization
Metals stones of the corpse
~~Fetish and Prayer to Light [?] (Seraph and fetish)~~
Sensitive penetration of death (Poe)

Baudelaire's relationship to his own work
the failures
Necessity for an author to put himself on the market
Eclectic way of proceeding: George
Catholic outlook: de Reynold, Rodenbach, Furnat[?]
"temporal" and "eternal" part of the work

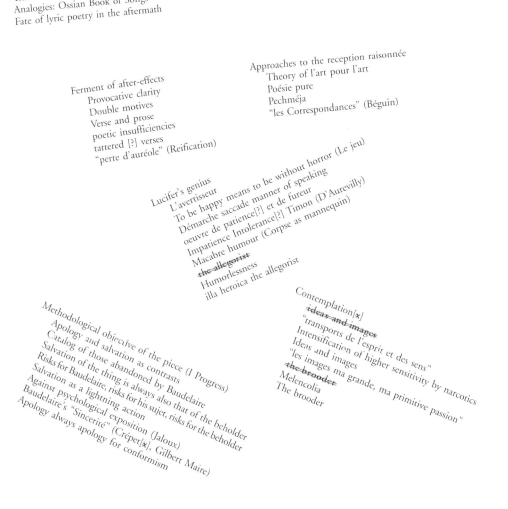

Baudelaire's literary reception
Edition statistics
Translation statistics
Analogies: Ossian Book of Songs
Fate of lyric poetry in the aftermath

Approaches to the reception raisonnée
Theory of l'art pour l'art
Poésie pure
Pechméja
"les Correspondances" (Béguin)

Ferment of after-effects
Provocative clarity
Double motives
Verse and prose
poetic insufficiencies
tattered [?] verses
"perte d'auréole" (Reification)

Lucifer's genius
L'avertisseur
To be happy means to be without horror (Le jeu)
Démarche saccade manner of speaking
oeuvre de patience[?] et de fureur
Impatience Intolerance[?] Timon (D'Aurevilly)
Macabre humour (Corpse as mannequin)
~~the allegorist~~
Humorlessness
illa heroica the allegorist

Contemplation[*]
~~ideas and images~~
"transports de l'esprit et des sens"
Intensification of higher sensitivity by narcotics
Ideas and images
"les images ma grande, ma primitive passion"
~~the brooder~~
Melencolia
The brooder

Methodological objective of the piece (I Progress)
Apology and salvation as contrasts
Catalog of those abandoned by Baudelaire
Salvation of the thing is always also that of the beholder
Risks for Baudelaire, risks for his sujet, risks for the beholder
Salvation as a lightning action
Against psychological exposition (Jaloux)
Baudelaire's "Sincerité" (Crépet[*], Gilbert Maire)
Apology always apology for conformism

Benjamin-Archiv
Ms 431

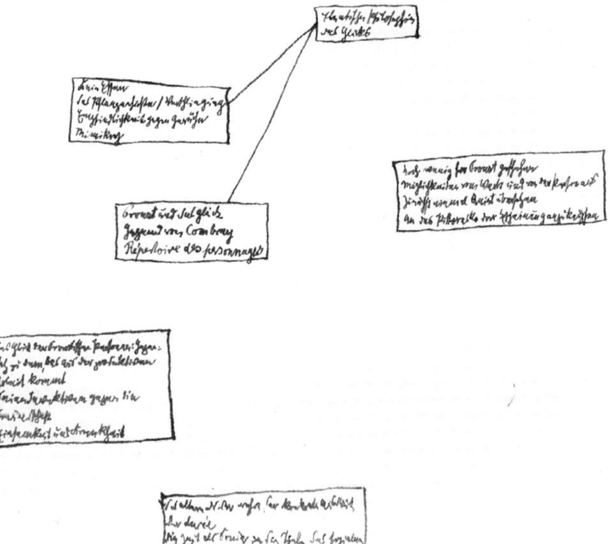
Mimikry
Jugend von Combray
Répertoire des personnages

Fig. 9.2

Fig. 9.2

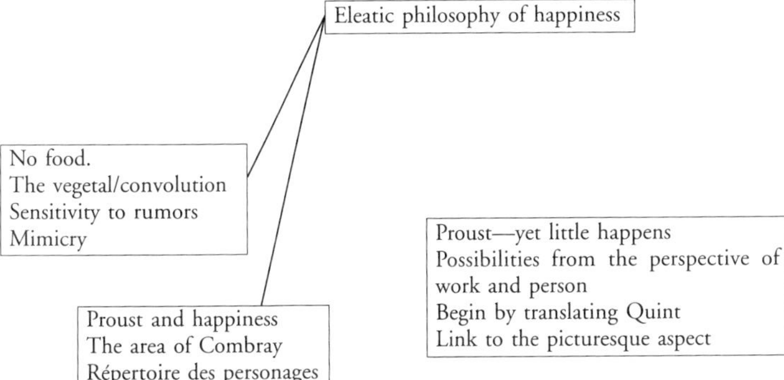

Eleatic philosophy of happiness
No food.
The vegetal/convolution
Sensitivity to rumors
Mimicry
Proust and happiness
The area of Combray
Répertoire des personages
Proust—yet little happens
Possibilities from the perspective of work and person
Begin by translating Quint
Link to the picturesque aspect

The happiness of the Proustian cast: contrast to that which results from productive work
His invectives against friendship
Loneliness and illness

Aging is the genuine, concrete expression of durée
Time as a probe into the depths of social appearance

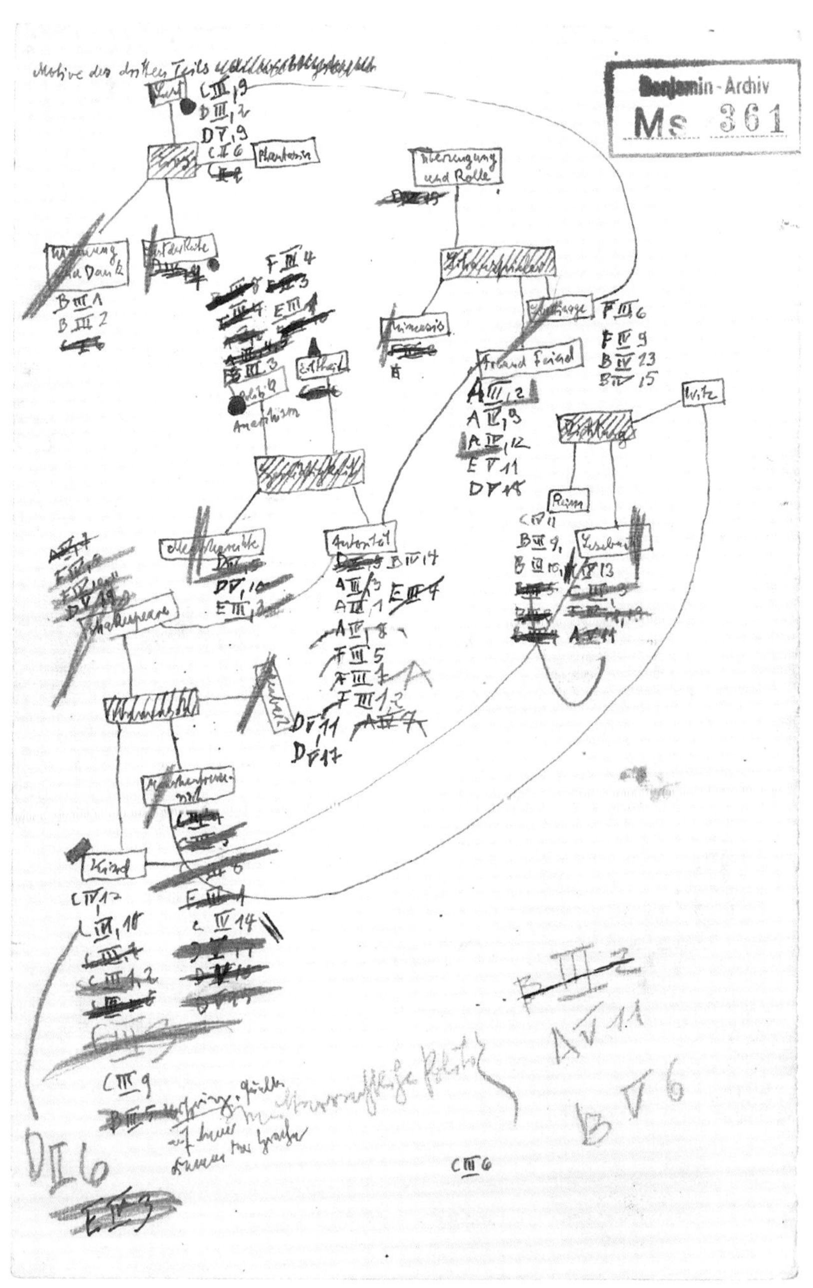
Motive des dritten Teils
Benjamin-Archiv
Ms 361
Phantasie
Überzeugung und Rolle
Mimesis
Witz
Reim
Autorität
Shakespeare
Kind

Fig. 9.3

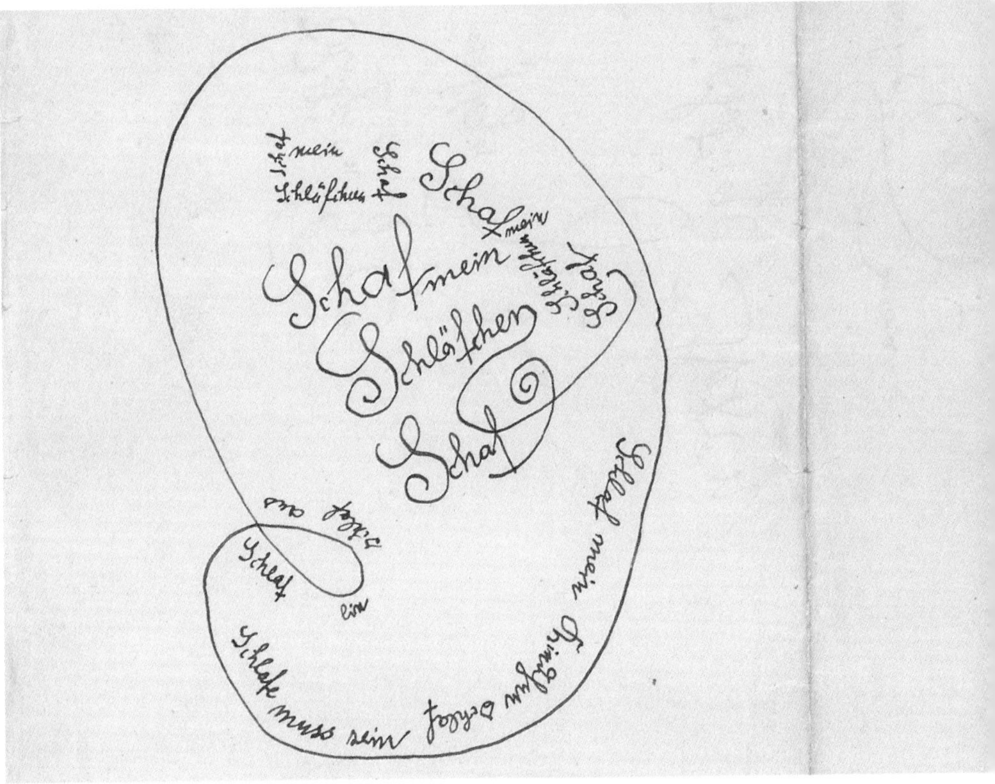

Fig 9.4

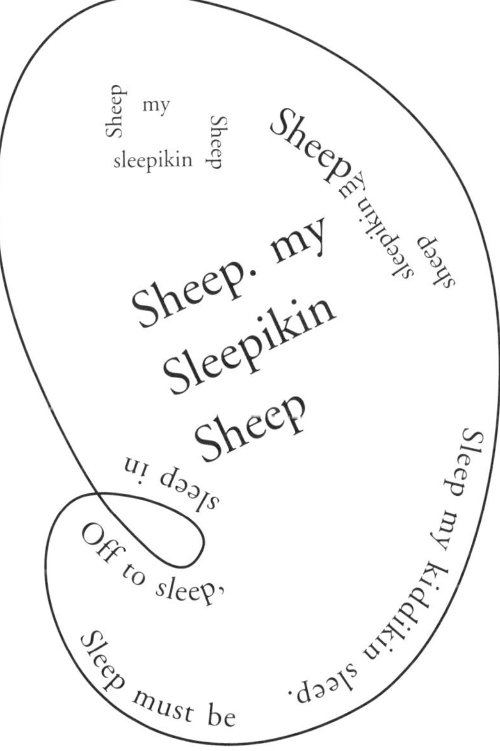
Sheep
my
sleepikin
Sheep
Sheep
my
sleepikin
sheep
Sheep. my
Sleepikin
Sheep
sleep in
Off to sleep,
Sleep must be
Sleep my kiddikin sleep.

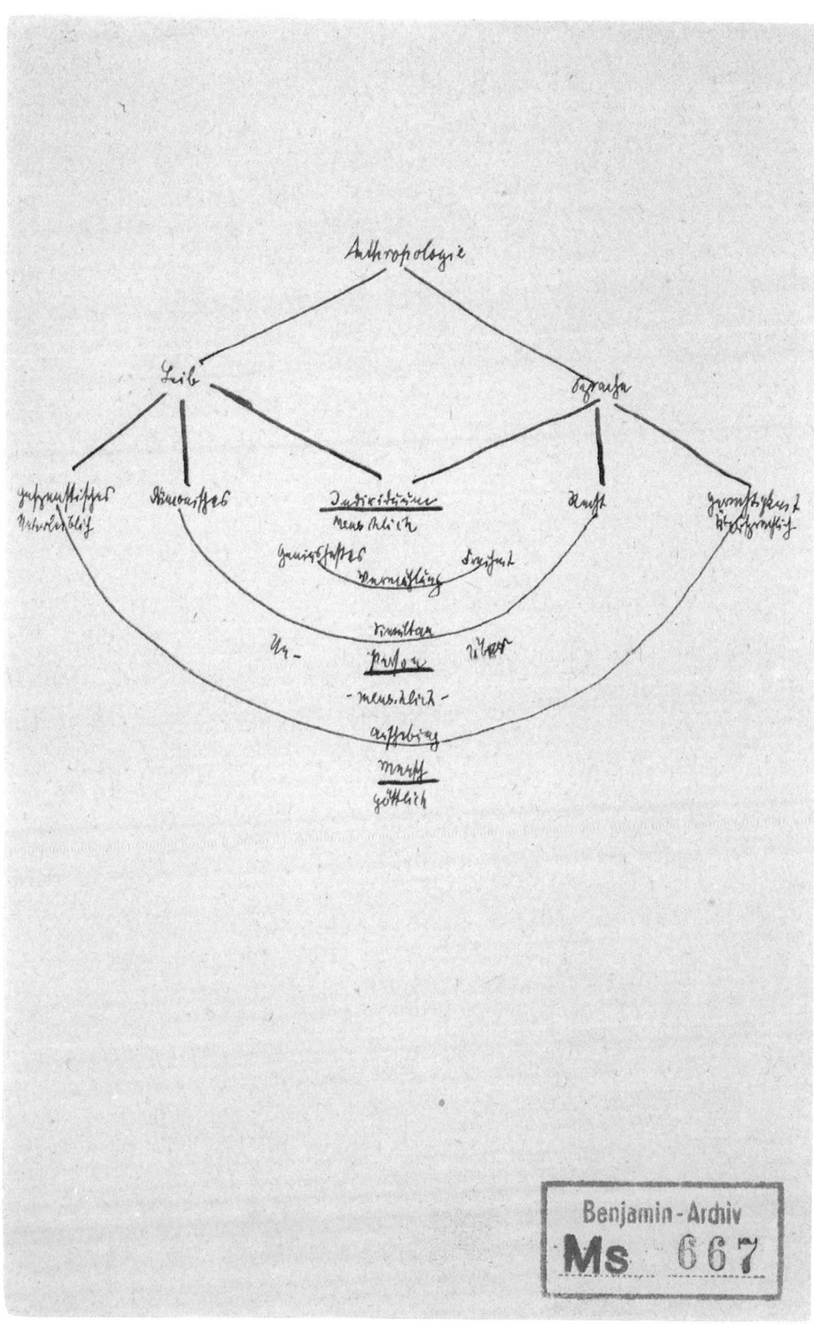
Anthropologie
Leib
Sprache
Individuum
menschlich
Un-
Über
Person
- menschlich -
göttlich
Benjamin-Archiv
Ms 667

Fig. 9.5

Fig. 9.5

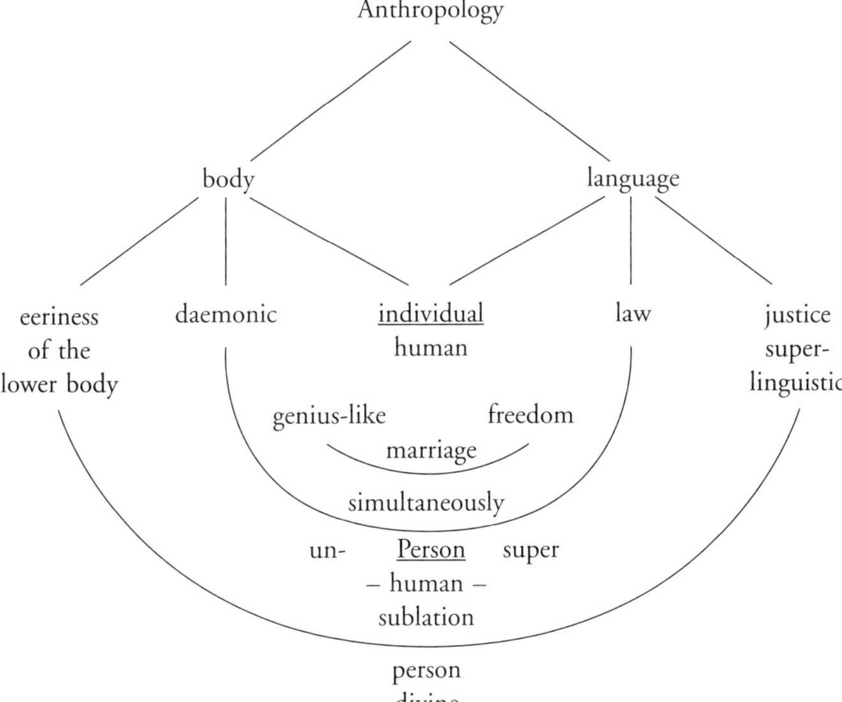
Anthropology
body
language
eeriness
of the
lower body
daemonic
individual
human
law
justice
super-
linguistic
genius-like
freedom
marriage
simultaneously
un-
Person
super
– human –
sublation
person
divine

Dämon

Dialektik

Ich
Lust Witz
Name Reim
Seele

Lust Witz
Name Reim
Seele

Kommentar zu den „Verlassenen"
L III 4 Gewohnheiten ablegen
Reim und Name: Platonische Liebe
B III 12 Tränenwolken
„Den Verlassenen"
Widmung die einzige Form der Selbstentäußerung
B III 3 Reim und platonische Liebe

Platonische Liebe –
aus der Sprache – „je näher man ein Wort ansieht, desto ferner blickt es zurück"
daher Widmung
Erfüllung der Gestalt
im Namen und Geschlecht
Schuld ermisst die Spannung zwischen den beiden
Dank an das Allerberühmteste – den Namen

Prostitution – Naturphänomen
Keine soziologische Analyse
hat ihr Gegenstück in der Sprache: da das Wort an Huren denen in den Mund genommen wird, denen es nicht Name ist

Onanist –
welche Bedeutung die Phantasie ihm hat.
die Phantasie – und die Schuld
Schuld ist das Aussetzen der Phantasie

Sprache : Geist = Eros : Sexus
Erotik: das Prisma der Lust, ihre Entfaltung
Sprache: die Sprengung des Geistes, seine Zerstörung
Dialektik ist das Verhältnis der Sprache zum Eros, zweideutig das des Geistes zur Sexualität

Fig. 9.6

Fig. 9.6

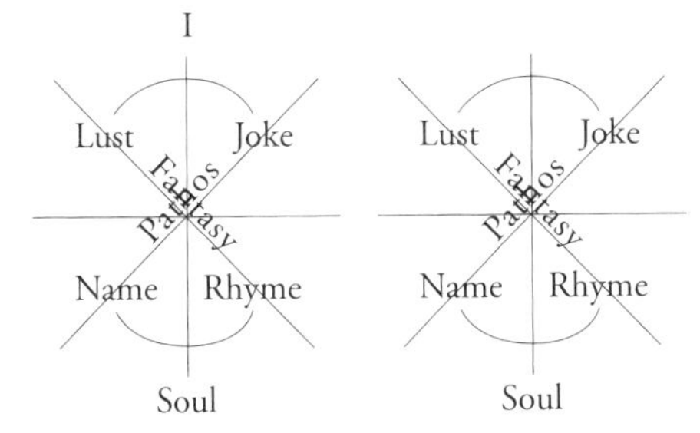

Commentary on the "Forsaken"

CIII 4	Discarding habits
	Rhyme and name: Platonic love
BIII 12	Clouds of tears
	"The Forsaken"
	Dedication the only form of self-renunciation
BIII 3	Rhyme and Platonic love

Platonic love—
From the language—"the more closely you look
at a word, the more distantly it looks back"
hence dedication

Breaking down of the figure
In name and sex
Guilt measures the tension between the two
Giving thanks to the most unmoved—the name

Prostitution—natural phenomenon
Pure sociological analysis
has its counterpart in language: since the word
is also taken into the mouth of those
whose name it is not

Onanist
What significance does fantasy have for him
Fantasy—and guilt
Guilt is the suspension of fantasy

Language: Mind[3] = Eros; Sexus
Eroticism: the prism of lust, its unfolding
Language: the detonation of spirit, its destruction
The relation of language to Eros is dialectical, ambiguous
That of mind is so to sexuality

3 The word is *Geist*, which also means intellect and spirit.

Fig.. 9.7

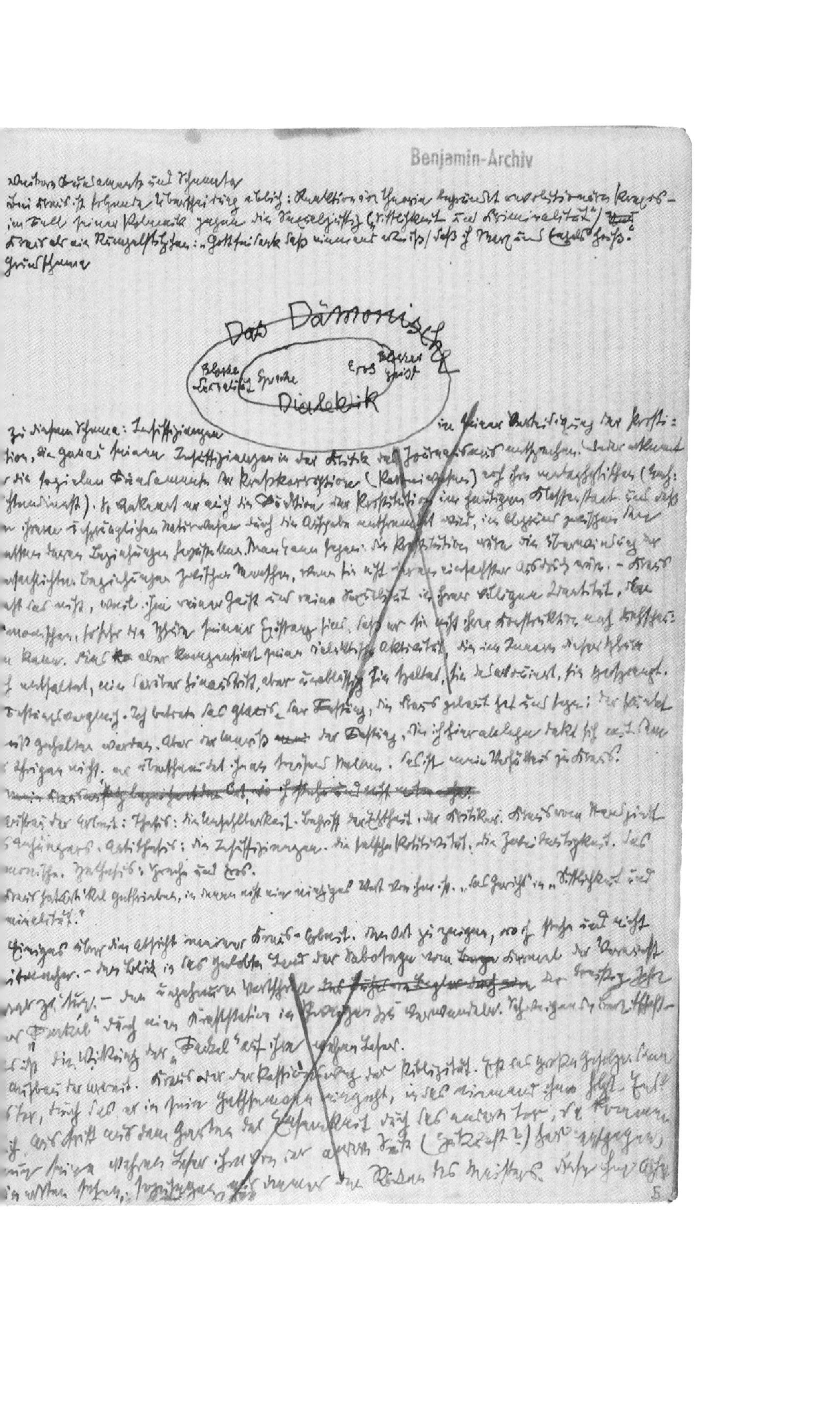

[illegible]

Das Dämonische

Blasse Sexualität

Sprache

Eros

Blasser Geist

Dialektik

[illegible]

Fig. 9.7

Diagrams for Karl Kraus

{"By Night"—this does not mean Mother Night, or a romantic, wistful night, but rather how many pieces attest to the mood between sleep and waking, the zone of falling asleep, whose daemonic powers form the great transformation station, out of which emerges the production of this man.

"I work day and night. So I have a lot of free time. In order to ask a picture in the room how it likes work; in order to ask the clock whether it is tired, and the night how it has slept."

Above all here night is the station where mere mind transforms into mere sexuality, mere sexuality into mere mind and where these two absolutes that are hostile to life find salvation, in exhibiting their inner identity under the light of the day. But in the face of this reality of mere mind, which Kraus recognizes in the guise of his opponent as satanic, by the same token, which he himself wields as a deadly weapon against himself, the pure mind that his followers worship in the master's activity is revealed as a mere chimera. And even if Kraus himself can sometimes cite it too without punishment, because the fire compound of his thousand denials protect him, it still devours the enthusiasts' hair and skin, destroying their enthusiasm and itself.

The different aggregated states of loneliness that Kraus knows: night, the café. On the café as a daemonic form of loneliness see Polgar's *Café Central*. Incidentally love too is also a refuge for his loneliness. Loneliness as a process of self-poisoning, whose anti-toxins lie in the creative attitude.}

"In my half-sleep I managed to attend to a lot of work. A phrase appears, sits on the edge of the bed and speaks to me ..."

{For Kraus the mimetic plays a decisive role in relation to the objects of his polemics. He imitates his opponents, in order to place in the smallest splices of their attitude, which show themselves to him[?] alone, the crowbar of his interpolations. Lessing's famous sentence—If God held out to me all truth in one hand, and in the other the persistent striving for it, I would choose the second; Kraus posed the counterpart to this sentence: if God held out to me in one hand the abolition of all evil and in the other its eternal destruction and asked me to choose, I would choose the second. Physiognomically this attitude of the polemicist stands in the closest connection to the pronounced courteousness with which Kraus thanked[?] his audience. Both this cruelty in his polemics and his courteousness in thanking[,] is actually Chinese. Chinese courteousness is mimetic: to creep inside the other. Mimicry of courteousness and hatred. This too, and not simply his humility, is Chinese.

Supplementary diagram. Glück pointed out to me that Kraus lacks any concept of the true effect of his work. He sees only the community of hysterics, who attract attention to themselves at readings or by writing to *The Torch*. He has absolutely no experience of even a small number of those in whom his work has its actual effect.}

I am missing the conversations with Glück at Schlichter's.

Further groundwork and plans

In Kraus the following intersection is common: reactionary theories are at the basis of revolutionary praxis, such that in the case of his polemic against sexual law ("Morality and Criminality") Kraus appears as Rumpelstiltskin: "God be thanked that no one rumbles / that my name is Marx and Engels."

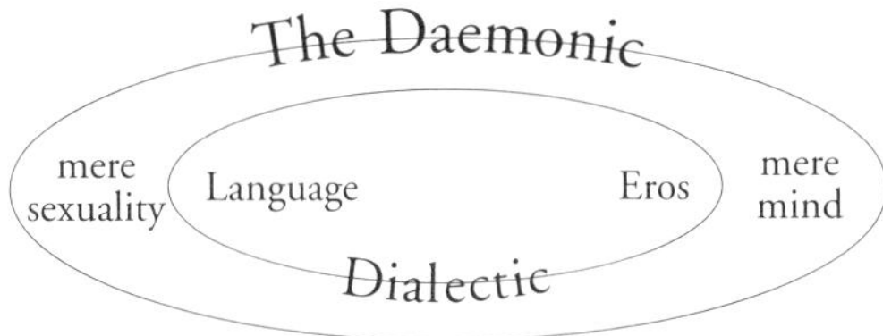

About this plan: Insufficiencies in his defense of prostitution, which correspond exactly to the insufficiencies in his critique of journalism. He neither recognizes the social foundation of the corruption of the press (party system), nor its metaphysical one (intelligence service). Likewise he misapprehends the function of prostitution in the contemporary class state and the fact that it is alienated from its original natural form by the task of producing relations between classes in the abyss. It could be said: prostitution would be the overcoming of objectified relationships between people, if it were not its simplest expression.—Kraus does not perceive this, because for him pure mind and pure sexuality in their full identity, in the daemonic, are so completely the sphere of his existence, that he is unable to penetrate through to their construction. But his dialectical activity compensates for this, unfolding at the core of this sphere, never stepping outside of it, but relentlessly splitting itself, disavowing it, dispersing it.}

Analogy to a fortification. I step onto the slope of the fortification that Kraus has built and say: the spot must be held. But the outline of the fortification, which I set down here[,] does not coincide with your own; it cuts across it in a thousand places. That is my relationship to Kraus.

{My Kraus essay describes the place where I stand and do not participate.}

Construction of the work: thesis: infallibility. Concept of genuineness. The critic. Kraus from the perspective of the follower. Antithesis: insufficiencies. False positivity. Ambiguity. The daemonic. Synthesis: language and Eros.

Kraus wrote articles in which not a single word stemmed from him. "The Court" in "Morality and Criminality."

Something on the aims of my work on Kraus. Show the place where I stand and do not participate.—To cast a look into the Promised Land of Sabotage from the Karmel {mountain} of reason.—{The enormous tirade of the book by Liegler [two indecipherable words] Transform the thirty years of *The Torch* into silence with a power station. Silent readiness—that is the effect of *The Torch* on its genuine readers.}

{Construction of the work. Kraus or the Passion Path of publicity.

First the great retinue. Then the gate through which he goes into his Gethsemane, into which no one follows him. Finally exit from the Garden of Loneliness through the other gate. Then his genuine readers come towards him from the other side (future?), the first of them only see the back of the master, as it were. This, without eyes [?; breaks off]}

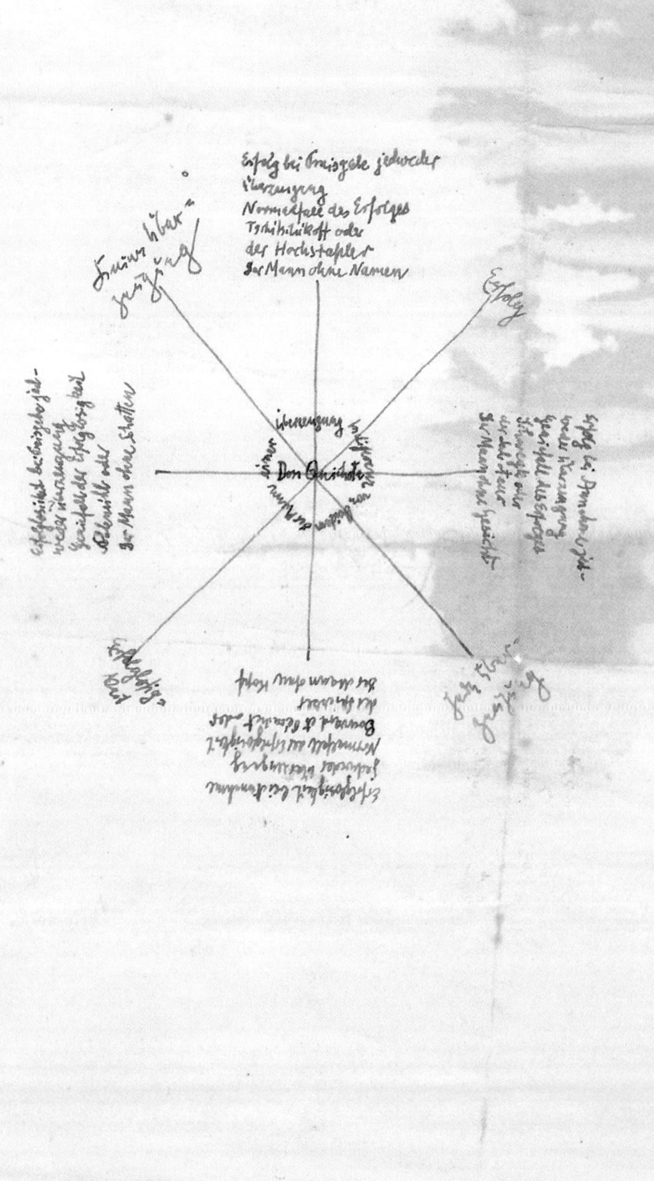
Erfolg bei Preisgabe jedweder Überzeugung
Normalfall des Erfolges
der Hochstapler
der Mann ohne Namen
Erfolg
Don Quichote

Fig. 9.8

Fig. 9.8

The Wind Rose of Success

Success at the cost of any sort of conviction. Normal case of success: Chlestakoff or the confidence trickster.—The confidence trickster allows himself to be led by the situation like a medium. *Mundus vult decipi.* He even chooses his name in order to please the world.

Success by adopting any sort of conviction. Mastermind case of success. Schweik or the lucky beggar.—The lucky beggar is an honorable bloke, who wants to do right by everyone. Lucky Hans[4] trades with anyone who fancies it.

Lack of success by adopting any sort of conviction. Normal case of lack of success: Bouvard and Pécuchet, or the philistine.—The philistine is the martyr of all sorts of convictions from Lao-tze to Rudolf Steiner. But to each he only devotes "just a quarter of an hour."

Lack of success by abandoning any sort of conviction. Mastermind case of lack of success: Chaplin or the unlucky devil.—The unlucky devil takes offence at nothing; he simply trips over his own feet. He is the only angel of peace who is accommodated by the earth.

This wind rose determines all of the good and ill winds that play their games with human existence. Nothing remains but to determine its center, the crossing-point of the axes, the place of complete indifference for success and failure. At this center Don Quixote finds his home, *the man of just one conviction*, whose story teaches that in this best or worst of all possible worlds,—and this is simply not thinkable—the conviction that what is in the books of chivalry is true makes a thrashed fool blessed, even if it is his only one.

GS IV.1, pp. 405f. See also *SW* 2:2 p. 590

[4] A fairytale by the Brothers Grimm.

10

Rag Picking

The Arcades Project

> "Here we have a man whose job it is to gather the day's refuse in the capital. Everything that the big city has thrown away, everything it has lost, everything it has scorned, everything it has crushed underfoot he catalogues and collects. He collates the annals of intemperance, the capharnaum of waste. He sorts things out and selects judiciously: he collects like a miser guarding a treasure, refuse which will assume the shape of useful or gratifying objects between the jaws of the goddess of Industry." This description is one extended metaphor for the poetic method, as Baudelaire practised it. Ragpicker and poet: both are concerned with refuse
>
> *SW* 4, p. 48

> Method of this project: literary montage. I needn't say anything. Merely show. I shall purloin no valuables, appropriate no ingenious formulations. But the rags, the refuse—these I will not inventory but allow, in the only way possible, to come into their own: by making use of them.
>
> *AP*, p. 460

Prompted by Louis Aragon's description of the Passage de l'Opéra in *Paris Peasant*, Benjamin and his friend Franz Hessel began preliminary work for a magazine article on the arcades. It was never finished. From the middle of 1927, Benjamin took notes for a piece on the Paris arcades in a small black notebook with a leather cover (fig. 10.1). At the beginning, Benjamin had intended only to write an essay on these themes, but the plan expanded as he reconceptualized the project subsequently. In May 1935 he noted in a letter to Alfred Cohn that, after an interruption of several years, he was returning to the project "known as the *Paris Arcades*, which since its beginnings seven or eight years ago has never been so keenly pursued as now and which has been through a large-scale and, I believe, beneficial process of fusing, in which the whole mass of thoughts, which were originally organized in an immediate metaphysical fashion, has been transferred into a state of aggregation more befitting of its contemporary existence. There now exists a comprehensive exposé of this work [see fig. 10.2], which allows traits of the actual book to be perceived. Whether this will ever get written is, of course, more doubtful than ever before. The only thing that is fairly certain is that to a much greater degree than I might have suspected earlier, it will become a counterpart to the baroque book. The old title *Paris Arcades* is discarded. The book is now called: *Paris, The Capital of the Nineteenth Century*" (*GB* V, p. 102). Just as the tragic drama book unrolled the seventeenth century from Germany, so too this new book was to reel the nineteenth century out of Paris. By interpreting concrete historical phenomena—architecture, fashion, advertising, prostitution or photography—Benjamin hoped to develop a historico-philosophical construction of the century from which he stemmed.

What the planned book tenders, for the most part, is a collation of quotations. The large manuscript of notes and materials for *The Arcades Project*, a collection of excerpts as well as Benjamin's fragmentary theoretical considerations, is crammed with findings drawn together from dispersed, frequently arcane sources in the Bibliothèque Nationale in Paris. From between the covers of books he attempted recovery: the pages of *The Arcades Project* provide a space for collection. Benjamin excerpted, copied down in his own manuscript, and compiled snatchings taken from a mass of books, essays, and pamphlets—the bibliography comprises 850 titles. Sheet after sheet (426 in total) was filled up with quarried citations, intermingled with his own reflections, programmatic notes, fragments that make comments and interpret.

In one of the fragments Charles Baudelaire's description of the *chiffonier* is quoted: " 'Voici un homme chargé de ramasser les débris d'une journée de la capitale. Tout ce que la grande cité a rejeté, tout ce qu'elle a perdu, tout ce qu'elle a dédaigné, *tout ce qu'elle a brisé, il le catalogue, il le collectionne*. Il compulse les archives de la débauche, le capharnaüm des rebuts. Il fait un triage, un choix intelligent; il ramasse, comme un avare un trésor, les ordures qui, remâchées par la divinité de l'Industrie, deviendront des objets d'utilité ou de jouissance' (Du vin et du haschish *Oeuvres I*, pp. 249–50). As may be gathered from this prose description of 1851, Baudelaire recognizes himself in the figure of the ragman" (*AP*, pp. 349–50). And Benjamin also recognized himself in the figure of the ragman or ragpicker. Benjamin underlined the words "everything it has crushed underfoot he catalogues and collects" in the French quotation (fig. 10.4). The archival work of the ragpicker is related to his own: *The Arcades Project* wishes to pick up the refuse of history. Like a poor and burdened man cleverly picking through the rubbish of the previous day, the materialist historian selects from amongst all that is disregarded and from the residues of history. At the library he is unconcerned with what has been accredited as precious and valuable, but rather is drawn towards historical refuse. Waste materials are to enter into significant connections and fragments are used to gain a new perspective on history. Benjamin conceived his work on the nineteenth century as an appropriation of rags.

The handwritten manuscript of notes and citations was probably begun in the autumn or winter of 1928. At the beginning of 1929 Benjamin discontinued the work, and only resumed it at the beginning of 1934. He wrote to Gretel Karplus from his Paris exile: "Now I have a small and bizarre request regarding the arcades papers. Since the first setting-up of the numerous sheets on which the notes are to reside, I have always used one and the same type of paper, namely a normal letter pad of white MK [Max Krause] paper. Now my supplies of this are exhausted and I would very much like to preserve the external uniformity of this bulky and elaborate manuscript. Would it be possible for you to arrange for one of those pads to be sent to me?" (*GB* IV, p. 330). The sheets of paper that make up the manuscript do indeed exhibit a thoroughly consistent uniformity. Benjamin folded them in the middle, making of them double sheets, and in each case he wrote on the first and third side in the left-hand column. The principle of construction insists that the right-hand column—flagged by Benjamin with a crease—remains devoid of writing (except when epigraphs were placed there). Each side with writing on it bears an alphanumeric classmark in the top left corner (e.g. J68, see fig. 10.4).

In preparing the earlier book on *The Origin of German Tragic Drama* Benjamin meticulously gathered copious quotations in a similar fashion: "I have at my disposal about six hundred quotations and, in addition, they are so well organized that you can get an overview at a glance" (*Correspondence*, p. 236). This time, though, an assemblage of numerous excerpts, accumulated to various ends, needed to be arranged in such a way that everything was easily locatable. Benjamin set up files or convolutes that pre-sorted the material along thematic lines. Each one was allocated a letter of the alphabet, which reappears in the classmark. The first letter of the classmark indicates the respective convolute—J, for example (in the classmark J68) indicates the one on Baudelaire. In the end there were over thirty files of material that arose via this method. Benjamin put together an overview (figs 10.5 and 10.6) that lists each one and thus, simultaneously, outlines a catalog of themes for the work in process. It assigns capital and lower-case letters of the alphabet—ordered in two columns—to the convolutes' titles. Empty spaces alongside some of the small letters are noticeable: these were clearly placeholders for possible further convolutes.

The Arcades Project never made it as far as composition. It fell through, disintegrating in the collector's hands. The more he collected, the further away shifted any possibility of finding some presentational form for the material. Around 1937 the focal point of the work concentrated on Baudelaire. A book about the poet was planned as a "miniature model" of the arcades study. To this end, Benjamin read through the arcades manuscripts and put colored marks on those notes that struck him as relevant for the Baudelaire project. Using colored pencils, he developed a code, a system of symbols, which were then associated with themes that were to be dealt with in his study of Baudelaire. One example of this is the solid green oval with a black cross on page J68, which indicates the theme of *Allegory*. This aspect was to be dealt with in the first part of the planned work. Benjamin never wrote it up—the book on Baudelaire remained a fragment too.

Figures

10.1 First notes for *Paris Arcades* (1927)—Manuscript in the black leather notebook, shown here page 16r. Compare *AP*, pp. 827–9.

10.2 Exposé of *Paris, The Capital of the Nineteenth Century* (1935)—Typescript (carbon copy), twenty-one sides; shown here, page 1. Compare *AP*, p. 3.

10.3 Gisèle Freund, "Walter Benjamin in the Bibliothèque Nationale" (Photographer's dating on the reverse, 1939)—Photograph, Theodor W. Adorno Archive, Frankfurt am Main.

10.4 Notes and materials for *The Arcades Project* (1928–1940)—426 double pages; shown here, J68. Compare *AP*, pp. 349–50.

10.5 and 10.6 Overview of *The Arcades Project* convolutes—Manuscript, two sides. Compare *AP*, p. 29.

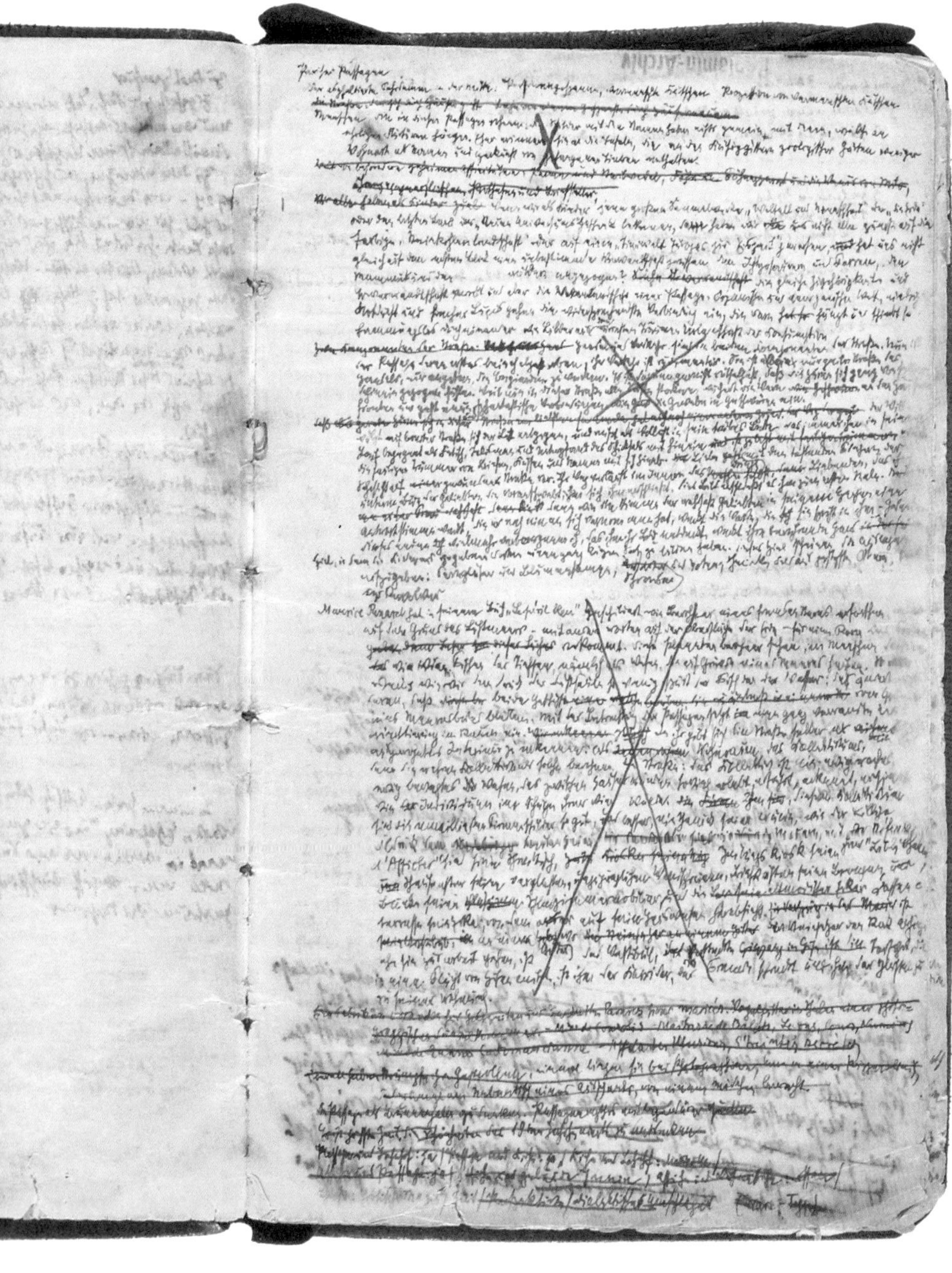

Fig. 10.1

Fig. 10.1

Paris Arcades

The asphalt roadway in the middle: teams of harnessed humans, human carriages. Procession of human carriages.

The street that runs through houses. Track of a ghost through the walls of houses.

People who inhabit these arcades: the signboards with the names have nothing in common with those that hang beside respectable entryways. Rather, they recall the plaques on the railings of cages at the zoo, put there to indicate not so much the dwelling place as the name and origin of the captive animals.

World of particular secret affinities: palm tree and feather duster, hairdryer and Venus de Milo, champagne bottles, prostheses, and letter-writing manuals, <broken off>

When, as children, we were made a present of those great encyclopedic works—*World and Mankind* or *The Earth* or the latest volume of the *New Universe*—wasn't it into the multicolored "Carboniferous Landscape" or "European Animal Kingdom of the Ice Age" that we plunged first of all, and weren't we, as though at first sight, drawn by an indeterminate affinity between the ichthyosaurs and bisons, the mammoths and the woodlands? Yet this same strange rapport and primordial relatedness is revealed in the landscape of an arcade. Organic world and inorganic world, abject poverty and insolent luxury enter into the most contradictory communication; the commodity intermingles and interbreeds as promiscuously as images in the most tangled of dreams. Primordial landscape of consumption.

Trade and traffic are the two components of the street. Now, in the arcade the first of these has all but died out: the traffic there is rudimentary. The arcade is a street of lascivious commerce only; it is wholly adapted to arousing desires. Thus, there is no mystery in the fact that whores feel spontaneously drawn there. Because in this street all the juices slow to a standstill, the commodity proliferates along the house fronts and enters into new and fantastic combinations, like the tissue in tumors.

The will turns down the wide street into the teeth of pleasure and, as lust, drags with it into its gloomy bed whatever it finds in the way of fetish, talisman, and gage of fate across its path, drags with it the rotting debris of letters, kisses, and names. Love presses forward with the inquisitive fingers of desire down the winding street. Its way leads through the interior of the lover, which opens up to him in the image of the beloved who passes lightly before him. This image opens up his interior to him for the first time. For, as the voice of the truly beloved awakens in his heart an answering voice which he has never before heard in himself, the words which she speaks awaken in him thoughts of this new, much more hidden ego that reveals to him her image, while the touch of her hand awakens <broken off>

Game in which children have to form a brief sentence out of given words. This game is seemingly played by the goods on display: binoculars and flower seeds, screws and musical scores, makeup and stuffed vipers, fur coats and revolvers.

Maurice Renard, in his book *Le Péril bleu*, has told how inhabitants of a distant planet come to study the flora and fauna indigenous to the lower depths of the atmosphere—in other words, to the surface of the earth. These interplanetary travelers see in human beings the equivalent of tiny deep-sea fish—that is to say, beings who live at the bottom of a sea. We no more feel the pressure of the atmosphere than fish feel that of the water; this in no way alters the fact that both sets of creatures reside on an ocean floor. With the study of the arcades, a closely related reorientation in space is opened up. The street itself is thereby manifest as <x> well-worn interior: as living space of the collective, for true collectives as such inhabit the street. The collective is an eternally awake, eternally agitated being that—in the space between the building fronts—lives, experiences, understands, invents as much as individuals do within the privacy of their own four walls. For it, for this collective, enameled shop signs are a wall decoration as good as, if not better than, the inexpensive oleograph above the hearth. Walls with their "Post No Bills" are its writing desk, newspaper stands its libraries, display windows its glazed inaccessible armoires, mailboxes its bronzes, benches its bedroom furniture, and the café terrace is the balcony from which it looks down on its household. As with a railing where pavers hang their coats before going to work, the vestibule is the hidden gateway which gives onto a row of courtyards—is, for it, the corridor that daunts the strangers and serves as the key to its dwelling.

A factory of 5,000 workers for weddings and banquets. Attire for bride and groom. Birdseed in the fixative pans of a photographer's darkroom.—Mme. de Consolis, Ballet Mistress. Lessons, Classes, Routines.—Mme.de Zahna, Fortuneteller. Possession by spirits, Illusions, Secret Embraces.

Everywhere stockings play a starring role. They are found in the photographer's studio, then in a doll hospital, and, one day, on the side table of a tavern, watched over by a girl.

The arcade may be conceived as mineral spa <*Brunnenhalle*>. Arcade myth, with legendary source.

It is high time the beauties of the nineteenth century were discovered.

Arcade and railroad station: yes / Arcade and church: yes / Church and railroad station: Marseilles /

Poster and arcade: yes / Poster and building: no / Poster and <x>: open /

Conclusion: erotic magic / Time / Perspective / Dialetical reversal (commodity—type).

I. Fourier oder die Passagen.

"De ces palais les colonnes magiques
A l'amateur montrent de toutes parts
Dans les objets qu'étalent leurs portiques
Que l'industrie est rivale des arts."

Nouveaux tableaux de Paris. Paris 1828, p.27

Die Mehrzahl der pariser Passagen entsteht in den anderthalb Jahrzehnten nach 1822. Die erste Bedingung ihres Aufkommens ist die Hochkonjunktur des Textilhandels. Die magasins de nouveauté, die ersten Etablissements, die grössere Warenlager im Hause unterhalten, beginnen sich zu zeigen. Sie sind die Vorläufer der Warenhäuser. Es war die Zeit, von der Balzac schrieb: "Le grand poème de l'étalage chante ses strophes de couleur depuis la Madeleine jusqu'à la porte Saint-Dénis". Die Passagen sind ein Zentrum des Handels in Luxuswaren. In ihrer Ausstattung tritt die Kunst in den Dienst des Kaufmanns. Die Zeitgenossen werden nicht müde, sie zu bewundern. Noch lange bleiben sie ein Anziehungspunkt für die Fremden. Ein "Illustrierter Pariser Führer" sagt: "Diese Passagen, eine neuere Erfindung des industriellen Luxus, sind glasgedeckte, marmorgetäfelte Gänge durch ganze XXXX Häusermassen, deren Besitzer sich zu solchen Spekulationen vereinigt haben. Zu beiden Seiten dieser Gänge, die ihr Licht von oben erhalten, laufen die elegantesten Warenläden hin, so dass eine solche Passage eine Stadt, ja eine Welt im Kleinen ist." Die Passagen sind der Schauplatz der ersten Gasbeleuchtung.

Fig. 10.2

Fig. 10.2

I. Fourier, or the Arcades

> The magic columns of these palaces
> Show to the amateur on all sides,
> In the objects their porticos display,
> That industry is the rival of the arts.

Nouveaux Tableaux de Paris (Paris, 1828), vol. 1, p. 27

Most of the Paris arcades come into being in the decade and a half after 1822. The first condition for their emergence is the boom in the textile trade. *Magasins de nouveautés*, the first establishments to keep large stocks of merchandise on the premises, make their appearance. They are the forerunners of department stores. This was the period of which Balzac wrote: "The great poem of display chants its stanzas of color from the Church of the Madeleine to the Porte Saint-Denis." The arcades are a center of commerce in luxury items. In fitting them out, art enters the service of the merchant. Contemporaries never tire of admiring them, and for a long time they remain a drawing point for foreigners. An *Illustrated Guide to Paris* says: "These arcades, a recent invention of industrial luxury, are glass-roofed, marble-paneled corridors extending through whole blocks of buildings, whose owners have joined together for such enterprises. Lining both sides of these corridors, which get their light from above, are the most elegant shops, so that the *passage* is a city, a world in miniature." The arcades are the scene of the first gas lighting.

Fig. 10.3

J68

„La destruction" über den démon: „Je… le sens qui brûle mon poumon / Et l'emplit d'un désir éternel et coupable." [illegible] Vgl. [illegible] fleurs invisible [illegible] Bénédiction.

Von allen baudelaireschen Gedichten enthüllt die „destruction" [illegible] allegorischen Intention. Der appareil sanglant, [illegible] ist der Hof der Allegorie: [illegible]

Zum vin des chiffonnier ist „dans ce cabriolet" von Sainte-Beuve (Poésies de Joseph Delorme Paris 1863 II p 193) zu vergleichen: et Jansels(?)

„Dans ce cabriolet de place j'examine
L'homme qui me conduit, qui n'est plus que machine,
Hideux, à barbe épaisse, à longs cheveux collés:
Vice et vin et sommeil chargent ses yeux soûlés.
Comment l'homme peut-il ainsi tomber? pensais-je,
Et je me reculais à l'autre coin du siège." [illegible] Baudelaire nennt dieses Gedicht in seinem Brief vom 15 Janvier 1866 an Sainte-Beuve.

Der chiffonnier ist die [illegible] Figur menschlichen Elends. [illegible] „Voici un homme chargé de ramasser les débris d'une journée de la capitale. Tout ce que la grande cité a rejeté, tout ce qu'elle a perdu, tout ce qu'elle a dédaigné, tout ce qu'elle a brisé, il le catalogue, il le collectionne. Il compulse les archives de la débauche, le capharnaüm des rebuts. Il fait un triage, un choix intelligent; il ramasse comme un avare un trésor, les ordures qui, remâchées par la divinité de l'industrie deviendront des objets d'utilité ou de jouissance." (Du vin et du haschisch Oeuvres I 249/50) Baudelaire [illegible] 1851 [illegible] „On voit un chiffonnier qui vient, hochant la tête / Buttant, et se cognant aux murs comme un poète, / Et sans prendre souci des mouchards, ses sujets, / Épanche tout son coeur en glorieux projets."

143

Fig. 10.4

Fig. 10.4 (previous page)

"La Destruction" on the demon: "he fills my burning lungs / with sinful cravings never satisfied." The lung as the seat of desire is the boldest intimation of desire's unrealizability that can be imagined. Compare the invisible stream in "Bénédiction." [J68,1]

Of all the Baudelairean poems, "La Destruction" comprises the most relentless elaboration of the allegorical intention. The "bloody retinue," which the poet is forced by the demon to contemplate, is the court of allegory—the scattered apparatus by dint of which allegory has so disfigured and so unsettled the world of things that only the fragments of that world are left to it now, as object of its brooding. The poem breaks off abruptly; it itself gives the impression—doubly surprising in a sonnet—of something fragmentary. [J68,2]

Compare "Le Vin des chiffonniers" with "Dans ce Cabriolet," by Sainte-Beuve (<*Les Consolations*,> vol. 2 [Paris, 1863], p. 193):

> Seated in this cabriolet, I examine the man
> Who drives me, the man who's little more than machine,
> Hideous with his thick beard, his long matted hair:
> Vice and wine and sleep weigh down his sottish eyes.
> How far then, I thought, can humanity sink?
> And I draw back to the other corner of the seat.

The poet goes on to ask himself whether his own soul is not just as unkempt as the soul of the coachman. Baudelaire mentions this poem in his letter of January 15, 1866, to Sainte-Beuve. [J68,3]

The ragpicker is the most provocative figure of human misery. "Ragtag" *Lump-enproletarier* in a double sense: clothed in rags and occupied with rags. "Here we have a man whose job it is to pick up the day's rubbish in the capital. He collects and catalogs everything that the great city has cast off, everything it has lost, and discarded, and broken. He goes through the archives of debauchery, and the jumbled array of refuse. He makes a selection, an intelligent choice; like a miser hoarding treasure, he collects the garbage that will become objects of utility or pleasure when refurbished by Industrial magic" ("Du Vin et du haschisch," *Oeuvres*, vol. 1, pp. 249–50). As may be gathered from this prose description of 1851, Baudelaire recognizes himself in the figure of the ragman. The poem presents a further affinity with the poet, immediately noted as such: "a ragpicker stumbles past, wagging his head / and bumping into walls with a poet's grace, / pouring out his heartfelt schemes to one / and all, including spies of the police." [J68,4]

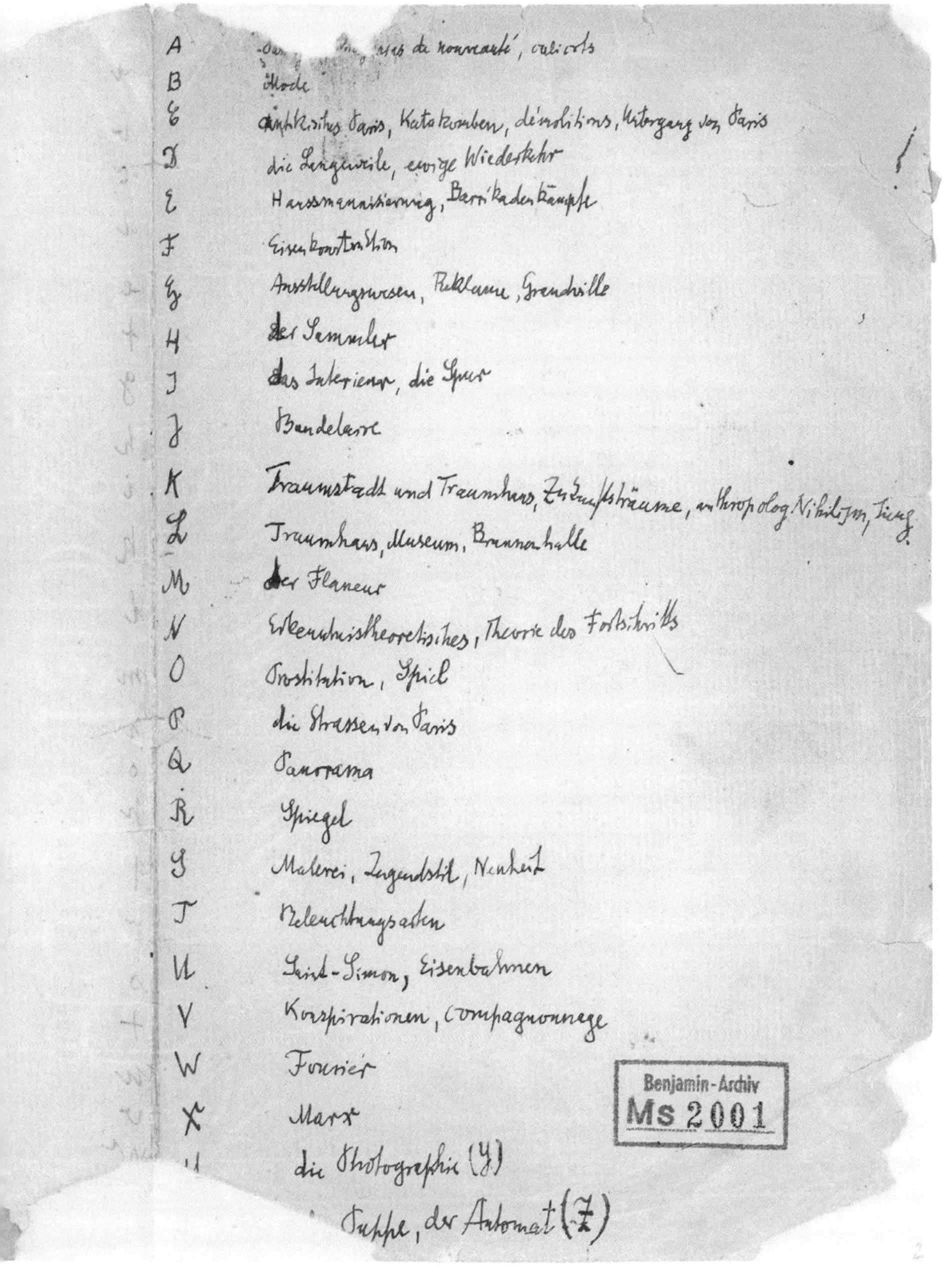

A Passagen, magasins de nouveauté, calicots
B Mode
C antikisches Paris, Katakomben, démolitions, Untergang von Paris
D die Langeweile, ewige Wiederkehr
E Haussmannisierung, Barrikadenkämpfe
F Eisenkonstruktion
G Ausstellungswesen, Reklame, Grandville
H der Sammler
I das Interieur, die Spur
J Baudelaire
K Traumstadt und Traumhaus, Zukunftsträume, anthropolog. Nihilismus, Jung
L Traumhaus, Museum, Brunnenhalle
M der Flaneur
N Erkenntnistheoretisches, Theorie des Fortschritts
O Prostitution, Spiel
P die Strassen von Paris
Q Panorama
R Spiegel
S Malerei, Jugendstil, Neuheit
T Beleuchtungsarten
U Saint-Simon, Eisenbahnen
V Konspirationen, compagnonnage
W Fourier
X Marx
die Photographie (Y)
Puppe, der Automat (Z)

Fig. 10.5

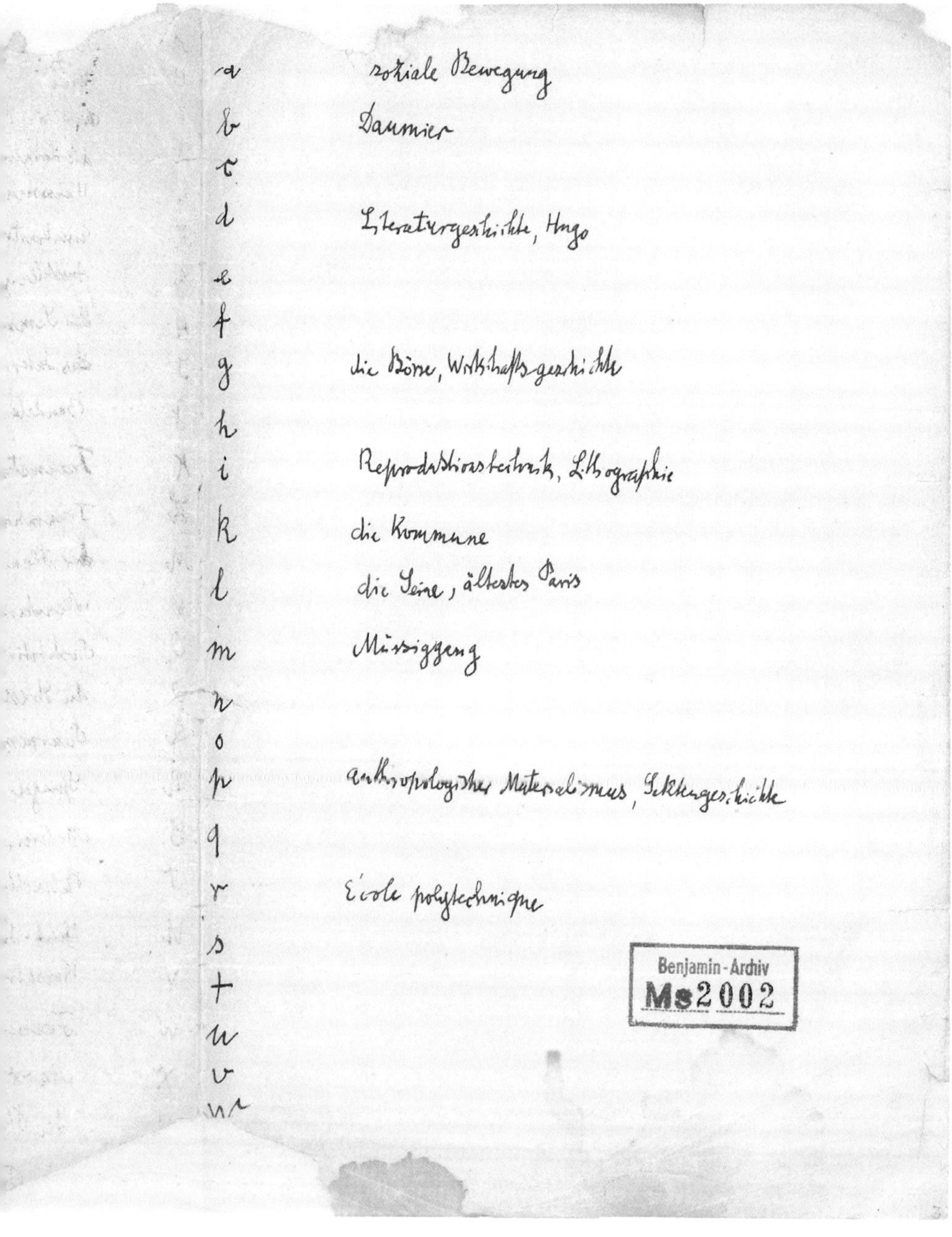

a soziale Bewegung
b Daumier
c
d Literaturgeschichte, Hugo
e
f
g die Börse, Wirtschaftsgeschichte
h
i Reproduktionstechnik, Lithographie
k die Kommune
l die Seine, ältestes Paris
m Müssiggang
n
o
p anthropologischer Materialismus, Sektengeschichte
q
r École polytechnique
s
t
u
v
w

Fig. 10.6

Fig. 10.5

Overview

A Arcades, *Magasins de Nouveautés*, Sales Clerks
B Fashion
C Ancient Paris, Catacombs, Demolitions, Decline of Paris
D Boredom, Eternal Return
E Haussmannization, Barricade Fighting
F Iron Construction
G Exhibitions, Advertising, Grandville
H The Collector
I The Interior, The Trace
J Baudelaire
K Dream City and Dream House, Dreams of the Future, Anthropological Nihilism, Jung
L Dream House, Museum, Spa
M The Flâneur
N On the Theory of Knowledge, Theory of Progress
O Prostitution, Gambling
P The Streets of Paris
Q Panorama
R Mirrors
S Painting, Jugendstil, Novelty
T Modes of Lighting
U Saint-Simon, Railroads
V Conspiracies, *Compagnonnage*
W Fourier
X Marx
Y Photography
Z The Doll, The Automaton

Fig. 10.6

a Social Movement
b Daumier
c …
d Literary History, Hugo
e …
f …
g The Stock Exchange, Economic History
h …
i Reproduction Technology, Lithography
k The Commune
l The Seine, The Oldest Paris
m Idleness
n …
o …
p Anthropological Materialism, History of Sects
q …
r Ecole Polytechnique
s …
t …
u …
v …
w …

11

Past Turned Space

Arcades and Interiors

Here, the Paris arcades are examined as though they were properties in the hand of a collector.

AP, p. 205

The collector is the true resident of the interior.

AP, p. 9

"I needn't *say* anything. Merely show" (*AP*, p. 860)—that could be a photographic slogan. It could even be Germaine Krull's (1897–1985). Benjamin became acquainted with her in 1926 or 1927. A close friendship appears to have developed only in 1937 (in April of that year Benjamin requested that Friedrich Pollock convey his address to the photographer). Preserved in the archive are a number of letters from Krull to Benjamin—his ones to her are, with one sole exception, lost. These letters date from October 1937 to October 1938 and, for the most part, they report on her travails with *Chien-fou*, a novel with autobiographical elements, for which Krull hoped to find a publisher in Paris.

Germaine Krull came to public attention in 1928 following the publication in Paris of her album *Métal*, a series of industrial photos, of factories, cranes, bridge-constructions and iron girders (belonging to the Eiffel Tower). Benjamin mentions her for the first time in 1930 in a short report on *Surrealist Magazines* (*GS* IV.1, pp. 595–6). He counted Krull amongst the photographic avant-garde. One paragraph in *Little History of Photography* names her in the same breath as August Sander and Karl Blossfeldt. Sander, Krull, and Blossfeldt represent a photography grounded in the "physiognomic, political, and scientific interest" (*SW* 2:2, p. 526) in reality. When *Little History of Photography* appeared in the *Literary World* in 1931 reproductions of photographs accompanied the article, amongst them two by Krull (fig. 11.14). Neither of these photographs, of which Benjamin presumably had copies, have been preserved in the archive. In total the archive holds thirteen images of Paris by Germaine Krull. Nine of them, taken in 1928, are photographs of arcades, dressed shop windows or shop fronts. There are four others (figs 11.10 to 11.13), which present unadorned excerpts of the material reality of the city: a building façade and street, a dilapidated rear courtyard, damaged walls, oppressive corners—and lost within all of this some lone individuals. The images sample the details of a petrified world. They record urban grayness, austerity, and ordinary existence and capture the melancholy traces of decay and deterioration.

Peeling courtyards, worn out façades, displays of wigs or corsets—Eugène Atget (1857–1927) had already documented the same subjects as Krull. These are motifs that the Surrealists rediscovered in the twenties. In 1926 some of Atget's photographs were published in *Le Révolution Surréaliste*. Just a couple of years later Krull's shop-window dummies appeared in the Surrealist magazine *Variétés*. A number of them were placed right next to similar ones by Atget. Her display windows present alienated images of fashion, dreamlike scenes: brashly made-up dolls, amusingly and unsettlingly identical at one and the same time, carcasses, loose heads, severed body parts.

Krull's Parisian arcades are imaged as an extinct architecture—a past building form, antiquated and passé. The photographer attempts to find new aspects in the vanishing and the old-fashioned, in everything that conjures up nostalgia. Her arcades, in which people (or their strolling shadows) are only seldom found, turn into spaces crammed with signs, or even enigmatically confusing forests of symbols. Unusual perspectives are deployed, most strikingly perhaps in the photograph of the Imprimerie de l'Horloge (fig. 11.4), which is taken at an extreme angle and is further defamiliarized by the decisions reached in cropping the image. The clock appears dominant in this image. And clocks appear several times in these photographs. They show the hour that struck for the arcades: images of time stilled.

Benjamin regarded arcades and private interiors as corresponding spatial formations. Along with the arcades photos, he also held on to a few photos of a bourgeois interior. Three are present in the bequest (figs 11.15 to 11.17); they were taken by his friend Sasha Stone (Aleksander Serge Steinsapir, 1895–1940), who also designed the dust jacket for *One-Way Street*. In one passage in that book—"Manorially Furnished Ten-Room Apartment"—Benjamin describes just such an interior. The three photographs that have been preserved show, from contrasting perspectives, and, in one case, exposed in a stark back light, the same opulently cluttered and cushioned space, in which there is barely room between all the amassed things for its inhabitant: "knickknacks, knickknacks everywhere" (*SW* 2:1, p. 141).

Figures

11.1 Germaine Krull, Entrance to the Passage du Ponceau—Photograph.

11.2 Germaine Krull, Passage du Ponceau—Photograph.

11.3 Germaine Krull, Passage du Ponceau—Photograph.

11.4 Germaine Krull, Passage des Deux-Soeurs—Photograph.

11.5 Germaine Krull, Passage—Photograph.

11.6 Germaine Krull, Passage du Caire—Photograph.

11.7 Germaine Krull, Shop-window dummies—Photograph.

11.8 Germaine Krull, Display with corsets—Photograph.

11.9 Germaine Krull, Shop front in an arcade—Photograph.

11.10 Germaine Krull, Rear courtyard in Paris—Photograph.

11.11 Germaine Krull, Corner between houses—Photograph.

11.12 Germaine Krull, Building façades in Paris—Photograph.

11.13 Germaine Krull, Entrance to an arcade—Photograph.

11.14 *Little History of Photography*. In *Literary World*, September 18 and 25 and October 2, 1931—shown here: extract from the installment in the issue published on September 25, 1931 (No. 39), page 3. Compare *SW* 2:2, pp. 514–15.

11.15 to 11.17 Sasha Stone, Bourgeois interior—Photographs.

MACHINES
ECRIRE
Circulaires
BANDAGES
ORTHOPEDIE
PLACEMENT

Fig. 11.1

LIBRAIRIE
en SOLDE
G. TAFI
CORSETS CEINTURES
ORTHOPEDIE
MACHINES
A ECRIRE
VETEMENTS
POUR
HOMMES

Fig. 11.2

Fig. 11.3

Fig. 11.4

Fig. 11.5

Fig. 11.6

Fig. 11.7

Grossesse
Ceintures
Corsets
en Tissu Elastique
opération
CORR
DEVIA

Fig. 11.8

ETIQUET
IMPRIMÉS
"LA LITHORELIEF"
ETIQUETTES d'ETALAGES
97
SOLDES
RABAIS
Voyez — Prix
SOLDES
RÉCLAME
Défense
FUMER
Meubles
CASIOL
SPORA

Fig. 11.9

Fig. 11.10

Fig. 11.11

Fig. 11.12

Fig. 11.13

KLEINE GESCHICHTE DER PHOTOGRAPHIE

Von Walter Benjamin (Fortsetzung)

Man muß im übrigen, um sich die gewaltige Wirkung der Daguerreotypie im Zeitalter ihrer Entdeckung ganz gegenwärtig zu machen, bedenken, daß die Pleinairmalerei damals den vorgeschrittensten unter den Malern ganz neue Perspektiven zu entdecken begonnen hatte. Im Bewußtsein, daß gerade in dieser Sache die Photographie von der Malerei die Staffette zu übernehmen habe, heißt es denn auch bei Arago im historischen Rückblick auf die frühen Versuche Giovanni Battista Portas ausdrücklich: „Was die Wirkung betrifft, welche von der unvollkommenen Durchsichtigkeit unserer Atmosphäre abhängt (und welche man durch den uneigentlichen Ausdruck ‚Luftperspektive' charakterisiert hat), so hoffen selbst die geübten Maler nicht, daß die camera obscura" — will sagen das Kopieren der in ihr erscheinenden Bilder — „ihnen dazu behilflich sein könnte, dieselben mit Genauigkeit hervorzubringen." Im Augenblick, da es Daguerre geglückt war, die Bilder der camera obscura zu fixieren, waren die Maler an diesem Punkte vom Techniker verabschiedet worden. Das eigentliche Opfer der Photographie aber wurde nicht die Landschaftsmalerei, sondern die Porträtminiatur. Die Dinge entwickelten sich so schnell, daß schon um 1840 die meisten unter den zahllosen Miniaturmalern Berufsphotographen wurden, zunächst nur nebenher, bald aber ausschließlich. Dabei kamen ihnen die Erfahrungen ihrer ursprünglichen Brotarbeit zustatten und nicht ihre künstlerische, sondern ihre handwerkliche Vorbildung ist es, der man das hohe Niveau ihrer photographischen Leistungen zu verdanken hat. Sehr allmählich verschwand diese Generation des Uebergangs; ja es scheint eine Art von biblischem Segen auf jenen ersten Photographen geruht zu haben: die Nadar, Stelzner, Pierson, Bayard sind alle an die Neunzig oder Hundert herangerückt. Schließlich aber drangen von überallher Geschäftsleute in den Stand der Berufsphotographen ein, und als dann späterhin die Negativretusche, mit welcher der schlechte Maler sich an der Photographie rächte, allge-

Photo Germaine Krull

mein üblich wurde, setzte ein jäher Verfall des Geschmacks ein. Das war die Zeit, da die Photographiealben sich zu füllen begannen. An den frostigsten Stellen der Wohnung, auf Konsolen oder Gueridons im Besuchszimmer, fanden sie sich am liebsten: Lederschwarten mit abstoßenden Metallbeschlägen und den fingerdicken goldumrandeten Blättern, auf denen närrisch drapierte oder verschnürte Figuren — Onkel Alex und Tante Riekchen, Trudchen wie sie noch klein war, Papa im ersten Semester — verteilt waren und endlich, um die Schande voll zu machen, wir selbst: als Salontiroler, jodelnd, den Hut gegen gepinselte Firnen schwingend, oder als adretter Matrose, Standbein und Spielbein wie es sich gehört, gegen einen polierten Pfosten gelehnt. Noch erinnert die Staffage solcher Porträts mit ihren Postamenten, Balustraden und ovalen Tischchen an die Zeit, da man der langen Expositionsdauer wegen den Modellen Stützpunkte geben mußte, damit sie fixiert blieben. Hatte man anfangs mit „Kopfhalter" oder „Kniebrille" sich begnügt, so folgte bald weiteres Beiwerk wie es in berühmten Gemälden

Fig. 11.14

Fig. 11.14 (previous page)

Little History of Photography
by Walter Benjamin

To appreciate the full impact made by the daguerreotype in the age of its discovery, one should also bear in mind that *plein air* painting was then opening up entirely new perspectives for the most advanced painters. Conscious that in this very area photography had to take the baton from painting, even Arago, in his historical review of the early attempts of Giovanni Battista Della Porta, explicitly commented: "As regards the effect produced by the imperfect transparency of our atmosphere (which has been loosely termed 'atmospheric degradation'), not even experienced painters expect the camera obscura"—i.e., the copying of images appearing in it—"to help them to render it accurately." At the moment when Daguerre succeeded in fixing the images of the camera obscura, painters parted company on this point with technicians. The real victim of photography, however, was not landscape painting but the portrait miniature. Things developed so rapidly that by 1840 most of the innumerable miniaturists had already become professional photographers, at first only as a sideline, but before long exclusively. Here the experience of their original livelihood stood them in good stead, and it is not their artistic background so much as their training as craftsmen that we have to thank for the high level of their photographic achievement. This transitional generation disappeared very gradually; indeed, there seems to have been a kind of biblical blessing on those first photographers: the Nadars, Stelzners, Piersons, Bayards all lived well into their eighties and nineties. In the end, though, businessmen invaded professional photography from every side; and when, later on, the retouched negative, which was the bad painter's revenge on photography, became ubiquitous, a sharp decline in taste set in. This was the time photograph albums came into vogue. They were most at home in the chilliest spots, on occasional tables or little stands in the drawing room—leather-bound tomes with repellent metal hasps and those gilt-edged pages as thick as your finger, where foolishly draped or corseted figures were displayed: Uncle Alex and Aunt Reikchen, little Trudi when she was still a baby, Papa in his first term at university … and finally, to make our shame complete, we ourselves—as a parlor Tyrolean, yodeling, waving our hat before a painted snowscape, or as a smartly turned-out sailor, standing rakishly with our weight on one leg, as is proper, leaning against a polished door jamb. The accessories used in these portraits, the pedestals and balustrades and little oval tables, are still reminiscent of the period when, because of the long exposure of time, subjects had to be given supports so that they wouldn't move. And if at first head clamps and knee braces were felt to be sufficient, "further impedimenta were soon added, such as were to be seen in famous paintings

Figs 11.15 and 11.16

Fig. 11.17

12

Hard Nuts to Crack

Riddles, Brainteasers, Word Games

Puzzles[1]

1) If I steal the beginning of the middle from him
He follows the beauties through halls and rooms,
Instead of a rolling cloud of glowing dust
He only trails a little dusty cloud.

Answer: Samum, Saum [*simoom, hem*]

2) Once sought-after and desired,
Died out and devastated,
It now appears across the old spot
with a new word.
And from its middle spits
A glimmer; whoever extinguishes it,
Finds that in the rolls of rubble
An ancient riddle sounds.

Answer: Ruine, Rune [*ruin, rune*]

3) An animal turns its tail into its head and so transforms itself into a bunch of angry people? What is it called?

Answer: Otter, Rotte [*otter, mob*]

4) If the last syllable shows itself clearly
Then the first one offers itself inside it.
Yet it brought death to the man,
Who took it as the first,
And the area, where it occurred,
Stands before you as a whole.

Answer: Bodensee [*Lake Constance—in German it literally means "ground lake"*]

---

[1] The following puzzles are word games, most of them rhyming, that do not translate. In each instance, the German solution is given, followed by the English translation in italics in brackets.

5) The names of a contradictory pair
present themselves:
The first one doesn't budge from its spot,
The other one is easy to displace.
The first one generally brings joy,
The second ones remain uncertain.

Answer: Fest, Lose [*fixed/festival, loose/lots (as in a lottery)*]

6) With P *one* animal, with R a mass.

Answer: Pudel, Rudel [*poodle, herd*]

7) What happens first of all to the building plan happens last of all to the house. What is it?

Answer: Das Überdachtwerden [*Being considered/being roofed*]

8) Saint Anthony shouts his
Words in his seclusion.
The borders of a large town
Are subsequently characterized in this way.

Answer: Weich' Bild!, Weichbild [*Be gone image!, municipal area*]

Only to the fleeting glance do they appear peripheral: the collection of riddles, brainteasers, and word games, which Benjamin published, included in his letters and preserved amongst his papers. This too is only a torso, less than three-score riddles and brainteasers have survived. But Benjamin resides in them—with his pleasure in playing games, his interest in theories of language, his passion for cogitation, his developed sense of the visual and shapes, his love of poetic sounds and wordplay. Benjamin shared his joy at discovering riddles with others: his brother Georg, his wife Dora, his son Stefan, Gershom Scholem, Gretel Karplus. These tiny forms demonstrate his capacity for humor, such as also impresses itself on Benjamin's letters and some of his writings—for example, the communications from the University of Muri, whereby he devised, together with the fictitious beadle Scholem, pastiches of academic life, ingenious and punning announcements of courses or library acquisitions.

There are three types of puzzles in the collection, even if the borders between them are quite fluid: word games, brainteasers, and rebuses. Benjamin was not only theoretically interested in the connections between the sound of a word and its meaning. In his study of Baroque tragic drama he mentioned the speculations about sounds on the part of Jacob Boehme, who conceived the language of creatures not "as a realm of words," but rather "as something resolved into its sounds and noises": "In his view A was the first letter which forces its way from the heart, I the center of the highest love, R possessed the character of the source of fire because it 'rasps, crackles, and rattles' and S was sacred fire" (*The Origin of German Tragic Drama*, p. 204). Likewise, in a review, Benjamin interpreted the name Rinaldo Rinaldini according to the sounds of the letters; it was "an onomatopoetic expression—not of the robber's life, but rather of the eternal longing for it. This name is inhabited by the forest echo of the *vieux souvenir*, of which Baudelaire wrote in a poem, it reaches us 'like a crying horn'. The leitmotifs 'loneliness,' 'justness,' and 'freedom' coalesce in this magical sound" (*GS* III, p. 185). On occasion, Benjamin attempted to voice his own magical sounds. Together with the poet Friedrich Heinle (1894–1914), a fellow student, he composed *Spirits of the Primeval Forest*, a number of verses whose linguistic joshing, inspired by the Expressionists, depends on alliteration and absurd rhymes at the end of the lines. Distortions of words and linguistic jokes play an important role in his notes on Stefan.

A series of rhyming riddles—of which two appeared in 1927, in *The Practical Berlin Woman*, a magazine edited by Dora Sophie Benjamin—are based totally on the principle of word formation: the solutions are words that are differentiated from each other by a single letter, palindromes or homonyms. For his birthday in 1938 he received some riddles from his sister-in-law Hilde Benjamin, thought up for him by his brother Georg who was in prison. Benjamin expressed his gratitude: "His brain twisters are very tough nuts to crack and I still haven't managed it" (*GB* VI, p. 144), and, in response, he sent him a number of puzzles called "daldals": "The end of the sentence must be substituted by homonymic groups of syllables. The number and writing mode of the dal—how many and whether written separately or conjoined—[indicates] how many syllables are to be appended and how they group together as words" (*GB* VI, p. 144). One of the examples goes like this: "Jimmy was a rude drunkard, who never went to the bank and so developed the habit of always paying with unsecured cheques. As they entered a new pub, the final stop of a long beery binge with his friend Tommy, the friend said to Jimmy: Your turn to cough up at the dal dal daldal." The solution: "bar bar Barbar" (*GS* VI, 145), with "bar" permutating in meaning from "bar," where one drinks, "bar" as "cash" and "Barbar" meaning "barbarian." Benjamin also deploys the assonance of syllables, on which the daldal puzzle depends, in a verse in the *Spirits of the Primeval Forest*. And he devised alphabetic experiments with his own name, for example, forming anagrams that could be used as pseudonyms, such as Anni M. Bie, Jann Beim, or Jemabinn (fig. 12.1).

As a writer for radio and a presenter Benjamin knew how to deliver punchlines and how the tone of a voice could be put to best use. He not only possessed the necessary talent for communication, but also—as his radio lectures for children demonstrate—had at his disposal pedagogical skills. On July 6, 1932 Benjamin confronted his young radio listeners with thirty "Hard Nuts to Crack" and three brainteasers that might be characterized as especially "Tough Almonds": number puzzles, geometrical questions, exercises in logic, and teasers with words and letters (compare *GS* VII, pp. 305–15). Since the eighteenth century puzzles have been collected under the rubrics "Nuts", "Tough Nuts", "Hard Nuts" or "Tough Almonds". These terms were very familiar to a child growing up around 1900. Perhaps Benjamin even knew the book from 1918 called *Children's Delight*, which contained "Tough Almonds" and riddles; the editor of the volume was Frida Schanz, who, as Scholem attested, represented "W.B.'s favorite example of literary vacuity" (Scholem, *Correspondence*, p. 194). One brainteaser is preserved amongst Ruth Berlau's literary remains, because Margarete Steffin transcribed it and furnished it with her own suggested solution. It follows a pattern that is still favored today, which allows lots of variants but only one combination that works (fig. 12.3). Such a training for the brain finds its correspondence in criminal ambitions, which Benjamin possessed as a reader—and, for a period, even as the author of a detective novel, which he planned to write with Brecht. An exercise in sleuthing—his own invention?—which he sent to Stefan on May 28, 1936, has not been preserved. In contrast, an "Ariadne Puzzle", whose author is unknown, is found in his bequest. Benjamin cannot be ruled out as the originator, because the text has been typed on the same typewriter as other puzzles by him that he managed to get into print (fig. 12.4). During the First World War Dora and Walter Benjamin delved into techniques of encryption, in order to advise Scholem, who was under observation in the army, about the possibility of an encrypted letter exchange. They decided that the "most ingenious" secret code was one that depended on a change in the code number, such that, for example, in the case of 42345, first the fourth word, then the second, then the third, etc., is meaningful, while the other words are filler, even though they appear to make sense. A similar encryption code is mentioned in some notes for a detective story. One of Benjamin's pseudonyms owes its existence to his desire for anonymity. In exile he wanted to sign his works as O.E. TAL, reversal of the Latin phrase "lateo" (I am hidden).

In July 1929 Benjamin published a piece on picture puzzles in the *Illustrierte Blatt*, with the title "What Our Grandparents Racked Their Brains Over" (fig. 12.2). He included some rebuses in the article. "The picture puzzle is not quite as old as those obscure and lofty riddles of folklore, the best known of which is that of the Sphinx," he writes. "Perhaps man's awe when confronted by the word had to decline a little, before he dared to loosen the connection of sound and meaning—which had seemed so strong—and invited them to play with each other" (*GS* IV.2, p. 622). Benjamin compared the picture puzzles of his ancestors with the perceptual world of his day, the standardized architecture, statistical schemes, the unambiguousness of neon advertising signs and traffic symbols. "The actualities of another epoch deposit themselves in other signs" (*GS* IV.2, p. 623). Benjamin read a window display in the Paris arcades as a rebus. He included picture puzzles in letters: for the Vierwaldstättersee—the German name for Lake Lucerne which includes the number 4 and the word forest and a homonym for *Städter*, city dweller, in its name—he used the number 4, trees, and a citizen. A diploma made for Scholem's fiancée, Elsa Burchhardt, is replete with symbols and Hebrew letters. There is a *Figure Puzzle* in the bequest, which has been typed on the same typewriter as the *Ariadne Puzzle* mentioned earlier (fig. 12.5).

One of his contributions to the 100th anniversary of Hebbel's death is subtitled *Picture Puzzle* and it is as just such a thing that one of the photographs in Benjamin's bequest functions. It is an image of washing lines full with laundry, just as one sees stretched across Neapolitan alleys. But these ones happen to hang in a hilly landscape, which does not seem to tally with a south Italian town (fig. 12.6). Where might it be? Who took the photograph? Why did Benjamin hold on to it?

The meaningful figurativeness of a rebus is a good match for Benjamin's thinking. It corresponds to the architectonic construction of his thought's arrangement and the significance that he accorded the graphic form of his manuscripts. In addition, Benjamin took pleasure in the poetological and aesthetic dimensions of puzzles, for example, in 1926, in a review of the novel *Bella* by Jean Girandoux. He characterized it as "the loveliest updating of the crossword puzzle," because it is "written to all intents and purposes in such a pattern": "If in that form words are cut up into letters, here are images that among themselves traverse each other in the thing, the name, and the concept. A puzzle whose resolved image presents the wildest features of political and erotic struggle in its breathtaking intersections" (*GS* III, p. 37). The aesthetic dimension can also be found in notes on the Paris Arcades and is a continuation of considerations in the book on Baroque tragic drama. An entry in convolute J of *The Arcades Project*, on Baudelaire, begins: "Allegory recognizes many enigmas, but it knows no mystery. An enigma is a fragment that, together with another, matching fragment, makes up a whole" (*AP*, p. 365). Puzzles, like fragments, are incomplete. They hold something open, demand a counterpart—the solution. They are schools for "mental exercises" (*GS* IV.2, p. 622), which instigate the cultivation of the brain, the forsaking of paradigms and the detonation of boundaries.

Figures

12.1 Draft anagrams. Reverse of a manuscript page with notes for *On the Concept of History*.

12.2 "What Our Grandparents Racked Their Brains Over." In *Das Illustrierte Blatt*, July 1929 (No. 28), p. 95. Compare *GS* IV.2, pp. 622–4.

12.3 Brainteaser. Transcription by Margarete Steffin—Typescript. Ruth-Berlau Archive, one side.

12.4 "Ariadne Puzzle"—Typescript (carbon copy), one side.

12.5 "Figure Puzzle"—Typescript (carbon copy), one side.

12.6 Unknown photograph, untitled.

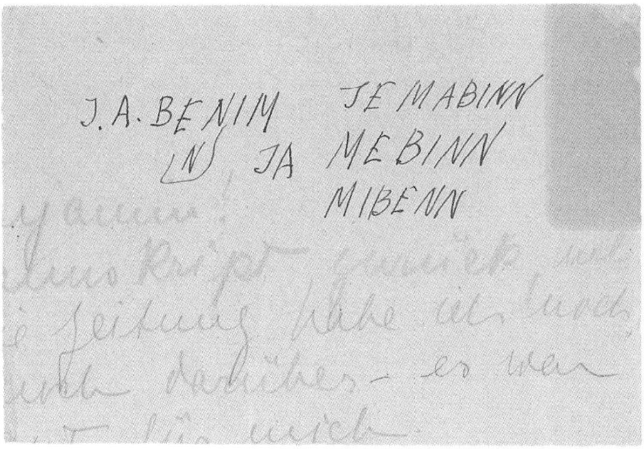

Fig. 12.1

Das Illustrierte Blatt Nr. 28 Seite 795

Ein sehr beliebter Rebus, der in den verschiedensten Formen wiederkehrte:

Erster Rebus.

Ss S ſ s ſſ ß S ſ s ß ſſ S ſ s ſſ S ſ s ſſ ß

„Es kann doch nicht immer so bleiben hier unter dem wechselnden Mond."

Worüber sich unsere Großeltern den Kopf zerbrachen

Von Walter Benjamin

Ein Normal-Rebus als Beweis dafür, wie man sich über die Autorität der Rechtschreibung hinwegsetzte:

„Frauenschönheit, das Echo im Wald Und Regenbogen vergehen bald".

Das Bilderrätsel ist nicht ganz so alt wie die dunklen vornehmen Rätselfragen der Völker, von denen die der Sphinx die berühmteste ist. Vielleicht mußte die Ehrfurcht des Menschen vor dem Wort schon ein wenig geschwunden sein, ehe er es wagen konnte, den scheinbar so festen Zusammenhang von Laut und Bedeutung zu lockern und sie zum Spiele miteinander einzuladen. Das haben sie sodann „Nach Feierabend" im „Daheim", im Schoße des „Familienfreundes", der „Rätselecke" des „Bazar" anmutig getrieben. Aber so gut wir die Faszination der Kreuzworträtsel, des „Golf mit Worten" und ähnlichen Denksports verstehen, der ihnen heute in der Gunst der Modejournale gefolgt ist, so kurios und entlegen scheint uns dieser vergangene. Wenn wir noch begreifen, wie unsere Großeltern daran Spaß hatten — wie sie diesem ausgemergelten Corps de ballet der Geräte und Lettern sein Geheimnis abzugewinnen wußten, das bleibt uns dunkel. Doch nur solange wir von unserer Merkwelt, der das Kreuzworträtsel so gut entspricht, von den normierten Architekturen, den Schemata der Statistik, der eindeutigen Sprache unserer Lichtreklame und unserer Verkehrszeichen ausgehen.

Die Aktualitäten einer anderen Zeit schlugen sich in anderen Zeichen nieder. Man denke nur an den Stil der politischen Karikatur in der Mitte des vorigen Jahrhunderts, der wir heute nichts ähnliches an die Seite zu setzen haben. Und eben damals blühte das Bilderrätsel, das sich über die Autorität der Rechtschreibung genau so hinwegsetzte wie ein Cham oder Daumier über die Autoritäten des Ministeriums. Der eigentliche Patron dieser Rebus aber war der geniale Illustrator Grandville, dessen zeichnerische Demagogie nicht nur Himmel und Erde, sondern Möbel, Kleider und Instrumente gegen den Herrn der Schöpfung mobil machte und noch den Buchstaben die Gliedmaßen und den Uebermut lieh, mit denen sie hier den Leser mystifizieren.

Ein klassischer Rebus:

„In den Ozean schifft mit tausend Masten der Jüngling, Still, auf gerettetem Boot, treibt in den Hafen der Greis".

Ein „überspannter" Rebus:

„Ein Gelehrter am Arm eines überspannten Frauenzimmers".

Ein Rebus, auf dem die Seine in Polen fließt:

„Wer macht seine sämtlichen Reisen im Bett? – die Flüsse!"

Bilder aus alten Jahrgängen des „Bazar" und des „Deutschen Hausschatz" (Preuß. Staatsbibliothek, Berlin).

Fig. 12.2

Fig. 12.2

What Our Grandparents Racked Their Brains Over

The picture puzzle is not quite as old as those obscure and lofty riddles of folklore, the best known of which is that of the Sphinx. Perhaps man's awe when confronted by the word had to decline a little, before he dared to loosen the connection of sound and meaning—which had seemed so strong—and invited them to play with each other. This is what they did so charmingly in "At the Close of the Working Day" in *The Fireside* journal, in the lap of the *Family Friend*, in the "Puzzle Corner" of *Bazaar*. But as well we might understand the fascination of the crossword puzzle, the interest in this "golf with words" and the other mental exercises that have followed them and won over the fashion magazines, these ones from the past appear most curious and remote. We might yet be able to recognize that our grandparents amused themselves with these—but what remains obscure to us is how they knew the ways to steal the secrets of this emaciated *corps de ballet* of devices and letters. But this is so only for as long as we proceed from our own perceptual world, which corresponds to the crossword puzzle so well, its standardized architecture, statistical schemes, the unambiguousness of neon advertising signs and traffic symbols.

The actualities of another epoch deposit themselves in other signs. One need think only of the style of political caricature in the middle of the last century, of which we have nothing to set alongside it today. It was precisely then that the picture puzzle flourished, flouting the authority of orthography, just as a Cham or a Daumier flouted the authority of the government. The real patron of the rebus, though, was the brilliant illustrator Grandville, whose graphic demagogy made not only heaven and earth, but also furniture, clothing, and instruments mobile against the Lord of Creation and lent letters the limbs and high spirits with which they mystify the reader here.

Walter Benjamin:

6 Autoren sitzen im Eisenbahnwagen erster Klasse, je 3 auf einer Seite. Müller, Schulze, Schmidt, Becker, Meier, Lehmann. Sie sind - nicht eben in der gleichen Reihenfolge; Essayst, Historiker, Humorist, Romancier, Dramatiker und Dichter.

Jeder hat ein Buch geschrieben, das ein anderer von den Mitreisenden gerade liest.

Müller liest Essays, Becker liest das Buch seines Gegenübers. Schulze sitzt zwischen dem Essaysten und dem Humoristen. Meier ist der Nachbar des Dramatikers. Der Essayst sitzt dem Historiker gegenüber. Schmidt liest ein Stück. Schulze ist der Schwager des Romanciers. Müller, der in einer Ecke sitzt, interessiert sich nicht für Geschichte. Schmidt sitzt dem Romancier gegenüber. Meier liest das Buch des Humoristen. Lehmann liest die Gedichte.

Jedem Autor ist sein Name zu geben.

Dr. Benjamins Verfahren:

Ich habe mir 4 Schemata gemacht. In das erste habe ich eingetragen, was Müller, Schulze usw. nicht verfasst haben können. In das zweite habe ich eingetragen, wie Essayist, Historiker usw. nicht heissen können.

Diese beiden negativen Schemata habe ich durch zwei positive ergänzt, beides Lagepläne der Sitze im Eisenbahnwagen. In den ersten habe ich eingetragen, wo Müller, Schulze usw. sitzen, in den zweiten, wo Essayist, Historiker usw. sitzen.

Jedes dieser vier Schemata kann nur ganz unvollständig ausgefüllt werden. Die Lösung, die aus ihrer Kombination hervorgeht, sieht so aus:

Schmidt Humorist	Müller Romancier
Schulze Dichter	Becker Dramatiker
Lehmann Essayist	Meyer Historiker

Steffins Lösung:

Humorist Schmidt liest ein Stück	Dramatiker Schulze liest hist. Roman	Essayist Meyer liest Humoresken
romancier Müller liest Essays	Dichter Becker liest Dramen	Historiker Lehmann liest Gedichte

Fig. 12.3

Fig. 12.3

Walter Benjamin:
Six authors are sitting in a first-class railway carriage. Three of them sit on each side. Müller, Schulze, Schmidt, Becker, Meier, Lehmann. Their professions are—though not in the same order—essayist, historian, humorist, novelist, playwright, and poet.

Each one has written a book, which another one of the party is currently reading.

Müller is reading essays. Becker is reading the book by the person sitting opposite him. Schulze is sitting between the essayist and the humorist. Meier is next to the playwright. The essayist is sitting opposite the historian. Schmidt is reading a play. Schulze is the brother-in-law of the novelist. Müller, who is sitting in the corner, is not interested in history. Schmidt is sitting opposite the novelist. Meier is reading the book by the humorist. Lehmann is reading poems.

Give each author his name.

Dr Benjamin's procedure:
I made four diagrams. In the first one I set down everything that Müller, Schulze, etc., can not have written. In the second one I set down who can not be an essayist, historian, etc.

These two negative diagrams are supplemented by my two positive ones, both of which are position plans of the seats in the railway carriage. In the first one I set down where Müller, Schulze, etc., are sitting, in the second one where the essayist, historian, etc., sit.

Each of these four diagrams can only be incompletely filled in. The solution emerges from their combination and is as follows:

Schmidt Humorist	Müller Novelist
Schulze Poet	Becker Playwright
Lehmann Essayist	Meyer Historian

Steffin's solution:

humorist Schmidt reads a play	playwright Schulze reads a hist. novel	essayist Meyer reads a humorous book
novelist Müller reads essays	poet Becker reads plays	historian Lehmann reads poem

Ariadnerätsel

Viele von uns erinnern sich wohl noch aus ihrer Schulzeit der"Labyrinthe", die sie oder ihre Mitschüler ~~xxxx~~ waehrend der Schulstunden auf Löschblätter oder an den Rand ihrer Hefte malten. In der griechischen Sage bekommt nun Theseus, der so ein Labyrinth durchwandern muss von seiner Freundin , der Ariadne, einen Faden mittels dessen er wieder zum Ausgang zurückfindet. In Erinnerung an dieses Griechenmädchen nannten unsere Grosseltern gewisse Rätsel, deren Lösung in seltsam gewundenen Linienzügen besteht,Ariadnerätsel. Wir setzen unseren Lesern eins hierher, über dem sie vieilleicht nicht ungern ein Weilchen nachdenken.

Der innere Raum unserer Zeichnung ist von einer Mauer eingeschlossen. A,B und C sind drei Häuser, welche an die Mauer angebaut sind; leider können ihre Bewohner einander nicht ausstehen. Zum Unglück ist es nun so, dass der zum Hause A gehörige Brunnen sich bei a, der zum Hause B gehörige bei b und der zum Hause gehörige sich bei c befindet. Die Brunnen bei a und c stehen frei, während der bei b hart an der Mauer liegt und nicht umgangen werden kann. Es will nun jeder Hausbesitzer zu seinem Brunnen gelangen, ohne den Weg seines ärgerlichen Nachbarn zu überschneiden. Das kann er auch. A b e r w i e ?

L ö s u n g :

Fig. 12.4

Fig. 12.4

Ariadne Puzzle

Many of us can probably still remember the "labyrinth" from our school days, which you or your classmates sketched on blotting paper or on the margins of your school notebooks during lessons. In the Greek legend, Theseus, who had to wander through just such a labyrinth, receives from his girlfriend Ariadne a thread by means of which he is able to find his way back to the exit. Our grandparents named certain puzzles, whose solution consists in strange, meandering, and zigzag lines, Ariadne Puzzles, in memory of this Greek girl. Here we place just such a one before our readers, and perhaps you might like to spend some moments considering it.

The inner space of our drawing is enclosed in a wall. A, B, and C are three houses, which are built into the wall; unfortunately their inhabitants cannot stand each other. Unhappily too, it happens that the well that belongs to house A is at a, that which belongs to house B is at b and the one belonging to house [C] is at c. Wells a and c are free-standing, but well b is right on the wall and it is impossible to go round it. Each house owner wants to get to his well, without cutting across the path of his neighbor. And it is possible. But how?

Figurenrätsel

Wie kann man diese beiden Figuren so in je vier Teile zerlegen, dass jeder Teil mit den drei anderen mindestens eine Linie gemeinsam hat?

Lösung

Fig. 12.5

Fig. 12.5

Figure Puzzle

How can one divide each of these figures into four parts, such that each part shares at least one line with the three others?

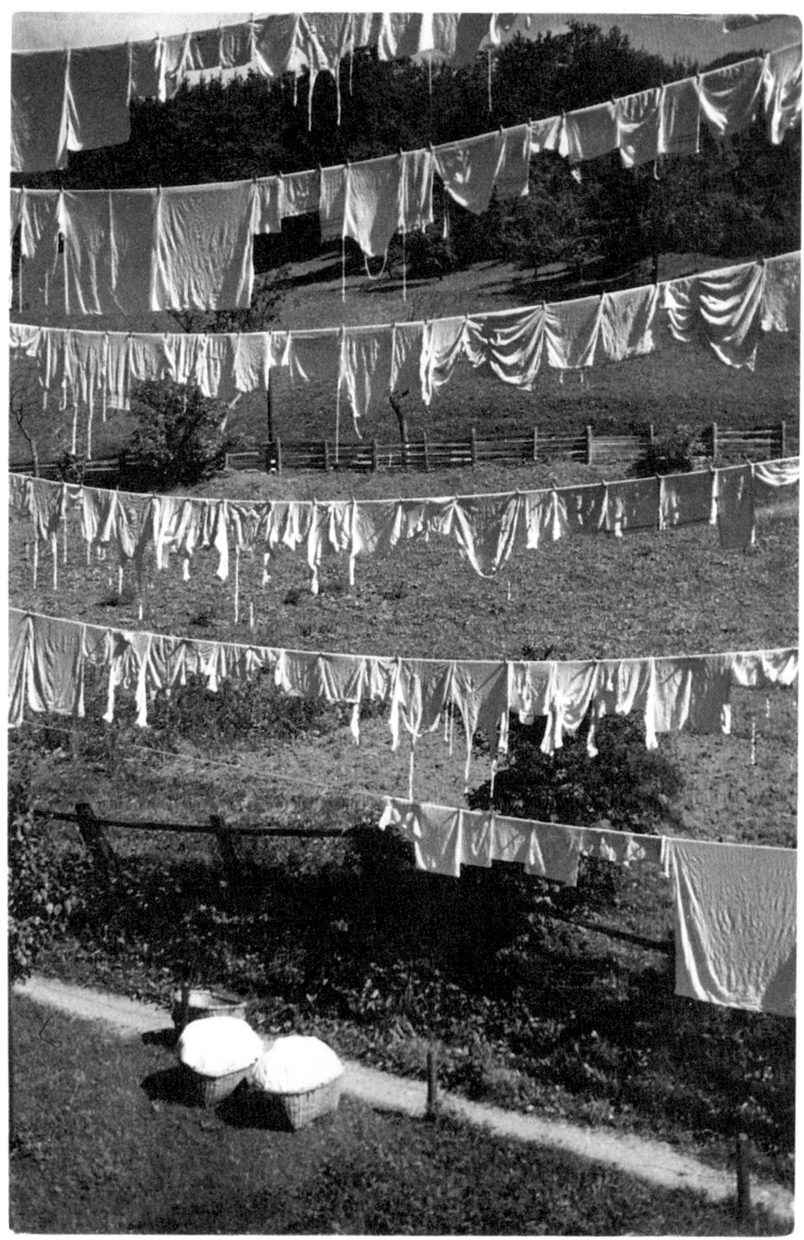

Fig. 12.6

13

Sibyls

Mosaics in Siena

Easy the way that leads into Avernus.

Virgil, *The Aeneid*

It is the unique provision of Baudelaire's poetry that the image of the woman and the image of death intermingle in a third: that of Paris. The Paris of his poems is a sunken city, and more submarine than subterranean. The chthonic elements of the city—its topographic formations, the old abandoned bed of the Seine—have evidently found in him a mold. Decisive for Baudelaire in the "death-fraught idyll" of the city, however, is a social, a modern substrate. The modern is a principal accent of his poetry. As spleen, it fractures the ideal ("Spleen et idéal"). But precisely the modern, *la modernité*, is always citing primal history.

AP, p. 10

Eight postcard-sized art prints with representations of sibyls have been preserved in Benjamin's bequest. These cards depict the mosaics that are embedded in the floor of the two nave aisles in the cathedral at Siena. The eight sibyls are shown on slabs that appear like giant woodcuts, with outlines picked out in black on white marble. We know from his letters that Benjamin was in Siena in 1929: "Tomorrow I am going to Siena. Time will be rather tight there," he wrote to Gershom Scholem on July 27, 1929 (*Correspondence*, p. 354). In contrast to his reports from other Italian towns, he is extremely elliptical when it comes to Siena. He wrote not a single word on the mosaics in the cathedral there, at least none that have been passed on. We do not even know if he went to the cathedral and actually saw the sibyl mosaics. What more can be said then? On December 6, 1937 Benjamin wrote to Horkheimer: "It is sometimes necessary to make the reader clearly aware of the difficulties that stand in the path of the author" (*GB* V, p. 624). Our difficulties are the how and the why of these art postcards, their secret, the riddle of their presence in the bequest. Can the riddle be solved? Benjamin himself, a fan of puzzles, gives us one clue: "for this reason many puzzles can be solved simply through an image, but they can be saved only through the word" (*SW* 1, p. 268).[1] The postcards can be fathomed; we can label them, discover the names of the sibyls, find out the various roles that history and stories have ascribed them. We know who created the Siena mosaics. But for the solution to the riddle of how and why they found their way into Benjamin's collection we are lacking the key words.

And so we search amongst his texts and notes for words that might help us to solve this riddle. In the exposé *Paris, the Capital of the Nineteenth Century* (1935) Benjamin places Virgil's "Facilis descensus Averno" above a section on *Baudelaire, or the Streets of Paris*. Why? What secret is buried here before the eyes of the ignorant? Is he reliant on the experts, those for whom Virgil's words are not unknown and who therefore recognize the context? Avernus is a lake and the entrance to the underworld, guarded by the Cumaean Sibyl. It is she who utters the words "Facilis descensus Averno" ("Easy the way that leads into Avernus") to Aeneas. What is the purpose of these sibylline words? What meaning does Benjamin intend them to generate? He begins his text with images of "woman" and "death." In Virgil's verses it is the Sibyl who descends with Aeneas into the underworld—the realm of death. Without her he would be lost, for only she has a connection with the realm of the dead and can bring the hero back to the world above once more. While in the underworld she leads him through the past, through all that has been lost and forgotten, and thereby she helps him to behold a new realm; she leads him into the past, in order to show him the future. Avernus and Sibyl are, for Benjamin, accordingly ciphers pointing to the connection of old and new, death and life.

These images are connected to a third, the image of Paris as an underworld. He lets himself be guided through this particular underworld by Baudelaire's poems, which delineate the past, present, and future of the city. For whoever desires to discover the new, must descend and turn his back on the present. This is how to understand "the phrase about the historian as a prophet turned backwards": "the historian turns his back on his own time, and his prophetic gaze ignites on the peaks of earlier generations that fade ever further into the past. It is to just such a prophetic gaze that an epoch is more clearly present than to the contemporaries who 'keep pace with it'" (*GS* I.3, p. 1237). In the mythic image of the descent with the Sibyl—the prophetess—Benjamin develops a formula which looks forwards and backwards, pointing back to the origin and forwards to new possibilities of understanding in the reformulation of the old.

[1] The translation has been modified here from that in the *Selected Works* in order to render Benjamin's play with the words *lösen* and *erlösen* (solve and redeem).

Sibyls stand at the crossing point of primitive history, antiquity, and Christianity. Their origins reach right back into primitive culture. Originally they were oracle-priestesses, who served various goddesses: the Sumerian-Persian sibyl the goddess Ishtar, the Cumaean sibyl Demeter, Delphica, and Hellespontica served the Greek Gaia, and the Phrygian sibyl served Cybele; these figures were mentioned by a variety of writers in antiquity, and thus word of them was passed on (Altenhöner, Sibylle, *p. 103). Usually they lived in a cave, the sibyl's grotto. The existence of such enclosures has been verified archaeologically, for example in Erythrai, an ancient town in Asia Minor. And nowadays one is still able to visit the Sibyl's Grotto in Cumae, in the coastal region of Campania in Italy. In the Old Testament Sibyls appeared as Jewish prophetesses—such as, for example, the judge Deborah (Judges 4, verse 4) or the Witch of Endor (1. Samuel 28, verses 5–25). In antiquity the sibyls augured at the behest of Apollo, and in early Christianity they proclaimed the birth and ministry of Jesus Christ. In many church buildings sibyls are represented in paintings or mosaics, as in the cathedral at Siena.*

Figures

13.1 Sibyl Delfica (Delphica), also known as Pythia, augured in the Temple of Apollo at Delphi. The name Delphi is derived from the Greek word δελφυϑ (delphys) for "womb" and indicates an old veneration of the Earth Goddess Gaia.

13.2 The Sibyl of Cumae was the most significant sibyl in the Roman Empire. The nine famous sibylline books, which described the fate of the Romans, belonged to her; they were destroyed in the fire at the temple in Rome in 83 BC. She is known through Virgil's *Aeneid.*

13.3 The Sibyl Cumana. Cumana is another name for the Sibyl of Cumae.

13.4 The Sibyl of Erythrai was the most famous Hellenic Sibyl. She is supposed to have foretold the fall of Troy.

13.5 The Sibyl Persica, also known as a Chaldean-Jewish sibyl, with the name Sabba or Sambethe, appears in Euripides as well.

13.7 Sibyl Frigia (Phrygia) belongs in the cultural area of the Assyrians, Hittites, (1950–1180 BC) and the Phrygians (900–620 BC) in contemporary Turkey. She foretold the deeds of Alexander the Great (300–100 BC).

13.8 Sibyl Hellespontica is the oldest Hellenic Sibyl and is supposed to have been endowed with the ability to presage by Apollo. Her domain of influence was Alexandria, west of Thessalonica; according to legend, she died in Troy.

8 La Sibilla Delfica (G. di Biagio o V. di Marco)

ET MORTIS FATVM FINI
ET TRIVM DIERVM SO
MNO SVSCEPTO TVNC
AMORTVIS REGRESSVS
IN LVCEM VENIET PRIM
VM RESVRRECTIONIS
INITIVM OSTENDENS
2 La Sibilla Cumea (L. di Ruggero o V. di Marco)
Sab. Sadun - Siena
Dettaglio del pavimento

VLTIMA CVMAEI VENIT IAM
CARMINIS AETAS MAGNVS
AB INTEGRO SAECLORVM
NASCITVR ORDO IAM RE
DIT ET VIRGO REDEVNT
SATVRNIA REGNA IAM
NOVA PROGENIES CAELO
DEMITTITVR ALTO
10 La Sibilla Cumana (Giov. di Maestro Stefano)
Sab. Sadun - Siena
Dettaglio del pavimento

SIBYLLA LYBICA
CVIVS MEMINIT
EVRIPIDES
7 La Sibilla Libica (Guidaccio Cozzarelli)
Sab. Sadun - Siena
Dettaglio del pavimento

Figs 13.1 to 13.4

Figs 13.5 to 13.8

Bibliography and Abbreviations

Walter Benjamin

The Arcades Project. Edited by Rolf Tiedemann, Cambridge, MA: Belknap Press of Harvard 1999—abbreviated: *AP*

The Correspondence of Walter Benjamin 1910–1940. Edited by Gershom Scholem and T.W. Adorno, Chicago: University of Chicago 1994—abbreviated: *Correspondence*

The Correspondence of Walter Benjamin and Gershom Scholem 1932–1940. Edited by Gershom Scholem, New York: Schocken 1989—abbreviated: *Benjamin/Scholem Correspondence*

Gesammelte Briefe, volumes 1–6. Edited by Christoph Gödde and Henri Lonitz, Frankfurt am Main: Suhrkamp 1995–2000—abbreviated: *GB* [I–VI]

Gesammelte Schriften, volumes I–VII. With the assistance of T.W. Adorno and Gershom Scholem, edited by Rolf Tiedemann and Hermann Schweppenhäuser, Frankfurt am Main: Suhrkamp 1972–1989—abbreviated: *GS* [I–VII]

Moscow Diary. With an Afterword by Gary Smith [originally an edition of the journal *October*], Cambridge, MA: Harvard University Press 1986—abbreviated: *Moscow Diary*

On Hashish. Cambridge, MA: Belknap Press of Harvard 2006—abbreviated: *On Hashish*

Selected Writings, Volume I: 1913–1926. Edited by Marcus Bullock and Michael W. Jennings, Cambridge, MA: Belknap Press of Harvard 1996—abbreviated: *SW 1*

Selected Writings, Volume 2:1 and 2:2: 1927–1934. Edited by Michael W. Jennings, Cambridge, MA: Bellknap Press of Harvard 1999—abbreviated: *SW* 2:1 and 2:2

Selected Writings, Volume 3: 1935–1938. Edited by Howard Eiland and Michael W. Jennings, Cambridge, MA: Belknap Press of Harvard 2002—abbreviated: *SW* 3

Selected Writings, Volume 4: 1938–1940. Edited by Howard Eiland and Michael W. Jennings, Cambridge, MA: Belknap Press of Harvard 2002—abbreviated: *SW* 4

Other Sources

Theodor W. Adorno, "Benjamin the Letter-Writer," in *On Walter Benjamin*. Edited by Gary Smith, Cambridge, MA: MIT 1991, pp. 329–37.

Ingrid Altenhöner, *Die Sibylle als literarische Chiffre bei Johann Georg Hamann—Friedrich Schlegel—Johann Wolfgang Goethe*. Frankfurt am Main: Peter Lang 1997—abbreviated: Altenhöner, *Sibylle*

Charles Baudelaire, *The Mirror of Art*, London: Phaidon 1955.

Davide Giuriato, *Mikrographien. Zu einer Poetologie des Schreibens in Walter Benjamins Kindheitserinnerungen (1932–1939)*, Paderborn: Fink 2006.

Markus Krajewski, *Zettelwirtschaft. Die Geburt der Kartei aus dem Geiste der Bibliothek*. Berlin: Kulturverlag-Kadmos 2002.

Werner Morlang, *Im Tarnzauber der Mikrographie*. In *Du. Zeitschrift für Kultur*. No. 730 (October 2002), pp. 58–63 and p. 88—abbreviated: Walser, cited from Morlang

Ingrid Scheurmann, *Neue Dokumente zum Tode Walter Benjamins*, Bonn: AsKI 1992.

Gershom Scholem, "Walter Benjamin," in *On Jews and Judaism in Crisis*, New York: Shocken 1976—abbreviated: Scholem, "Benjamin"

——"Walter Benjamin and his Angel," in *On Walter Benjamin*, edited by Gary Smith, Cambridge, MA: MIT 1991, pp. 51–89—abbreviated: Scholem, *Angel*

—— *Walter Benjamin: The Story of a Friendship*. New York: NYRB 2003—abbreviated: Scholem, *Friendship*

Jean Selz, "Benjamin in Ibiza," in *On Walter Benjamin*, edited by Gary Smith, Cambridge, MA: MIT 1991, pp. 353–66—abbreviated: Selz

Kim Sichel, *Germaine Krull. Photographer of Modernity*, Cambridge, MA: MIT 1999.

Über Walter Benjamin. With contributions from Theodor W. Adorno, Ernst Bloch, Max Rychner, Gershom Scholem, Jean Selz, Hans Heinz Holz, and Ernst Fischer. Frankfurt am Main: Suhrkamp 1968.

Virgil [Publius Vergilius Maro], *Aeneid*. Facing-page Latin–English edition: Virgil: *Eclogues, Georgics, Aeneid* 1–6 (Loeb Classical Library, No. 63) H. R. Fairclough (trans.), Cambridge, MA: Harvard 1916.

Virgil [Publius Vergilius Maro], *Aeneid. Books 7–12, Appendix Vergiliana* (Loeb Classical Library, No. 64) H.R. Fairclough (trans.), Cambridge, MA: Harvard 1918.

Walter Benjamin. 1892–1940. An exhibition of the Theodor W. Adorno Archive, Frankfurt am Main in association with the German Literature Archive, Marbach am Neckar. Edited by Rolf Tiedemann, Christoph Gödde, and Henri Lonitz (*Marbacher Magazin* 55). Third revised and expanded edition, Marbach am Neckar 1991.

Erdmut Wizisla, "*Verzettelte Schreiberei*," *Walter Benjamins Archiv*. In *Sinn und Form*, No. 2 (March/April 2006), pp. 265–73.

Irving Wohlfarth, "Et Cetera? The Historian as Chiffonnier," *New German Critique* 39 (Fall 1986): 147–86.

About the book

The German edition of this book was published to coincide with the exhibition *Walter Benjamin's Archives*, which ran from October 3 to November 19, 2006 in the Academy of Arts, Berlin, supported by the Kulturstiftung des Bundes. As in the exhibition, the volume collates *Images, Texts, and Signs* from Benjamin's bequest. The originals of materials reproduced in this book may be found in the Walter Benjamin Archive (abbreviated: WBA). One exception to this is the *Wind Rose of Success*; this is in the possession of Jörg Leinweber (Marburg an der Lahn). The brainteaser reproduced in the twelfth chapter originates from the Ruth-Berlau Archive of the Academy of Arts.

The transcriptions of Benjamin's manuscripts in this book do not follow the positionings and line breaks of the handwritten originals. They are not strict topographical transcripts. Any deletions in Benjamin's manuscripts are given—in as far as they can still be read. Any crossed-out words and parts of words that can no longer be deciphered are marked by a [x], in the case of multiple crossings out a [x]. Longer passages that have been crossed out are denoted by curly parentheses. Additions on the part of the editors are within square brackets in sans serif.[1] Uncertain words and passages are marked by a [?]. Any missing quotation marks in the manuscript are not supplemented.

The prefaces to chapters 1, 3, and 8 are by Ursula Marx, while those to chapters 2, 6, and 12 are by Erdmut Wizisla. Prefaces to chapters 4, 5, and 9 to 11 are by Michael Schwarz, and those to chapters 7 and 13 are by Gudrun Schwarz.

[1] Some notes in square or angled brackets in translations of the manuscripts stem from the editorial apparatus in Benjamin's *Gesammelte Schriften*.